# Strangers in a Strange Land

# Contemporary Societies Series

Jeffrey C. Alexander, Series Editor

Andrew Abbott *Methods of Discovery: Heuristics for the Social Sciences*

Michael Schudson *The Sociology of News*

Steven Seidman *The Social Construction of Sexuality*

Judith Lorber *Breaking the Bowls: Gender Theory and Feminist Change*

Douglas Massey *Strangers in a Strange Land: Humans in an Urbanizing World*

Bryan Turner *The New Medical Sociology: Social Forms of Health and Illness*

## Forthcoming

Craig Calhoun *The Public Sphere*

Arne Kalleberg *The Mismatched Worker*

Saskia Sassen *A Sociology of Globalization*

Mike Shanahan *The Life Course*

David Snow and Sarah Soule *A Primer on Social Movements*

# STRANGERS IN A STRANGE LAND

## Humans in an Urbanizing World

Douglas S. Massey

CONTEMPORARY SOCIETIES
Jeffrey C. Alexander
SERIES EDITOR

W. W. NORTON & COMPANY NEW YORK LONDON

W. W. Norton & Company has been independent since its founding in 1923, when William Warder Norton and Mary D. Herter Norton first published lectures delivered at the People's Institute, the adult education division of New York City's Cooper Union. The Nortons soon expanded their program beyond the Institute, publishing books by celebrated academics from America and abroad. By mid-century, the two major pillars of Norton's publishing program—trade books and college texts—were firmly established. In the 1950s, the Norton family transferred control of the company to its employees, and today—with a staff of four hundred and a comparable number of trade, college, and professional titles published each year—W. W. Norton & Company stands as the largest and oldest publishing house owned wholly by its employees.


Printed in the United States of America.

The text of this book is composed in Garamond.
Composition by PennSet, Inc.
Manufacturing by Quebecor World—Fairfield Division.
Drawn art by John McAusland.
Production manager: Benjamin Reynolds.

**ISBN 0–393–92727–X**

W. W. Norton & Company, Inc., 500 Fifth Avenue, New York, N.Y. 10110–0017
www.wwnorton.com

W. W. Norton & Company Ltd., Castle House,
75/76 Wells Street, London W1T 3QT

1 2 3 4 5 6 7 8 9 0

To my friend and mentor, G. Edward Stephan

# Contents

# Acknowledgments

Thanks to Susan T. Fiske for reading and commenting on the first draft of this book, and to Princeton University for granting me the sabbatical time to write it.

# Strangers in a Strange Land

# Chapter One
# The Structure of Social Change

Human beings are the last survivors of a long line of bipedal primates, known as hominids, who once walked the earth. The path of descent from the first bipeds to ourselves resembles not so much a tree as a bush with many branches, some drifting off to extinction and others continuing to the present. Over the course of 6 million years of hominid evolution, however, one thing has been constant: The apes and their descendants who eventually became human beings always lived in groups. Hominids never lived or acted alone; they were always enmeshed in social networks that were themselves embedded within larger social structures.

Humans beings are fundamentally social creatures—in the words of the social psychologist Susan T. Fiske, "social to the core" (Fiske 2003:169). For members of the human species, survival is impossible outside the group. As an organism, we are characterized by an unusually long period of helplessness and dependence early in life. For years after birth, human young are incapable of feeding, clothing, and maintaining themselves without help from adults. Left alone, human infants and children quickly die. Even as adults, survival outside the group is tenuous, at best. Before agriculture—that is, for most of human existence—no single adult could possibly secure enough calories day after day, year after year, to support himself or herself and reproduce. One individual's bad luck at the hunt or limited success at gathering would have left that person without sufficient nourishment. Moreover, all humans are inevitably incapacitated for significant spans of time by injury, illness, immaturity, and senescence; and females are routinely burdened by the demands of pregnancy, childbirth, and child rearing. As a result, food sharing characterizes all known human societies. For human beings, eating is as much a social as a biological endeavor.

The importance of social integration continues even in contemporary, post-industrial societies characterized by low mortality and long life expectancies. Even given assured access to food, shelter, and modern medicine, adults who are socially disconnected from others get sick and die at much higher rates than those who are socially integrated. Across all cultures the harshest punishment that is imposed on a human being short of death is estrangement from the group. Whereas foraging societies impose banishment, we subject our evil-doers to solitary confinement in prisons. Given our social nature, depriving a human being of the company of other people represents a harsh punishment in and of itself. Try as they might, human beings cannot escape the presence—real or imagined, concrete or symbolic—of other people. They don't like to be alone, at least not for very long.

Although individual human beings are inevitably embedded within social networks that bind them into larger communities, the size, structure, and organization of human society have changed dramatically over the course of 6 million years of evolution. The societies that now span the globe contain vastly more people living together in higher concentrations than ever before. The denizens of today's societies live in much larger settlements of higher density and interact far more intensely across a wider array of social categories than was true just a century ago. In the words of one social historian, small-scale settlements where everyone knows everyone else constitute "a world we have lost" (Laslett 1971).

The process by which human societies evolve and change over time has long attracted the attention of social thinkers. From the dawn of history, philosophers have speculated about the nature of the ideal relationship between the individual and society. More recently, social scientists have endeavored to observe and catalogue the diversity of social forms across time and space and, on the basis of these observations, to describe generalized patterns of social structure and to formulate universal models of change.

Since the emergence of the social sciences in the late nineteenth century, thoughtful observers have proposed numerous models of social evolution. Some of them are *unilinear*, viewing social change as an unbroken, monotonic line of progress stretching from past to present. Others are *multilinear*, conceiving of social change as manifold, with different branches moving forward at different rates at different times, some reaching dead ends and others progressing toward the present. Many theories are *unicausal*, positing that the impetus for change and development lies in one or another overriding factor—population growth, technological innovation, environmental transformation, social reorganization. Other models are *multicausal*, viewing change as stemming from a complex interplay of many different factors that influence one another in convoluted, often nonlinear ways.

## THE ELEMENTS OF SOCIAL CHANGE

After years of investigation and study across a variety of domains, most social scientists have abandoned simple unilinear and unicausal models of change and now conceive of societal evolution as a complex of multicausal, multistranded social processes with nonlinear feedbacks that affect one another nonrecursively over time (see Bogucki 1999; Sanderson 1999; Johnson and Earle 2000). Although such a system is inherently complicated and unstable, its basic organization and feedbacks may be simply summarized. Figure 1.1 offers an illustrative diagram of societal change as the outcome of interactive feedbacks among three important clusters of factors: those defining the physical environment (environmental cluster); those characterizing social relations among humans at the micro level (microsocial cluster); and those affecting the social organization of human societies at the macro level (macrosocial cluster).

Across different epochs of human existence, the relative strength and importance of the various intercluster pathways (e.g., those linking environment with microsocial relations, macrosocial structure with environmental conditions, and macrosocial structure with microsocial relations) vary considerably; but over the long run of human evolution, all have come into play. Only their relative influence, not their existence, varies over time. Each cluster in Figure 1.1 is composed of three constituent elements that form a subset of relationships determining the nature, form, and relative importance of that cluster at any particular historical moment.

Figure 1.1

Schematic Model of Social Change in Human Society

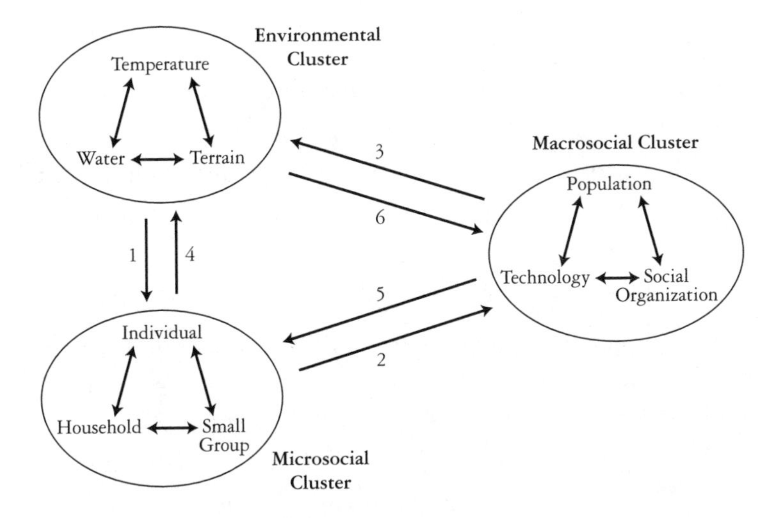


*The Environmental Cluster*

The ultimate arbiter of all human behavior at both the micro and macro levels is the environment. In the absence of appropriate amounts of oxygen, water, nutrients, and warmth, human beings cannot survive. The environment to which humans must adapt is defined by a set of prevailing temperatures (which may vary seasonally); degree of access to water (in the form of precipitation and in liquid and frozen concentrations); and a particular terrain (defined by the degree and variability of elevation). In any location at any point in time, the elements of temperature, water, and terrain combine to define a particular ecological niche; if humans are to survive, they somehow must organize themselves into a combination of micro-level relationships and macro-level social structures that enable them to persist and reproduce within that niche.

The environment, of course, varies across both space and time. Temporal change may be seasonal (occurring in short, orderly cycles throughout the year) or evolutionary (occurring in long phases that persist for decades, centuries, and even millennia). Environmental change has at various historical junctures functioned as the wellspring for change in human social organization. During the earliest phases of hominid evolution, for example, the ancestral environment shifted from forest to grassland during an evolutionary cycle of global warming, which selected for genes that enabled organisms to stand upright and look over tall vegetation, to move quickly about on two legs, and to devote the hands to rooting for food (Wrangham 2001).

Similarly, the period during which human brain size increased most rapidly was one of abnormal climate oscillation that caused very abrupt changes in habitat over short periods (in the form of successive ice ages), thereby favoring an adaptive tool that could change quickly (i.e., culture), rather than one that shifted slowly across generations (i.e., genetic evolution—see Bogucki 1999). With the final expansion of the prefrontal cortex around 150,000 years ago, the *genetic adaptation* of humans to the environment effectively ceased and was replaced by *cultural adaptation*. After being confined for millions of years to Africa, southern Europe, and southern Asia, within a few thousand years the new hominids—Homo sapiens—were able to use culture to adapt to virtually all of the world's ecological niches, no matter how hot or cold, wet or dry, high or low.

With the emergence of culture rather than genetic evolution as the primary means of human adaptation to ecological variation, the relative influence of the environment on social affairs

(Pathways 1 and 6 in Figure 1.1) began to wane and the effect of human behavior on the environment grew (Pathways 3 and 4). Indeed, shortly after the arrival on the scene of modern humans, dozens of species of megafauna (bison, mammoths, sabertooth tigers, and the like) suddenly disappeared from the fossil record, likely owing to over-hunting. More recently, human beings have turned forests into fields, fields into deserts, and deserts into gardens; and with evidence for human-induced global warming growing stronger (Watson 2002), one could say that completion of the circle is under way, whereby human actions affect the environment in so powerful a fashion that it mandates changes in both interpersonal behavior and social organization.

### *The Microsocial Cluster*

By far the greatest amount of waking time in the life of any human being is spent in the company of small numbers of other people assembled within some narrowly circumscribed location. At most times and in most places in the course of human evolution, the total number of people with whom individuals interacted either directly or indirectly numbered in the dozens or hundreds and did not exceed one thousand in a lifetime. From the advent of the hominid line around 6 million years ago, through the emergence of Homo sapiens some 150,000 years ago—indeed, until just 10,000 years ago—all human beings lived together in small groups, moving about the environment in small bands that survived by scavenging, hunting, and gathering, a way of life generally known as foraging.

Whatever else one can say about human beings, it is clear that we are adapted primarily to life in small social groups. No matter what the circumstances, we instinctively seek out, form, and endeavor to maintain social bonds with other people. As children we bond to people with whom we share living space, usually but not always close kin. We do not seek out parents, siblings, and other household members, of course; we are automatically bound to them by shared genetics and intimate association across space and time. As we grow older, however, we come to interact in culturally expected ways with other, more distant relations, and we are instinctively motivated to form emotional bonds of friendship and trust with nonrelatives. Upon adolescence, we are socially programmed to seek out and form attachments to sexual partners, usually but not always members of the opposite sex. When social bonding does not occur for some reason, human beings generally develop severe physical, social, and psychological pathologies. (Bowlby 1982).

In dealing with other individuals as social actors, all human beings must face and overcome four inescapable and fundamental problems (Plutchik 1980). The first is *temporality*, which is imposed by the fact that life is ultimately finite. The existence of any organism is defined by the vital events of birth and death, between which unfold the sequential stages of infancy, childhood, adolescence, sexual maturity, adulthood, and senescence. Given mortality, time is always a limited good, and human beings and their social organizations generally operate to minimize its expenditure (Stephan 2004). The bookend events of birth and death make feelings of attachment and loss—the emotions of joy and sadness—intrinsic to the human condition (TenHouten 1999).

A second fundamental problem is *territoriality*. All interpersonal interactions must occur within or transcend physical space. In order to achieve safety and security, all organisms need to achieve a certain command and control over some territory, the boundaries of which they generally seek to mark in some fashion. A fundamental emotional compulsion in all mammals is to seek and explore one's environment (Panksepp 1998), which is in turn associated with the universal emotion of surprise (Eibl-Eibesfeld 1989).

A third fundamental issue faced by all human beings is *identity*: the nature of one's membership in a social group. As already noted, isolated individuals are unable to perpetuate their genes, and functioning within a group always involves solving issues of identity that determine (1) when and under what circumstances one engages in cooperative behavior with others, and (2) how the intent to cooperate with other social beings is communicated through words, facial expressions, gestures, and symbols. Associated with identity are characteristic emotional valances: Attraction brings about social bonding and acceptance; disgust yields avoidance and rejection.

The last fundamental problem of social life is *hierarchy*: how one is positioned within a graded classification ordered with respect to some attribute of social dominance such as power, influence, wealth, status, or prestige. Hierarchy is the vertical dimension of group life and position within a classification structure that determines the organism's degree of access to food, shelter, comfort, safety, and pleasure. The relevant emotions associated with hierarchy are rage and anger, which bring about aggressive behavior that establishes location in a graded social order, and fear and envy, which trigger submissive or deferential behaviors that acknowledge another actor's higher rank.

In foraging societies, individual human beings confront these issues almost exclusively at the microsocial level, innovating social structure from the bottom-up as they forge ties with other people in their social environment to create an interpersonal network of connections to relatives and friends (Gamble 1999). Individuals thus actively construct society as a network of interpersonal ties and alliances, building up social networks, improvising scripts, and creating social life as they move through life interacting with people they encounter, a process that Giddens (1984) has labeled "structuration." In fact, structuration is the fundamental activity carried out within the microsocial cluster.

Networks are structured sets of social ties that link human beings to one another across space and time. Humans establish social ties by exchanging one of three kinds of resources: emotional, material, or symbolic. *Multiplex ties* are those characterized by exchanges of multiple resources simultaneously, whereas *uniplex ties* are those involving the exchange of just one resource. Ties within one's immediate family are multiplex, as they involve the ongoing exchange of a variety of emotional, material, and symbolic resources. In contrast, interacting with a ticket-taker at a theater entrance—handing over the ticket and saying "thank you" after being told "first door to the right"—is a uniplex tie because it involves a narrow symbolic exchange (a ticket in return for a greeting, admittance, and simple direction) and does not include other emotional, material, or symbolic content.

The collection of social ties that constitute any given person's network may be characterized by a set of abstract properties (see Turner and Maryanski 1991). The *size* of a network is simply the number of ties it contains. *Density* involves the number of ties relative to the number that could possibly exist within any fixed set of people. For any collection of $N$ individuals, the number of possible ties is given by the formula $N!/[2(N-2)!]$. Density is defined as the number of observed social ties among $N$ individuals divided by the value of this expression (where $N!$ indicates the combinatorial $N \times (N-1) \times (N-2) \times (N-3) \ldots \times 1$). When density equals 1.0, it means that every person knows every other person in the social network. Another word for density is *connectivity*, suggesting the degree to which people within any social group are linked to one another.

In contrast, *centrality* refers to the location of a specific actor in a social network, and it is measured as the share of all network members to which that person is connected. A person who knows 19 out of 20 people in a social network is more central than someone who knows just 5 of the 20 people. Finally, *transitivity* is the extent to which a social relationship within a network transfers to another person with whom one has not heretofore interacted. Even though one may never have met one's first cousin, one can expect to be treated with more consideration and acceptance by that cousin than by a randomly selected individual who is also unknown, for kinship is transitive. Certain obligations pass through one's relationship to his or her parents through their siblings to the children of their siblings (one's cousins).

Networks that are characterized by a high degree of density, connectivity, and transitivity are said to confer a high degree of *social closure*: Information about any single individual will be widely diffused throughout the network, and any change in his or her status will quickly be apprehended by all. For most of the time that humans have walked on earth, networks have been established and maintained through face-to-face interactions involving other people within a narrowly circumscribed locale. Although the resulting social networks were relatively small and did not extend very far in space or time, they were composed of multiplex, transitive ties arranged in configurations of high density, yielding a very high degree of social closure. Everyone repeatedly exchanged a variety of emotional, material, and symbolic resources with everyone else on an ongoing basis.

Although opportunities to interact with people who were unknown and personally unfamiliar were infrequent in preagrarian foraging societies, they nonetheless existed, yielding a basic distinction between personal and global networks. The global network is defined by the characteristic of "otherness." A *global network* is the set of people "out there" somewhere, occupying a larger but unknown social world of strangers who are never or rarely encountered because of their removal in space and time (Gamble 1999). Given the fact that cultivating and maintaining a social tie requires time, and that time is limited, the larger the population within any defined territory, the larger the number of strangers—there are simply too many people to interact with on a meaningful basis.

Thus, a characteristic feature of human beings is their cognitive ability to exclude other people categorically from membership in social groups and networks (Colson 1978), minimizing the exchange of emotional, material, or interpersonal relations to limit the intensity of interpersonal interactions and to keep the total within manageable limits. For example, when a person attends a sporting event with 50,000 other fans, he or she cannot possibly engage in multiplex social relations with everyone who is present at that particular point in time. Instead, one relegates everyone but one's companions to the category of "other fans" and interacts with those encountered in only the most superficial way. Human encounters with strangers are universally governed by a principle of exclusion that must be negotiated away socially for the interaction to proceed (Mauss 1967).

In contrast to the global network of unknown others is one's *personal network*, which has three components (Gamble 1999). The *intimate network* consists of multiplex ties characterized by the intense exchange of emotional resources, in addition to material and symbolic resources. An intimate network can only be maintained through ongoing face-to-face interactions over an extended period. Given this intensity of emotional investment, the size of intimate networks is quite limited. In his crosscultural study of Western societies, Milardo (1992) found that intimate networks for adults generally ranged in size from three to seven people with an average of around five. In foraging societies, most members of an intimate network are close kin, and even in the contemporary Western societies considered by Milardo, 50% of those in intimate networks were immediate family members.

A person's *effective network* consists of the social ties that are created and maintained to deal with the logistics of everyday life, the interpersonal connections that one uses to pursue instrumental goals associated with survival, pleasure, and the accumulation of emotional, material, or symbolic resources. Ties within an effective network often involve the intense exchange of material and symbolic resources; but compared with ties in an intimate network, emotional exchanges are less frequent and less intense. In his crosscultural survey, Milardo (1992) found that effective networks ranged from 6 to 34 people and averaged around 20, only 40% of whom were immediate kin.

Finally, a personal network includes an *extended network* of social ties to people who are known to the individual and who may be brought into his or her effective network if necessary. The extended network consists of distant kin, passing acquaintances, and "friends of friends"—what Granovetter (1974) calls "weak ties." The size of extended networks is difficult to estimate and varies considerably among people, depending on the degree of transitivity and the number of passive ties that have been accumulated. In contemporary societies, extended networks are thought to vary from around 100 to around 400 persons (Gamble 1999).

Across all cultures, the size, density, and composition of personal networks vary by sex and age. In general, as people grow older the number and range of social ties increase. The increase is particularly rapid at phases of the life cycle associated with mate selection, when individuals (and their parents) explore a wide range of ties in search of a partner and then acquire a whole new set of relatives through marriage. Moreover, because women in most cultures marry at younger ages than men, and because in pre-industrial societies they usually have a lower life expectancy as well, the size and density of female personal networks peak at an earlier age and display lower averages compared with those of men (Gamble 1999).

Throughout most of human history, people lived in small groups, participating in intimate networks of 3 to 7 people and interacting within effective networks of 20 to 30 people who hunted, gathered, or scavenged together to produce enough calories and nutrients to survive another day. The extended networks of early foragers generally numbered no more than a few hundred and were at times even smaller. This combination of small intimate networks, modest effective networks, numerically limited extended networks, and sporadic, infrequent contact with global networks constitutes the social world to which we are adapted as organisms.

Central to the process of social change have been technological and social innovations that relax two fundamental constraints on human interaction (Gamble 1999). The evolution of human societies from small groups of foragers to postindustrial urban agglomerations has involved (1) a release from spatial proximity as a necessary condition for the exchange of emotional, material, or symbolic resources, and (2) a release from temporal promixity, the requirement that actors interact simultaneously in real time to form and sustain a social tie. The "stretching" of social relations across time and space (Giddens 1984:35) has occurred most importantly through innovations in transportation and communication (Hawley 1950).

Although we may be adapted physically and psychologically for life in small social groups, human beings in the twenty-first century will increasingly find themselves living in large, dense, and diverse agglomerations of population. But no matter how big the community or how extensive its social organization, in daily life we are still driven to form the same social bonds as our forager ancestors were, engaging in face-to-face interactions with the people we encounter. The major difference is that people now are brought together by macro-level social structures operating within a built environment containing millions of people rather than by being born into a small group of people that occupies a particular ecological niche.

Nonetheless, whether one considers workmates meeting for gossip around the water cooler, playmates jostling on the school ground, urbanites gossiping on the front stoop, or suburbanites gathering around the barbeque, humans are driven to create and maintain the same microsocial networks as our homminid ancestors were. Human beings are not and have never been atomized individuals. They may or may not be fully rational actors (an issue addressed in Chapter Three), but they are always social actors embedded in networks of kinship, friendship, and acquaintance within which emotional, material, and symbolic resources are exchanged.

*The Macrosocial Cluster*

Until quite recently in human history, social change occurred mainly through the interaction of the environmental and microsocial clusters. Small bands of foragers evolved kinship systems, household structures, and social relations that enabled them to survive and reproduce within a particular ecological niche. Beyond a changeable band of interrelated households, they formed relatively few larger social aggregates, and those that did form tended to be short lived and seasonal. As a result, the size of human populations was small and most influences of the macrosocial cluster on societal evolution were through technology—the application of cultural knowledge to create symbolic and material tools to enable a more successful adaptation to the environment.

Although it was once thought that only humans were capable of inventing and using tools, their use has now been amply documented among our closest living relatives, the chimpanzees (Marks 2002; Rumbaugh and Washburn 2003). Chimps have been observed to fashion small branches to "fish" for ants, to employ medium-sized branches as digging sticks, and to wield larger ones as weapons; and they have been shown to deploy stones as instruments to break open nuts and fruit as well as to hurl as projectiles (Goodall 1986, 1999; Dunbar 1988; de Waal 1998). No doubt our earliest hominid ancestors likewise employed similar tools, which left no trace in the fossil or archeological record.

The earliest durable tools were crudely fashioned stone choppers that appeared around 2.5 million years ago and were followed about a million years later by more finely worked hand axes, cleavers, and knives that were symmetrical in shape (indicating a preconceived design). Then around 300,000 years ago the tool kit changed once again, taking the form of flint blades set into wood handles; but it wasn't until the emergence of Homo sapiens around 150,000 years ago that tool invention became regularized as a process of steady, cumulative innovation rather than one of sporadic, unpredictable change. Once the hominid line acquired the ability, through culture, to invent and deploy new tools, the macrosocial cluster was poised to assume a larger role driving the process of social change (through Pathways 3 and 5).

The invention of spear throwers and the bow and arrow between 50,000 and 100,000 years ago, for example, made possible changes in social organization that permitted the routinized hunting of large mammals (R. Klein 1999); likewise, the invention of nets, baskets, hooks, and boats permitted fuller exploitation of the marine environment (Johnson and Earle 2000). As a result, the size and density of populations rose and human beings migrated and spread out to occupy the entire globe. Rising population densities, in turn, stimulated technological change and innovation (Boserup 1981), and increasing population size made possible new forms of social differentiation and led to the emergence of novel forms of social organization beyond small bands of interrelated foraging families (Bogucki 1999).

The technological change that unleashed the first true revolution in human settlement was the invention of agriculture, which in concert with the domestication of animals led to the advent of the first permanent settlements in the hills of Anatolia, the Levant, and Mesopotamia around 10,000 years ago (Burenhult et al. 1993). Wherever agriculture and animal husbandry took root, permanently settled villages emerged and then slowly grew into larger towns. Sedentary life made possible new occupational specialization and social stratification and led to the creation of novel organizational structures to maximize, manage, and distribute the resulting surplus of food (Bogucki 1999; Sanderson 1999).

Once agriculture spread from the hills of Mesopotamia onto the fertile, well-watered plains between the Tigris and Euphrates rivers, the stage was set for the emergence of cities—large, dense, and heterogeneous agglomerations of people—around 8,000 years ago. Cities for the first time concentrated at a particular place and at a single point in time a sizeable population of people who did not have to produce food for themselves or their immediate relatives (Chant and Goodman 1999). Rather, they could devote their full attention to nonfood-producing occupations such as ruling, worshiping, soldiering, and manufacturing. More important, cities gave rise to a leisured class of people with the time to think, imagine, and invent, leading to the emergence of an accelerating and self-perpetuating cycle of technological and organizational change that, with fits and starts, continues to the present day.

Since the advent of urban civilization 10,000 years ago, the process of social change has been dominated more and more by mutually reinforcing interactions among elements within the macrosocial cluster and the growing influence of that cluster on elements in the other two clusters (through Pathways 3 and 5). Over the past thousand years, in particular, technological inventions have made possible population growth and forms of social organization that have served to accelerate the pace of social and technological change and to move societal evolution forward at an exponential pace, with significant effects and increasingly powerful consequences for both the environment and microsocial relations. Indeed, the scale and rapidity of macrosocial change may now be pushing the limits of human and environmental adaptability, bringing about new and potentially powerful effects via Pathways 2 and 6.

The framework summarized in Figure 1.1 provides a way of conceptualizing the process of societal evolution over the long run of human experience, which stretches 6 million years from the emergence of the first hominids to the present. At different points in time, elements in one of the three clusters—environmental, microsocial, and macrosocial—have played more or less important roles in propelling social change. But since the system feeds back on itself through multiple pathways, it is inherently unstable; consequently, dynamism has tended to shift over time from the environmental to the microsocial and, lately, to the macrosocial cluster. However, given that the impetus for social change has increasingly come to reside in the macrosocial cluster, the rate of change has accelerated markedly as shifts in technology, population, and social organization feed off one another in a self-reinforcing cycle.

## SOCIAL CHANGE IN EVOLUTIONARY PERSPECTIVE

The foregoing heuristic model, which I will apply to interpret the evolution of human society in the ensuing chapters, builds upon foundations laid by earlier generations of social scientists. Figures such as Childe (1951), Steward (1955), Duncan (1964), Carneiro (1970), Service (1962, 1975), Boserup (1990), Sanderson (1999), and Johnson and Earle (2000) have all recounted the roles played by population, social organization, environment, and technology in accounting for social change. Most prior attention, however, has focused on links between and among elements within the environmental and macrosocial clusters, with less attention paid to the microsocial cluster. Recent advances in cognitive neuroscience and social psychology, however, make the time ripe for a reintegration of microsocial relations into the panorama of social change and societal evolution. When combined with new data and theories from anthropology and sociology, recent advances offer a new window on the human condition and a clearer vision of prospects for our shared urban future.

# Chapter Two
# Foraging as a Way of Life

As organisms, human beings evolved within the context of social groups. Society thus serves as the interface between the individual and the physical environment. In many important ways, we are more adapted to life in small groups than to survival within any particular physical habitat. The natural forces that bind us together into cohesive communities are very old and certainly predate our much-vaunted cognitive capacities for language and rational thought, which could be called "johnny-come-latelies" in the grand sweep of human evolution. Emotional bonds linking hominids together within stable social structures existed long before human beings were able to undertake any rational consideration of the costs and benefits of sociality. If we are to comprehend our place in the contemporary post-modern, post-industrial landscape, we must return to our emotional roots in the class of primates known as hominids.

## Early Stages of Human Society

What is today recognized as human society emerged slowly over millions of years and proceeded in four basic phases that unfolded in geological time at an accelerating pace. Owing to the accumulation of genetic and cultural changes over time, each phase was shorter than its predecessor and was characterized by a well-defined material regime, a particular set of cognitive abilities, and particular forms of social life shared by members of relatively small, mobile communities. The oldest and longest phase in human evolution was that between the emergence of the first bipeds and the earliest concrete evidence of tool usage.

### *Pre-Habiline Society*

Elsewhere (Massey 2002) I have labeled this period Pre-Habiline because it predates the emergence of stone tools (the root *habilis* means "tool-maker"). Recent archeological discoveries have pushed the origins of the hominid line back to a point around 6 million years ago, when Ardepithecus ramidus and then Australopithecus africanus came down from trees to spend their days walking upright, thereby becoming able to exploit an emerging ecology of mixed forest and grassland (Wrangham 2001). Our earliest ancestors were quite small, averaging just 1.5 meters in height and maybe 70 kilograms in weight, but with a pronounced sexual dimorphism that left males 60% larger than females. Among primates, such a high degree of dimorphism is associated with a pattern of female out-marriage into a group composed of a dominant male plus subordinate males, consorting females, offspring, parents, and siblings (Dunbar 1988; Turner 2000). As such, their way of life was probably very similar to that of modern-day chimpanzees, which is organized around gathering, scavenging, and the occasional hunting of small prey (Goodall 1986, 1999; de Waal 1998).

There is no evidence that early australopithecines manufactured permanent tools; but like modern-day chimps, they could very well have modified perishable materials and wielded unworked stones for a variety of purposes. The teeth of the australopithecines were large, their jaws were adapted for crushing, and their guts were capacious, suggesting a diet centered on vegetable matter. Some have argued that the australopithecines came down from trees precisely in order to exploit new, ground-based food sources (protein-rich roots and tubers) that were becoming available on the expanding savannahs (Wrangham 2001).

Groups of early hominids, like modern chimps, were probably loosely structured socially (Rodseth et al. 1991; Maryanski and Turner 1992). Chimpanzee communities are held together by emotional bonds among individuals differentiated by sex, age, and rank in a dominance hierarchy. Within groups, strong ties exist between mothers and offspring, and these may persist even after the latter are grown, especially for male offspring; weaker ties exist among adult males; and ties among other community members are generally weak or absent. Females transfer out of the group at puberty, preventing the formation of strong matrilineal structures. As among today's great apes, social structure for our last common ancestor was likely fluid, "leaving individuals at the micro level to seek out their own supportive 'friendships' that reflect personal likes and dislikes"; this type of relationship creates an overall sense of community and integration at the group level (Turner 2000:9).

Emotional bonds of kinship and friendship among present-day chimpanzees are maintained by mutual grooming, whereas rank is established by threat displays backed up periodically by force. Social relations are complex, requiring each individual to recognize and form alliances with others. In order to survive socially, chimps must cultivate webs of influence and mutual obligation, form coalitions to defeat common adversaries, remember the personal attributes and past behaviors of others, and know of relationships among others (Goodall 1999; de Waal 1998; Byrne 2001). Studies and field observations show that chimpanzees are self-aware, able to infer the intentions of others, and fully capable of social deception and manipulation (Yerkes 1943; Gallup 1970, 1982; Goodall 1986, 1999; de Waal 1998). It is quite likely that australopithecines possessed similar capacities (Maryanski 1987, 1992, 1993).

Compared with modern-day chimps, however, early hominids lived in slightly larger groups. Whereas chimps roam in groups of up to 50 individuals, calculations by Dunbar (1996) suggest that australopithecines customarily lived in groups of up to 60 or 70 individuals. Like chimpanzees, therefore, the earliest hominid species must have possessed a well-developed social intelligence. The number of dyads among any $N$ individuals is given by the formula $(N^2 - N)/2$, which is graphed as a function of group size in Figure 2.1. Whereas chimps (at $N = 50$) must keep track of 1,225 dyadic relationships, australopithicines (at $N = 65$) had to manage 2,080, which required more cognitive ability (Dunbar 2001). As a result, the average cranial capacity of australopithecines, around 450 cc, is greater than that of chimps, which averages around 400 cc (Napier and Napier 1985; Wood 1992).

The increase in cranial capacity occurred through an expansion of the neocortex, the outermost layer of the brain, yielding a higher degree of encephalization (Jerison 1973; Passingham and Ettlinger 1974). Despite their keen social intelligence, however, there is little evidence that australopithecines pos-

**Figure 2.1**

**Number of Dyadic Relationships by Group Size**

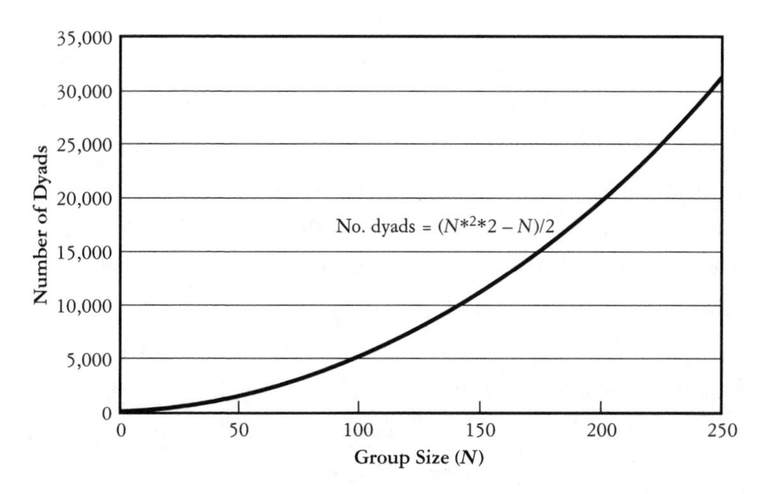


sessed much in the way of what we today would call "rationality." The frontal, temporal, and parietal lobes of the brain—the loci of abstract reasoning and language in humans—remained relatively undeveloped, and there is little evidence of any size asymmetry between the right and left hemispheres, a definitive characteristic of habitual tool manufacture and use. Expansion occurred mainly in portions of the cortex that dealt with sensory processing; such expansion probably involved a rewiring to enable greater cortical control of emotional expression through vocalization and facial display (Turner 1997, 2000).

Like modern chimps, the early australopithecines could probably solve simple practical problems and learn through observation and imitation, but their communication was restricted to vocalizations and gestures. Although modern chimps can be taught in the neighborhood of 150 to 200 symbols in the laboratory and can learn to string them together in sets of two or three (Snowdon 2001), they display no awareness of word order, and over millions of years they have never evolved symbolic language on their own (Lennenberg 1980). Chimps do not even engage in spontaneous pointing, a behavior displayed by the youngest human children (Bruner 1986).

Pre-Habiline cognition is associated with what Donald (1991) calls "episodic culture," in which perceptions and behaviors flow largely in the present moment. Individuals have memories of concrete past episodes, they can recall prior experiences and feelings, and they can perceive ongoing social situations; but they lack semantic memory and abstract reasoning. Pre-Habiline society and its episodic culture dominated human life for 3.5 million years. During all this time—around 175,000 generations—no stone tools were produced and hominid life was confined to a narrow habitat of savannah in eastern and southern Africa, yielding a population that numbered only in the tens of thousands, dispersed among a limited set of small foraging groups (Coale 1974). The essential features of Pre-Habiline society are summarized in the first column of Table 2.1.

*Oldawan Society*

The first true revolution in human affairs occurred with the appearance of stone tools about 2.5 million years ago and was associated with the appearance of a new genus of hominid. Homo habilis made crude stone artifacts that most of us today would not even recognize as tools unless we knew what to look for. Named for the East African gorge (Olduvai) where they were first discovered, Oldawan tools are pieces of rock that have been sharpened on one side by flaking to create crude choppers and

Table 2.1

Eras in the Evolution of Human Society

| | Pre-Habiline | Oldawan | Paleolithic | Neolithic |
|---|---|---|---|---|
| Beginning date | 6 million BP* | 2.5 million BP | 1.5 million BP | 50,000 BP |
| Duration | 3.5 million yrs. | 1 million yrs. | 1.5 million yrs. | 40,000 yrs. |
| Generations | 175,000 | 50,000 | 75,000 | 2,000 |
| Inhabitants | A. africanus | H. habilis | H. erectus | H. sapiens |
| Cranial capacity | 450 cc | 550 cc | 1,100 cc | 1,450 cc |
| Sustenance | Foraging | Foraging | Foraging | Foraging |
| Tools | Perishable | Crude stone | Refined stone | Flint & bronze |
| Kind of culture | Episodic | Episodic | Mimetic | Mythic |
| Settlement type | Mobile band | Butchering site | Base camp | Camp/hamlet |
| Community size (no. of individuals) | 65 | 75 | 140 | 155 |
| Human population | <50,000 | <100,000 | <1,000,000 | <6,000,000 |

*BP = before the present

scrapers. These simple tools are associated with the first evidence of patterned human living in the form of centralized butchering sites, which suggests a growing reliance on hunting over gathering and scavenging.

Although height did not change dramatically compared with the australopithecines, the weight of Homo habilis did increase as skeletons grew more robust and cranial capacity expanded to an average of around 550 cc (Stringer 1992), a 20% increase that is associated with an expansion of group size to 70 or 80 individuals (Dunbar 2001). Not only would the increase in group size require a greater cognitive capacity to monitor the increased number of interpersonal dyads (2,775 at $N = 75$), but it would also necessitate a concomitant increase in the amount of time spent grooming. Primates cultivate and maintain dyadic bonds through mutual grooming, which causes the release of a brain chemical known as oxytocin that promotes feelings of well-being, attachment, and attraction, leading to social cohesion (Keverne, Martensz, and Tuite 1989; LeDoux 2002).

Group size is limited by the amount of time individuals can afford to spend grooming rather than engaging in other essential behaviors such as sleeping, feeding, courting, and mating (Dunbar 2001). Across primate species, 20% seems to represent an upper threshold for time spent grooming. The group size characteristic of Homo habilis for the first time pushed grooming time well above this threshold, suggesting that other mechanisms must have come into play (Aielo and Dunbar 1993). Turner (2000) suggests these mechanisms involved a more complex communication of emotion to cement social bonds.

Beyond increased group size, the existence of stone tools, a larger brain, and more control over emotion, little else changed cognitively, culturally, or socially for hominids during the Oldawan period, which lasted around a million years or 50,000 generations. The total human population at the time still numbered in the tens of thousands, all in eastern or southern Africa, and there is no evidence of any use of language or expression of symbolic culture (see the characteristics of Oldawan culture summarized in the second column of Table 2.1). Hominid culture thus remained episodic, albeit with some increase in group size and social complexity, along with a concomitant expansion of cranial capacity to accommodate the greater demands on social intelligence.

*Paleolithic Society*

Somewhere around 1.5 million years ago, the appearance of another species and technology signaled the emergence of a new kind of society. The species was Homo erectus, and the technology was the Acheulean tool culture. The progression from habilis to erectus marked an abrupt and very important shift in human evolution (Donald 1991). Although individuals' upper heights changed relatively little, they became considerably more uniform (1.3 to 1.5 meters), and sexual dimorphism was reduced dramatically from a 60% male-female differential to one on the order of 15%—about the average for modern humans. Anatomically, full shoulder rotation disappeared, indicating a final, decisive break from arboreal life. Now there was no going back. Meanwhile, teeth and guts grew smaller, suggesting the increasing nutritional importance of meat. With the emergence of Homo erectus, one finds evidence for the first human use of fire (Brain 1983) and the apparent use of seasonal base camps as well (Donald 1991).

The sharp decrease in sexual dimorphism stemmed not from a reduction in the size of males, but from an increase in the size of females, thus raising the average height of hominids and reducing the variance. The increase in female size was necessary to accommodate the birth of new creatures with very large heads and sizeable brains, for the progression from Homo habilis to Homo erectus was accompanied by a remarkable doubling of cranial capacity into the range of 1,000 cc to 1,100 cc. The dome of the cranium rose, and the face flattened to accommodate expansion of the frontal, temporal, and parietal lobes of the brain.

Homo erectus also provides the first evidence of brain laterality—a differentiation in size between right and left brain hemispheres—which is associated with handedness and communication abilities (Donald 1991). Acheulean tools consist of symmetrically shaped, carefully worked hand axes, cleavers, and knives with sharper and more-effective cutting surfaces (Gamble 1999). Compared with the crude choppers of the Oldawan culture, the makers of this toolkit evinced considerable manual dexterity, which goes along with handedness. Chimpanzees, for example, do not exhibit strong laterality and are incapable of reliably flaking a rock even after intensive instruction and practice (Savage-Rumbaugh and Lewin 1994).

The decline in sexual dimorphism and the need to care for large-brained children who were helpless in infancy, vulnerable in childhood, and dependent through adolescence produced a radical change in human life cycle, social structure, and mating patterns (Ellison 2001; Bogin 2001). It was during this era that the human practice of pair bonding probably appeared, accompanied by a decline in inter-male conflict, the disappearance of rigid male dominance hierarchies, and a growing investment by fathers of time and resources in their mates and children (Lovejoy 1980). Male commitment to pair bonding was reinforced (though not guaranteed) by an entirely new reproductive biology in which females were continuously sexually receptive, breasts were enlarged and displayed, and the timing of estrus was hidden. The distinctively human and unprimate practice of copulating in private probably also emerged at this time.

The increase in brain size enabled another expansion in group size to 90–120 individuals, yielding somewhere in the neighborhood of 6,000 dyadic relationships ($N = 110$). Despite greater encephalization, however, evidence suggests that the intelligence of Homo erectus was still pre-linguistic. It was, however, quite different from the episodic intelligence that preceded it, for the basic cognitive function for Homo erectus was *mimesis*—imitation or mimicry—in which vocalizations, facial expressions, eye movements, body postures, and manual signs were used to communicate and to transmit emotion and simple information from being to being.

Even today, humans retain a remarkable ability and an expansive repertoire of gestures that enable them to communicate nonverbally (see Axtell 1998; Messing and Campbell 1999; De Jorio 2002). Using hand gestures, body language, and especially facial expressions, human beings are quite facile at nonverbal communication and can quickly and accurately convey emotional states and feelings to one another. The face constitutes the screen for the display of human emotions, and patterns of nonverbal facial expression recur across cultures and are interpreted similarly by humans in all societies, suggesting a "hard-wired" ability to read facially expressed emotions (Eibl-Eibesfeldt 1989; Goleman 1995; Ekman and Rosenberg 1997).

The emergence of gestural communication was accompanied by a significant increase in the range and complexity of the emotions expressed, as the cognitive bases for primary emotions such as fear, anger, disgust, happiness, and sadness were rewired and interconnected via the cortex to produce new and more complex sets of emotions conducive to social cohesion and solidarity (often called secondary emotions), leading to innovations such as shame, guilt, anticipation, love, and hope (Turner 2000). Learned physical abilities were also an essential adaptive resource and were passed from generation to generation by demonstration and imitation (Donald 1991).

Although mimetic culture remained concrete, visual, and episode-bound, it nevertheless brought about an increase in the sharing and accumulation of knowledge; this yielded a more stable social structure based on ritual and custom, which served to heighten the emotional content of social relationships and promote bonding (Turner 2000). Mimetic culture provided the new proto-humans with a powerful adaptive tool that enabled them to leave their ancestral homeland for the first time and survive in a wider variety of habitats. Around 1 million years ago, Homo erectus moved out of Africa and occupied the southern portions of Asia and Europe, bringing about the first significant growth of the human population (Coale 1974).

Late in the Paleolithic period, around 300,000 years ago, several new species of hominid arrived on the scene to compete with Homo erectus, which eventually disappeared. The new species were Homo heidelbergensis and their better-known cousins, Homo neanderthalensis, more widely known as the Neanderthals (Tattersall 1995, 1999). The latter approximated modern humans in height but were much heavier and more powerfully built, with thicker bones and a more robust musculature. The size of the cranium also expanded to reach volumes characteristic of our own species, although the physical organization of the brain remained distinct, with smaller and more constricted frontal lobes. Nonetheless, the increase in average cranial capacity to around 1,400 cc enabled group size to expand further, reaching 120–160 individuals, implying a need to manage some 9,730 separate dyadic relationships ($N = 140$; see Figure 2.1).

With groups this large, the maintenance of cohesion could not possibly have relied on mutual grooming, as servicing so many relationships would have required that around 40% of the group's entire time be spent in grooming, a percentage that is far too great to be feasible (Dunbar 2001). Culture, therefore, was clearly the central mechanism for creating and maintaining social cohesion. Nonetheless, both fossil and archeological evidence suggest that Neanderthal culture remained mimetic and that the species was nonverbal (Diamond 1992; Donald 1991). Specifically, their constricted frontal lobes and a skull flexure incapable of accommodating a modern vocal apparatus suggest that Neanderthals could not speak using fully formed words (Lieberman 1975, 1984).

The Neanderthals nonetheless evinced a more advanced material culture than their hominid predecessors, as indicated by the emergence of a new toolkit, the Mousterian, which consisted of flint or stone blades hafted onto wood or bone handles.

These represent the first instance of composite tools—those composed of at least three materials. This new toolkit yielded 10 times more cutting edge per kilo of raw material than the former Acheulean technology. With the Neanderthals, one also begins to observe stone hearths and postholes, indicating the first construction of permanent shelters (Mellars 1996). For the first time, beings in the human line had appropriated space and divided it up symbolically for social purposes, thereby coming to terms with temporality and territoriality in new ways. One also observes migration into the colder regions of northern Europe, where numerous bone middens indicate a heavy reliance on hunting. With the emergence of semi-permanent settlements of 120–160 persons, social structure began to expand beyond small bands differentiated by age and sex to encompass larger organizations based on extended kinship known as clans.

*Neolithic Society*

Recent compilations of genetic, archeological, and linguistic evidence all concur in suggesting that fully modern human beings emerged in eastern Africa somewhere between 200,000 and 100,000 years ago (Cavalli-Sforza, Menozzi, and Piazza 1994; Ruhlen 1994; Cavalli-Sforza and Cavalli-Sforza 1995; Relethford 2001; Klein and Edgar 2002). For convenience, I shall place the date of Homo sapiens' 'birth' at 150,000 years before the present (BP). From its African cradle, around 100,000 BP our species began to migrate outward to occupy the four corners of the earth, reaching Europe and Asia around 50,000 BP, Australia by 40,000 BP, the Arctic by 20,000 BP, the Americas by 10,000 BP, and most of the islands of Polynesia by 2,000 BP (Diamond 1997; Balter 2001; Gibbons 2001).

Demographers estimate that the prehistoric human population had grown to roughly 6 million persons by the time of the agricultural revolution around 10,000 years ago (Coale 1974; Livi-Bacci 1992; Landers 1992).

Whereas the australopithecines and habilines had remained in Africa for 5 million years without moving, and Homo erectus and the Neanderthals never expanded beyond southern Europe and Asia in over a million years, within the space of just 50,000 years the entire earth was successfully populated by Homo sapiens. Clearly, our species must have gained access to some remarkable new survival tools. In Homo sapiens the brain reached its final size, shape, and structure, with a full expansion of the frontal lobes that created the potential for a new and revolutionary kind of culture (Knight, Dunbar, and Power 1999; Watts 1999). The importance of the human brain as an adaptive organ is indicated by the fact that it constitutes 2% of body weight but uses 20% of the body's total energy (Donald 1991). Natural selection would never have favored such an energy sink unless it provided a powerful adaptive advantage.

Nonetheless, the appearance of anatomically modern human beings does not initially appear to have been accompanied by dramatic changes in culture. The crucial period of cultural change seems to have been around 50,000 years ago, an era that has variously been called "the great leap forward" (Diamond 1992), "the creative revolution" (Tattersall 1998), "the symbolic revolution" (Chase 1999), and the "creative explosion" (Pfeiffer 1982). From this point onward, technology began to undergo rapid changes that were disconnected from further modifications of brain size or anatomy. Whereas earlier technologies had prevailed for hundreds of thousands—even millions—of years and changed only with the arrival of a new species, after 50,000 BP material culture evolved rapidly and differentiated without any corresponding physical or genetic change.

With the emergence of Homo sapiens, human cognitive capacity had reached a state of dynamism whereby it could innovate and adapt ad infinitum with the neural biology it already possessed. The human brain is uniquely capable of changing itself chemically through experience to create, over a lifetime, novel synaptic structures and new neural pathways. These new circuits are passed on to succeeding generations not through heredity but through social learning; most remarkable, these socially inherited neural structures may themselves be modified by recipients in the next generation, who apply their own experiences and creative thinking to develop new concepts and categories (LeDoux 2002). This capacity to transmit information not only between people but across generations created new possibilities for the accumulation of knowledge.

In addition to hafted stone and wood tools characteristic of the Mousterian culture, the new cognitive abilities of Homo sapiens enabled humans to fashion a host of new and more delicate tools made from bone and antler, creating remarkably fine hooks, needles, awls, arrowheads, and harpoons. The earliest humans wove fibers into ropes and clothing, tanned hides for clothes and coverings, created jewelry and other forms of personal adornment, and built permanent shelters that included not only hearths but also lamps and kilns. They invented spear throwers and bows to facilitate effective hunting from a distance, thereby minimizing risks to personal safety. Eventually, human beings discovered how to smelt copper to produce sharper and more effective blades, and late in the Neolithic period they mastered the mixing of molten copper and tin to create a new and more durable alloy, thus ending the "stone age" to usher in the "bronze age" (Burenhult et al. 1993:103).

Perhaps not immediately, but sometime after the appearance of Homo sapiens, phonetic speech developed to give human beings a capacious verbal memory and new capacities for cognition and logical analysis (Gregory 1981). The development of language was made possible by important changes in the size, structure, and function of the brain. The expansion of an area located toward the bottom of the frontal lobes (Broca's area) permitted *phonology*, the making and controlling of sounds. The development of the temporal lobes (Wernicke's area) allowed *audition*, the ability to hear and differentiate sounds; and expansion of the parietal and frontal lobes permitted *conceptualization*, the ability to use and manipulate arbitrary sound symbols in meaningful ways—to think of words before uttering them and to organize them into larger and more abstract units of meaning. All these expanded brain functions were connected into a larger articulatory loop that functioned in a coordinated fashion to conceptualize, transmit, and process information (Panksepp 1998; Carter 1998).

Language emerged not to give humans a capacity for rational or abstract analysis per se—this was more of a byproduct. Rather, it evolved to enhance humans' *social intelligence* so as to get along more effectively in large groups (Dunbar 1996; Maryanski 1996). Language is the ultimate social arbiter for our species, enabling us to maintain interpersonal relationships through conversation, to monitor the social interactions of others through gossip, to reach collective decisions through discussion, and to enforce those decisions through the manipulation of pride, shame, and guilt. In Dunbar's (2001:181) words, "humans have bigger, more complexly organized groups than other species simply because we have a larger onboard computer (the neocortex) to allow us to do the calculations necessary to keep track of and manipulate the ever-changing world of social relationships in which we live."

As a means of maintaining social contact and monitoring interpersonal relationships, language is far more efficient than grooming for the simple reason that we can talk to and learn about more than one person at a time. The group size predicted for human beings from their cranial capacity is around 155 persons (see Figure 2.1). Comparing the group size of chimps to that of humans (55 to 155) suggests that whatever mechanism replaced grooming as a means of achieving group cohesion was about three times more efficient. Unobtrusive studies of conversations conducted across a variety of cultural and social settings reveal that human conversation groups naturally gravitate toward a configuration of one speaker and three listeners. Moreover, whereas chimps spend about 20% of their time grooming, humans spend around 20% of their time in social interaction, mostly in conversation (Dunbar 2001:190–91). Thus, language appears to have replaced grooming and built upon gesture as a means of ensuring social cohesion within large groups.

All human societies possess a spoken language, and all human beings are capable of learning any linguistic system. Indeed, as Chomsky (1975) and Pinker (1994) have suggested, human beings possess a "language instinct." Given appropriate exposure to linguistic stimuli in childhood, any person anywhere can learn any language with a minimal amount of effort and without formal instruction. Indeed, if people are deprived of a common language by circumstance, they quickly invent one, as demonstrated by the regular, patterned emergence of pidgins and creoles among divergent peoples undergoing initial contact (Sebba 1997) and by the recent innovation of an entirely new sign language by an abandoned, socially isolated group of deaf orphans in Nicaragua (Senghas 2003). In marked contrast, even after intensive training throughout childhood, chimpanzees cannot learn to speak any language with facility. Even though they can learn to recognize and manipulate up to 200 symbols, they cannot use them in grammatical fashion (Donald 1991; Diamond 1992).

Despite its evolution as an instrument of social intelligence, however, language also offered humans new possibilities for rational analysis. Through vocabulary, syntax, and grammar, languages create mental categories of perception for time, space, objects, and events in the real world. Languages inevitably build a conceptual model of the universe, permitting the invention of what Gregory (1981) calls "mind tools," categories of thought that facilitate other behavioral and mental operations. The emergence of language is thus associated with the emergence of a new kind of "mythic culture" in which humans developed symbolic metaphors to explain the universe and its operation (Donald 1991).

The appearance of musical instruments, rhythmic devices, lunar calendars, and various other symbolic artifacts in the millennia from 50,000 to 10,000 BP testifies to the growing importance of myth in society. Burial of the dead with ornaments indicates the importance of ritual, and interment along with utensils, food products, and jewelry indicates a belief in the afterlife (Donald 1991). The first symbolic art appears in the form of sculptures and cave paintings. Given the remote location of most cave art deep within the interior of almost inaccessible caverns, it obviously served some sort of symbolic, ceremonial purpose; it was not merely decorative (Tattersall 1998).

The emergence of mythic culture, for the first time in history, enabled humans to synthesize discrete, time-bound events and circumstances and to connect them into a single, coherent narrative account of the world. Mythic culture did not supplant episodic and mimetic culture, however. Rather, it was superimposed upon these earlier cultural forms and used to extend a pre-existing emotional infrastructure. Elaborate myths permeate daily life and, through verbal and nonverbal symbols, give meaning to everyday objects, circumstances, and events (Donald 1991). Myth constitutes a "symbolic web" that explains how people are supposed to behave, why cultural rules must be obeyed, and how they are to be enforced (Chase 1999). Deity myths, in particular, reflect a society's conceptualization of causality: where life comes from, what happens to people after death, and who or what controls events in the world (Campbell 1995).

Although possessing a capacity for rational thought, human beings took considerable time to develop fully the elements of rational cognition and logical culture. Indeed, the new cognitive apparatus created by words was more strongly connected to emotional centers of the brain through conditioning and learning that was reinforced by ritual, ceremony, and spirituality (Turner 2000). Foraging societies tend to classify people very simply according to age, gender, and kinship and have a symbolic structure based on opposites (good-evil, male-female, old-young, hot-cold, etc.). Their metaphoric narratives associate animal identities with those of humans, and action is infused emotionally through ritual (R. Collins 2004). The full flowering of cultural and social forms strongly connected to rational calculation required something that foraging peoples never achieved—a food surplus—and that only became possible with the domestication of plants and animals around 10,000 BP.

## The Foraging Spectrum

When European anthropologists first struck out to study and catalogue the world's so-called primitive peoples, they were searching for the lost way of life of our prehistoric ancestors. Because evolution was seen in cumulative, linear terms, the cultural meanings, technologies, and social structures uncovered in non-Western societies were assumed to be "survivals" from an earlier evolutionary stage and could therefore, in theory, be classified and placed along an ordered continuum from "primitive" to "civilized." In truth, the interpretations assigned by early Western anthropologists to the cultures they observed revealed more about their own obsessions and insecurities than they did about the people under study.

Beginning with a seminal conference on "Man the Hunter" held at the University of Chicago in 1966 (which could just as easily been called "Woman the Gatherer"), attention shifted from the search for ancient "survivals" to a consideration of how human beings went about adapting to an array of different natural environments using pre-agrarian, pre-industrial tools

(Lee and Devore 1968). Investigators soon realized that the sample of foraging peoples who had survived into the nineteenth century to be studied by Western anthropologists was not representative of all foraging peoples who had ever lived. Over the past 10,000 years, agriculturalists and then industrialists had confiscated most of the favorable habitats for their own purposes and had pushed hunter-gatherers into more difficult and marginal settings. Rather than being primitive relics from an earlier evolutionary stage, the basic technologies and simple social structures of foraging peoples were simply appropriate adaptations to the difficult and stingy environments to which they had been relegated.

As anthropologists began to pay greater attention to the diversity of cultures, technologies, and social forms exhibited by foragers across different habitats, their thinking coalesced under the banner of *behavioral ecology*, which explored the range of human adaptation to varying environmental conditions (Winterhalder and Smith 1981; Smith and Winterhalder 1992). Rather than looking for a single "hunter-gatherer lifestyle," anthropologists began focusing on the "foraging spectrum," a range of social and cultural adaptations to diverse ecological conditions (Kelly 1995). The range of observed human adaptations provides clues about the problems faced by our ancestors and the solutions they might have adopted to solve them in the roughly 140,000 years that elapsed between the emergence of Homo sapiens and the invention of agriculture.

The most systematic analysis of foraging as a cultural system and societal form is that of Kelly (1995), who assembled data for all foraging societies documented in the ethnographic literature (Table 2.2). Because different anthropologists docu-

Table 2.2

Average Variability and Range of Characteristics of Forager Societies Catalogued by Kelly (1995)

| Characteristic | *N* | Mean | Standard deviation | Minimum | Maximum |
|---|---|---|---|---|---|
| **Environmental** | | | | | |
| Biomass (g/m$^2$/yr) | 123 | 735.8 | 919.9 | 26 | 5,128 |
| Temperature (°C) | 123 | 13.7 | 3.8 | 8.5 | 24.9 |
| **Percentage of Diet from:** | | | | | |
| Hunting | 123 | 36.8 | 18.2 | 10 | 90 |
| Gathering | 123 | 32.4 | 21.0 | 0 | 85 |
| Fishing | 123 | 30.8 | 22.7 | 0 | 80 |
| **Hours per Day Spent:** | | | | | |
| Foraging (females) | 8 | 3.3 | 1.8 | 1.2 | 6.2 |
| Foraging (males) | 8 | 4.9 | 2.2 | 1.8 | 7.5 |
| Foraging (sex unspecified) | 7 | 7.1 | 3.8 | 3.5 | 13.7 |
| Working (sex unspecified) | 9 | 7.7 | 1.9 | 6.0 | 11.9 |
| **Geographic Mobility** | | | | | |
| Moves per year | 51 | 16.0 | 16.7 | 1 | 60 |
| Km traveled per year | 45 | 314 | 521 | 7 | 3,200 |
| Area of range (km$^2$) | 64 | 2,687 | 8,308 | 30 | 61,880 |
| **Demography** | | | | | |
| Sex ratio | 23 | 110 | 32.7 | 38 | 230 |
| Total fertility rate | 21 | 5.3 | 1.4 | 2.6 | 7.8 |
| Community size | 30 | 159 | 310 | 13 | 1,500 |
| Density | 120 | 33.8 | 55.4 | 0.2 | 281 |

Adapted from *The Foraging Spectrum: Diversity in Hunter-Gatherer Lifeways*, by Robert L. Kelly, 1995, Washington, DC: Smithsonian Institution Press, pp. 21, 67–69, 112–115, 206–208, 211, 222–226, 252, 263–264.

mented different characteristics in their published reports, the number of cases varies from trait to trait; but Table 2.2 draws upon these data to summarize the mean, standard deviation (variability), and the minimum and maximum (range) of selected characteristics exhibited by known foraging peoples.

As the top panel (Environmental Conditions) indicates, foragers occupy a variety of ecological niches characterized by different temperatures and patterns of vegetation, or biomass. One must bear in mind, once again, that these habitats constitute a subset of all those that were once occupied by foraging groups. Kelly (1995) measured temperature using composite index called "effective temperature" that takes into account seasonal variation between periods of cold and warmth. As can be seen, the ethnographic record contains information on foragers living in arctic climates with temperatures that go down to a seasonally weighted average of 8.5°C (47°F) as well as those dwelling in tropical climates with average temperatures of nearly 25°C (77°F). The overall average across the 123 forager groups Kelly considered was 13.7°C (56.7°F). The amount of vegetation—which Kelly (1995) measured in terms of grams of organic material available per square meter per year—ranged from 26 grams up to 5,128 grams and averaged nearly 736 grams. No other species has adapted successfully to life in such a range of distinct habitats.

Foraging peoples basically have three ways of meeting their daily needs for food: hunting, gathering (which includes scavenging meat killed by other predators or natural causes) and fishing. On average, the forager diet appears to be rather evenly divided among these methods of food acquisition, with average respective diet shares of 36.8%, 32.4%, and 30.8%; but these averages belie considerable diversity across groups, depending on local ecologies. Whereas all foragers rely to some extent on hunting (the observed range goes from 10% to 90% of diet), some groups consume no fish or foraged products. The range of reliance on fish goes from 0% to 80%, whereas reliance on gathering extends from 0% to 85%.

In general, foraging communities adopt whatever mix is most efficient in a given habitat—whatever combination of hunting, gathering, and fishing produces the most calories for the least effort (Smith and Winterhalder 1992). More vegetation and lower temperatures generally predict a greater reliance on hunting, whereas high temperatures and less vegetation predict more gathering; and whenever fish or other aquatic life are locally available in sufficient quantity, fishing expands to predict less reliance on either hunting or gathering (Kelly 1995).

Whereas early social scientists such as Thomas Hobbes viewed life among "primitive peoples" as "solitary, poor, nasty, brutish, and short," more recent investigations suggest that although the lives of foragers may have been short, their existence was hardly poor, nasty, or brutish. Indeed, in his analysis of hunter-gatherer subsistence patterns, entitled *Stone Age Economics*, Marshall Sahlins (1972) noted the remarkable lack of hard, sustained labor performed by hunter-gatherers, the slow pace of their lives, and the abundant leisure time they enjoyed. As a result, Sahlins labeled the foraging way of life as "the original affluent society," thereby making an ironic play on the then-popular conceptualization of postwar American society by John Kenneth Galbraith (1958).

Although there is clearly variation in the amount of work required in different ecological environments, on average

Sahlins's depiction appears to have been accurate. Although the number of ethnographic cases that have published reliable time budgets is rather small, on average adult females appear to spend 3.3 hours per day foraging or hunting, compared to 4.9 hours for males. In total, males and females together contribute only around 8 hours of daily labor to their sustenance, which compares quite favorably to the extended workday now commonly faced by contemporary working couples (Hochschild 2001, 2003).

Habitat also conditions patterns of geographic mobility. Although foraging communities move, on average, 16 times per year over an average distance of 314 km with a range of 2,687 $km^2$, these measures of central tendency once again obscure considerable diversity across groups. Some foraging peoples do not move very much at all (once per year), travel little (a total of just 7 km), and confine themselves to a narrow geographic range (just 30 $km^2$). In contrast, others move frequently (up to 60 times per year) over substantial distances (up to 3,200 km) within huge areas (a maximum of 61,880 $km^2$).

As one might expect, variations in the size of a foraging people's range and mobility are predicted by the kind of environment they inhabit and the food procurement strategy used within it. The first column of Table 2.3 estimates a simple statistical model (using ordinary least squares regression) to predict the number of moves made by foragers using independent variables of environment and food source. The numbers in the table are coefficients for an equation linking number of moves to unit changes in the variables. In general, the larger the coefficient, the greater the effect; the size of the apparent effect is indicated by sets of asterisks. No asterisk means that the effect

Table 2.3

Relationship of Food Procurement Strategies and Environmental Characteristics to Selected Mobility and Demographic Outcomes

| Predictor variable | Number of moves | Area of range ($km^2$) | Population density |
|---|---|---|---|
| **Environment** | | | |
| Biomass | 0.01** | -0.91 | 0.02* |
| Temperature | −3.92*** | −108.45 | −4.44 |
| **Food Source** | | | |
| % Hunting | 0.09 | 320.45** | −1.38*** |
| % Fishing | −0.47** | −0.79 | −0.45 |
| **Intercept** | 72.94*** | −4,328.26 | 141.59 |
| **$R^2$ (adjusted)** | 0.36*** | 0.24 | 0.11 |
| **N of Cases** | 32 | 38 | 99 |

*Note.* *$p < .10$ **$p < .05$ ***$p < .01$

is not statistically significant (it has no effect greater than one would expect from chance); one asterisk means that the effect is unlikely to have occurred by chance ($p < .10$), two means that it is very unlikely to have occurred by chance ($p < .05$); and three means that it is extremely unlikely to have occurred by chance ($p < .01$).

As is evident, the greater the amount of biomass and the lower the temperature, the fewer the moves made by a foraging group within any given year (see the significant negative coefficients). In addition, communities that derive large shares of their nourishment from fishing are particularly unlikely to move. In contrast, what predicts the area of a group's entire range is the degree to which it relies on hunting. For each additional percentage point that hunting accounts for in a people's diet, the area of the range increases by 320 $km^2$.

Going back to the bottom panel (Demography) of Table 2.2, one glimpses a snapshot of the demography of foraging societies. The average community size was 159 persons, with a sex ratio of 110 males to 100 females and a total fertility rate of 5.3 children per woman, meaning that the average woman gave birth to 5.3 children during her reproductive years. The resulting family size of around 7 persons lies within the size range from intimate networks mentioned above.

Once again, however, there is significant variation underlying these averages, and once more this variation can be related to the specifics of habitat and food source. Unfortunately, the number of documented cases is too small to produce statistically reliable estimates of the influence of these factors on sex ratio, community size, or fertility. But the third column of Table 2.3 shows the effect of habitat and food procurement method on population density, which is more widely catalogued in the ethnographic record. In general, habitats with more vegetation are associated with higher densities, whereas a reliance on hunting predicts much lower population densities.

In general, the largest populations and highest densities are observed within environments that combine a sizeable land-based biomass with an abundance of aquatic resources, as among the indigenous peoples of the northwestern coast of North America. In terms of the size and scale of non-agrarian societies, these foragers probably lie close to the ecological limits on foraging as a way of life. Among the Nootka Indians of Vancouver Island, for example, communities of 1,500 persons and densities of 77 persons per $km^2$ were documented. This group derived 60% of its diet from fishing, 20% from hunting, and 20% from gathering, permitting it a rather sedentary lifestyle within large settlements (Hayden 1981).

Although fertility rates are likewise variable, it is once again not possible with available cases to use statistical tools to link this variation reliably to environmental conditions or food-gathering strategies. Observed fertility rates range from 2.6 to 7.8 children per woman. This variation is "natural" in the sense that it does not stem from conscious efforts to influence the number or timing of births (Henry 1972). Rather, it reflects cultural variation in breast feeding, post-partum sexual customs, and the social regulation of sex and marriage (Meehan and White 1990; Kelly 1995). Cultures that normatively mandate extended and intense breast feeding after birth, promote marriage at later ages, prohibit the early resumption of sexual relations after childbirth, and discourage sex outside of socially recognized marriages are characterized by lower rates of fertility. Fertility rates are also depressed by poor nutrition during periods of food scarcity; the number of infants and children is also affected by infanticide, usually targeted to females (Howell 1979).

It is impossible to determine the rate of growth experienced by a human population without knowing both its mortality and fertility or knowing its population at two points in time. Unfortunately, Kelly (1995) provided little information on mortality and life expectancy among the foraging peoples he catalogued, and for this facet of demography I turn to the analysis of Pennington (2001). Among the 17 ethnographic cases she surveyed, life expectancy at birth ranged from 22 to 53 years and averaged around 35 or 36 years. Infant mortality rates were quite high, with an average of around one fifth of all births dying before age 1 and one third expiring before age 15.

For most of human prehistory, rates of population growth were only slightly above zero and the number of human beings expanded quite slowly. As Table 2.1 shows, during the 1.5 million years that separated the Paleolithic from the Neolithic periods, the human population grew from around 1 million to around 6 million persons, for an annual growth rate of one ten thousandth of 1% (0.00001%). With a life expectancy of 35 years, each woman must bear at least three children in her lifetime just to prevent population decline (to make up for the one third who die before reaching reproductive age).

Figure 2.2 shows the demographic structure that would result from a life expectancy of 35 years (the average reported by Pennington 2001) and a net reproduction rate of 1.07 (meaning that women in the population would produce an average of 1.07 daughters who survive to the midpoint of reproductive age). The resulting population pyramid depicts the age and sex structure that would result if mortality and fertility were held at these levels indefinitely, which would ultimately yield a stable population growing at just 0.2% per year. The figure shows the age-sex pyramid for a population of 159 people, the average community size among the cases studied by Kelly (1995). It thus summarizes the average social world experienced by our ancestors for more than 99% of human existence. It is the world for which we are ultimately adapted as biological organisms.

**Figure 2.2**

**Population Pyramid for a Typical Forager Community**

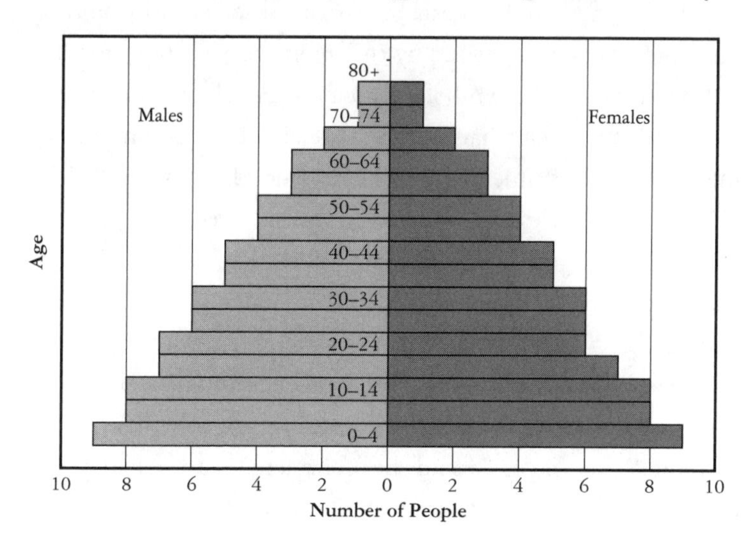


The distinguishing features of this demographic structure are its wide base and rapid tapering with rising age, yielding the prototypical pyramidal shape. Parents could expect to lose one fifth of their children to infectious disease by age 1, so death and the resulting sense of loss would have been a common experience among our foraging ancestors. Children who made it to their second year of life could expect to see about 19% of their peers die before puberty, so children too would know the pain of losing a close friend or relative. Within his or her foraging group, each child age 5 to 9 would have around 15 or 16 age-peers to play with, 2 or 3 of whom would probably die before reaching age 15. The total number of children below age 15 at any point in time would be around 50, and they would be supervised by some 64 adults of prime working age (20–49), assisted by another 30 people age 50 or over.

In such a society, everyone would know everyone else intimately on a face-to-face basis. Virtually all social ties would be multiplex and characterized by the intensive exchange of material, emotional, and symbolic resources. People would acquire an abundance of first-hand knowledge about other community members' temperaments, their likes and dislikes, and their skills and abilities in different domains. People would be closely related genetically to a large portion of the members of their local group, which would include one's parents, uncles, siblings, and assorted cousins. Consanguinity would be complete were it not for the fact that forager bands typically come together seasonally for ritual celebrations; during these larger meetings, marriages would be contracted and females exchanged across foraging groups. The most typical pattern in human societies is for the woman to join her husband's band (Kelly 1995).

Foraging societies of this size are generally characterized by a lack of hierarchy and interpersonal differentiation. Relations among people are egalitarian, and the division of labor is primarily along the lines of age and sex. Beyond a certain age, all able-bodied adults are expected to help produce food for the group by hunting, fishing, or gathering. Although women tend to specialize more in gathering and men in hunting, this gendered division of labor is not rigid; women opportunistically hunt small game while men frequently gather and scavenge. In habitats containing large mammals, however, big-game hunting is typically the province of men, and the longer men remain away on hunting expeditions, the more pronounced the group's pattern of gender stratification becomes (Sanday 1981).

Within foraging societies food is virtually always shared, although not always equally and not always willingly. Despite the lack of formal hierarchy, however, greater prestige does accrue to persons who contribute more to the common food supply, which in practice means that the greatest amounts of prestige accrue to males who hunt large game. In addition to the incentives for men to share meat in return for greater prestige (not to mention access to sex), children are taught by reward, punishment, and example from the earliest ages that hoarding is shameful and selfishness is dishonorable. Within foraging societies everyone pays close attention to who takes from whom and who contributes to the group's resources; foraging cultures characteristically employ leveling devices such as humor, ridicule, and ostracism to force compliance with collective behaviors and sentiments (Kelly 1995; Gamble 1999). People are always on the lookout for "free riders" who take but do not contribute and are highly sensitive to implicit notions of "fairness" (Cosmides and Tooby 1992).

Even though the advent of a spoken language offered foraging peoples great advantages in conceptualizing, organizing, and manipulating their social and physical environments, there were distinct limits to the total amount of knowledge that they could accumulate and pass on to successive generations, for all information had to be stored in human memory and passed on orally. Given high rates of mortality and small numbers, knowledge was constantly at risk of being eradicated from collective memory. After careful instruction and inculcation into the group's mythic culture over a period of years, a young person might die in his or her twenties before being able to pass anything on to his or her own children.

Because knowledge and experience accumulate over a lifetime, old people constitute a particularly valuable and scarce resource among hunter-gatherers, and for this reason they are typically accorded considerable influence and prestige in community affairs. In the population graphed in Figure 2.2, one can observe just eight people over the age of 65, constituting just 5% of the population; and none of these people are expected to reach age 80.

## Human Sociality in Envolutionary Perspective

Human beings were a long time in the making. The human story began around 6 million years ago with the divergence of the hominid line from that of the great apes, and it culminated with the emergence of modern Homo sapiens around 150,000 BP. Both events occurred in Africa, but within a very short time after Homo sapiens appeared, human beings left Africa and migrated outward to populate the remotest corners of earth, with the sole exception of Antarctica. Throughout the long period of human evolution, our ancestors lived in small social groups that gradually increased in size as cranial capacity grew to accommodate the expanded social intelligence that was required to keep track of a multiplying set of social relationships.

Most of the early brain expansion occurred in areas of the cerebral cortex connected with dexterity, hand-eye coordination, and emotion. The last region of the brain to expand was the prefrontal cortex, the frontmost part of the brain that is associated with logical reasoning and forward planning. Reflecting this evolutionary history, neurons in the human prefrontal cortex are the last to myelinate (i.e., to be covered with a layer of myelin that enables synaptic transmissions to travel efficiently and rapidly), a maturation process that is not complete until around age 20 or 21 (Restak 2001; LeDoux 2002).

During most of the time that hominids were evolving into modern human beings—some 300,000 generations—social communities were small and mobile, containing no more than 150 people whose most permanent settlement was a seasonal base camp. Only with the appearance of the Neanderthals around 300,000 years ago do the first signs of real permanence appear in the form of hearths, postholes, and burial sites. This foraging way of life largely continued for a long time after the appearance of Homo sapiens. Although the size of communities and the density of populations varied according to ecological circumstances, the average size among forager communities documented by anthropologists in recent historical times is around 159 individuals, with a range of 13 to 1,500; but in most habitats, mathematical models suggest that the optimal foraging party historically was around 25 to 30 people (Smith 1981).

The social world of our ancestors was one of intense intimacy based on kinship and large amounts of first-hand knowledge acquired through continuous, extended face-to-face encounters. People would meet very few strangers in their lifetime, and those that they did encounter would likely speak the same language and be "known" indirectly through some prior relationship with a member of one's own band or community or by virtue of extended kinship or a fictive kin relation. For human beings, microsocial networks constituted the principal adaptive interface between the individual and the physical environment. This world of the small group is the real environment to which we are ultimately adapted as organisms and which ultimately accounts for our "human nature."

# Chapter Three
# Human Nature and Social Organization

Western social thought has fought a long and bitter struggle against the idea of "human nature." Generations of philosophers, theologians, moralists, and, more recently, social scientists have opposed the idea that human beings possess a set of innate, genetically determined, hard-wired proclivities that condition the thoughts we have, the actions we take, and the social structures we build. From biblical times onward—through the Renaissance, the Enlightenment, the Protestant Reformation, and the various ideologies of modernism—we have told ourselves that we are endowed with "free will" and that by using our rational faculties we can "rise above" nature (Pinker 2002; Konner 2002).

For a variety of reasons we cling to the belief that at birth every human being is a "blank slate" without innate tendencies and inherited potentialities. The denial of human nature is rooted in deeply held beliefs about equality and human perfectability. We seem to fear that if we admit that we are biological organisms with innate physiological, psychological, and social traits and characteristics, then we condemn ourselves to a long slide down a slippery slope toward nihilistic social Darwinism.

Nothing could be further from the truth. Not only are these fears unfounded, but the persistent denial of human nature is increasingly untenable in light of accumulating empirical evidence. Ongoing studies in ethology (Eibl-Eibesfeldt 1989), genetics (Cavalli-Sforza and Cavalli-Sforza 1995), cognitive neuroscience (LeDoux 2002), linguistics (Ruhlen 1994), anthropology (Roughley 2000), and psychology (Barrett, Dunbar, and Lycett 2002) all point to the existence of a core set of human characteristics and proclivities that are deeply rooted in our physiology—and particularly in our neurophysiology. Given our common descent from a single "mitochondrial Eve" some 100,000 to 200,000 years ago, it should come as no surprise that a survey of the ethnographic literature yields a list of hundreds of "human universals"—behaviors, ideas, gestures, and social structures that are found across all human cultures (Brown 1991, 2000).

Many theoretical models in social science begin by assuming that human beings are rational, forward-looking, utility-maximizing agents. Although this assumption may enable social scientists to build sophisticated mathematical models of human behavior and social structure, it does not necessarily yield insight into the human condition. Increasingly, social scientists do not need to *assume* anything about human nature, for advances in neuroscience, molecular biology, and other fields now offer definitive *knowledge* about who we are and how we are cognitively wired. It is better, scientifically, to build theories on concrete premises that accurately reflect the reality of who we are than on the chimera of what we imagine ourselves to be. In coming to terms with human nature, the place to begin is with a clear understanding of the structure and organization of the human brain.

## THE BRAIN AND HUMAN COGNITION

As William Faulkner once noted, "The past is never dead. It's not even past" *(Requiem for a Nun*, Act 1, Scene 1). This observation certainly applies to the human brain. Our neural anatomy evolved over millions of years as a changing mixture of emotionality and rationality. As Chapter Two indicated, emotionality preceded rationality in the evolutionary sequence. As rationality developed, it did not replace emotionality as a basis for human action. Rather, the rational abilities of human beings were gradually added to pre-existing and simultaneously developing emotional capacities. Indeed, the neural anatomy essential for full rationality—the prefrontal cortex—is a very recent innovation, emerging only in the last 150,000 years of a 6-million-year existence, representing just 2.5% of humanity's total time on earth. To the extent that we possess rational cognition, therefore, it rests on a pre-existing emotional base that strongly conditions the thoughts we have, colors the actions we undertake, and infuses the social structures we create.

This evolutionary history is reflected in the basic organization of the human brain, which is summarized in Figure 3.1. Natural selection is always conservative: It does not build new features from scratch but acts upon structures and functions already in existence. As a result, human beings have come to possess what MacLean (1973, 1990) has called a "triune brain": three different layers of neural anatomy laid down on top of one another during different phases of evolution. The oldest and deepest layer consists of the *brain stem* and the *cerebellum*; it controls autonomic functions such as heartbeat, sleeping, and breathing, as well as instinctive behaviors such as the human sucking reflex. Known as the reptilian brain, it closely resembles the neural structure and organization found in reptiles today—and presumably in the past.

**Figure 3.1**

**Triune Structure of the Human Brain**

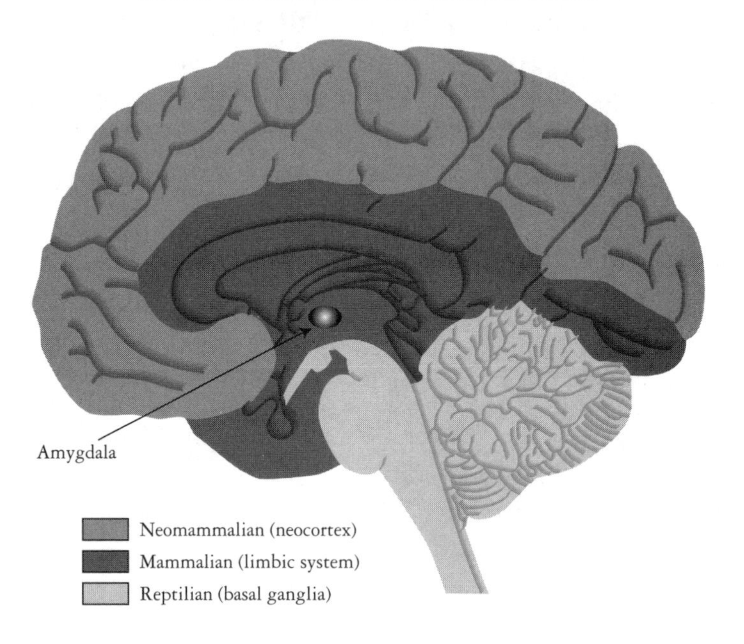


The next layer is the mammalian brain (Panksepp 1998). It surrounds the reptilian brain and consists of a set of neural structures collectively known as the limbic system. The most important organ in this system is the *amygdala*, which is crucial in registering and processing incoming emotional stimuli and in laying down emotional memories. Other limbic organs include the *thalamus*, which receives stimuli and relays them to other parts of the brain; the *hypothalamus*, which works with the pituitary gland to keep the body regulated and attuned to its environment; the *hippocampus*, which is responsible for laying down memory; and a surrounding layer of tissue known as the *cingulate cortex*. These cerebral organs work together, mostly subconsciously, to coordinate inputs from the senses and to generate subjective feelings and emotional states to influence both cognition and behavior (see Turner 1999, 2000, for a detailed account of the neurobiology of emotion).

The most recent addition to the brain is the neocortex, also known as the neomammalian brain (Panksepp 1998). It consists of an outer layer of gray matter mostly given over to the conscious processing of sensory stimuli. The neocortex has four basic sectors replicated symmetrically across two hemispheres of the brain. At the back, the *occipital lobes* do visual processing. Along the top and sides, the *parietal lobes* focus on movement, orientation, and coordination. Behind the ears, the *temporal lobes* deal with sound and vocalization; the lower part of the *frontal lobes* are devoted to taste and smell.

This pattern of organization is common to the brains of all mammals, although different lobes may be more or less developed in different species. Dogs, for example, have a better sense of smell than humans, and consequently the smell portion of their neocortex is more developed. The feature of brain anatomy separating humans from other mammals is the relative size of the prefrontal cortex—essentially the upper part of the frontal lobes. This is the portion of the brain that mushroomed so spectacularly over the course of hominid evolution, to the point where the prefrontal region now constitutes 28% of the entire cerebral cortex, 40% more than in our first hominid ancestors (Carter 1998).

The prefrontal region is the only region of the neocortex free from the demands of sensory processing, and as such it is the locus for abstract thinking, conceptualizing, and planning. This section of the brain is most clearly associated with human consciousness and volition, the place where we process and analyze information about the world and make plans for the future, which are then transmitted downward to the limbic system and basal ganglia along well-developed neural pathways for conversion into action. If the prefrontal lobes are damaged, human beings are unable to plan, to motivate themselves, or to recognize and act upon emotions (Goleman 1995; LeDoux 1996).

At the same time, however, if the underlying limbic system is compromised (e.g., through injury or surgery), then our much-esteemed rational faculties are fairly useless, for literally we cannot know what we want. A person whose amygdala has been damaged, for example, cannot learn to play simple card games, because winning feels exactly like losing (Konner 2002). Feelings that well up from the limbic system literally tell us what we want, what constitutes our subjective "utility"; then and only then can the rational capabilities embodied in the prefrontal cortex go about maximizing it through planning and action (Damasio 1994, 1999; Smith and Franks 1999). Indeed, "brains think with and through emotions" (Konner 2002:143).

Leaving aside the reptilian brain and its largely autonomic functions, evolution has bequeathed us two dynamic, interactive brains: one largely unconscious and emotional and located in the limbic system, and the other largely conscious and rational and centered in the outer cortex, especially the prefrontal region. These two neural systems are interconnected, but they operate in parallel to yield two different systems of perception and memory. Although neural pathways between the emotional and the rational brain carry information in both directions, the number of neural connections running from the limbic system to the cortex is far greater than the number connecting the cortex to the limbic system (LeDoux 1996; Carter 1998; Panksepp 1998).

As a result of this neural architecture, not only do unconscious emotional feelings exist independently of rational appraisals, but given the asymmetry in neural connections between the limbic system and the neocortex, it is much more likely that emotional impulses will dominate rational cognition than vice versa (Goleman 1995). To a great and unappreciated extent, therefore, our rational judgments about people and events reflect the influence of emotions that are stored unconsciously in the limbic system and transmitted to the cerebral cortex. In the words of Konner (2002:142), "the brain is a makeshift, inelegant, evolutionary pastiche. It is surely a parallel processor, but its structure of side-by-side or nested elements preserves ancient and outmoded chucks of circuitry forced to work in tandem with shiny, superfast new ones."

### *Emotional Cognition*

The emotional brain not only precedes the rational brain in evolutionary time, but it also precedes it in order of perception. Research in neuroscience shows that stimuli from the external world are perceived, evaluated, and acted upon by the emotional brain *before* the rational brain has received and processed the same information (LeDoux 1996). By the time the rational brain receives incoming sensory stimuli about an event, person, or object in the real world, the emotional brain usually has already swung into action and showered the neocortex with emotional messages that condition its logical calculations (Zajonc 1998).

Figure 3.2 presents a simplified schematic diagram illustrating how incoming stimuli are processed by the human brain. Sensory perceptions enter the brain and go to the thalamus, where the signal is dispatched to rational (sensory cortex) and emotional (amygdala) centers in the brain, which are connected to each other. But the timing of the neural signal's arrival in the emotional and rational brains is different, so that the former is activated first. The functioning of the two brains can be illustrated with a vignette.

**Figure 3.2**

**Schematic Representation of the Cognitive Processing of Sensory Stimuli**

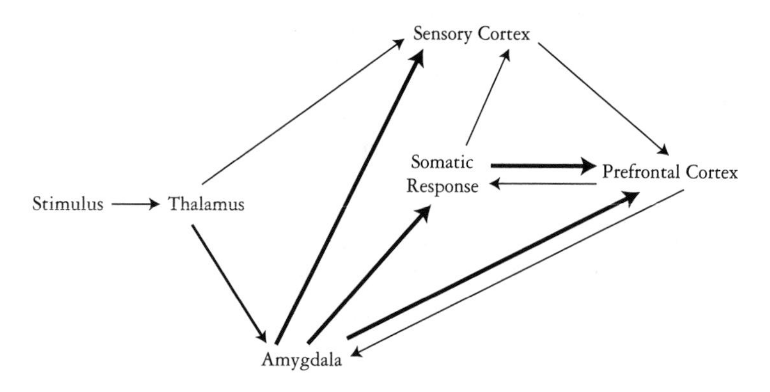

Imagine you are walking in a crosswalk and suddenly a car runs a red light and bears down upon you. The stimuli enter your eyes and ears. The perceptions travel along the optic and auditory nerves to the thalamus, which sends the signal in two directions. One is the "high road" to the neocortex: first to the appropriate sensory processing area, and then to the prefrontal cortex for rational consideration. There your rational brain will tell you that if you don't move quickly you will be run over by the car, resulting in serious injury or death, whereupon your frontal cortex issues instructions to motor areas in the parietal lobes to jump out of the way; the message is relayed down the brain stem to the outlying nerves, which cause your muscles to contract in such a way that you do indeed jump out of the way.

This vignette is consistent with a model of rational choice. Your brain made a quick cost-benefit calculation and decided it was worth the expenditure of energy to jump out of the way to avoid being run over by the car. Given what we now know about how the brain works, however, this account of human action is completely incorrect (Goleman 1995; LeDoux 1996; Panskepp 1998; Smith and Franks 1999), for by the time the rational brain has received the information about the oncoming threat, the emotional brain has already spurred your body into action and you will have begun to jump out of the way. Your heart will be pounding, your pulse will have quickened, and your breathing will have accelerated. If you later try to explain your behavior, you may say it all happened so fast that you acted "without thinking."

But the action was indeed a result of thinking; it was just unconscious thinking undertaken in the limbic system. At the same time that the thalamus sent the visual and auditory information to the cortex for high-order processing, it also dispatched it along a "low road" to the amygdala for what neuroscientist Joseph LeDoux (1996) calls "quick and dirty" processing. In contrast to the high road through the cortex, this lower route is much shorter, less complex, and consequently much faster. The amygdala immediately recognized the threat to survival posed by the oncoming car and sent a message to the hypothalamus to spur the body into immediate action in the form of an *allostatic response* (McEwan and Lasley 2002).

The response began when the hypothalamus sent a signal via neurons that connect it directly to the adrenal glands, which responded by releasing adrenaline into the bloodstream. Given this direct neural connection, the process is nearly instantaneous. The function of adrenaline is to prepare a person for action, either aggressive or evasive: It accelerates the heart, constricts blood vessels to the skin, expands the flow of blood to internal organs, and dilates bronchial tubes to increase the supply of oxygen. It also triggers the release of fibrinogen into the blood to facilitate clotting, and it mobilizes the body to release glucose and fatty acids from glycogen and stored fats, thereby providing ready sources of energy. Finally, it signals the brain to produce endorphins, the body's natural painkillers, thereby enabling the continuation of action despite potentially painful injuries.

At the same time that it sends these neural signals to the adrenals, the hypothalamus simultaneously secretes corticotropin-releasing factor into a special set of blood vessels that connect it to the pituitary gland. The pituitary then releases adrenocorticotropic hormone, which travels through the bloodstream to the adrenal glands, which then secrete cortisol into the blood. This hypothalamic-pituitary-adrenal (HPA) axis takes longer to operate than the adrenaline-release axis because it occurs via the bloodstream rather than through a direct neural connection.

The purpose of cortisol is to replace energy stores depleted by adrenaline. Cortisol accomplishes this replenishment in several ways: by converting food into glycogen and fat, by promoting the conversion of muscle protein to fat, and by blocking insulin from taking up blood glucose (leaving more for the body to use). Cortisol also causes a loss of minerals from bones and brings about a change in the texture of white blood cells, making them stickier so that they attach more readily to vessel walls and body tissue.

The allostatic response is nature's way of maximizing an organism's resources to meet an immediate, short-term threat. Long-term functions such as building and maintaining muscle, bone, and brain cells are temporarily sacrificed to put more energy into the bloodstream for evasive or aggressive action to ensure survival. It is an ancient mechanism that has been present in mammals for at least 400 million years; it has such a high survival value because it allows animals to escape or meet danger. After the threat has passed, an autonomic shutoff process takes over to return the organism to stability. This entire process occurs rapidly and unconsciously and is basically the same in rats and humans.

Laboratory studies indicate that information reaches the amygdala about a quarter of a second before it reaches the prefrontal cortex. Thus, the emotional brain perceives the danger and acts before the rational brain "knows" what is happening.

In the present case, evasive action actually derived from the workings of the older mammalian brain rather than the newer, more rational, but much slower neomammalian brain. If your frontal cortex were severed from the rest of your brain, thereby disabling your rational faculties, you would still jump out of the way.

In explaining human behavior it is thus crucial to distinguish between rationality and rationalization. In the previous vignette, a theoretical account that explains the act of jumping out of the way as the result of a rational cost-benefit decision is incorrect. This explanation is a rationalization of behavior whose trajectory had already been determined in the emotional brain. The limbic system, not the prefrontal cortex, was the locus of action. An innate feature of the rational brain, however, is to rationalize human behaviors. Even though the behavior in question stemmed from prerational cognition, we feel compelled to tell ourselves a logical story about what happened (Gazzaniga 1992).

The power of rationalization has been demonstrated by an experiment in which women were presented with a series of nylon stockings and asked to select the pair they liked best (Nisbett and Wilson 1977). When asked why they had made their decision, all subjects provided a lucid account referring to differences in quality, texture, color, size, workmanship, or style, even though the stockings were in fact identical. According to one neuroanatomist, "we like to think of . . . action as the result of a rational decision, but it is really just the fulfillment of an impulse" (Carter 1998:41). To an unappreciated degree, the prefrontal cortex helps us to maintain the illusion of agency and "free will" (Wegner 2002).

Not only does the emotional brain offer human beings a second, parallel system of perception and information processing, but it also provides a second system of memory in which emotional states and feelings are recorded independently of what is consciously stored in the neocortex (LeDoux 1996; Carter 1998). The fact that unconscious emotional memory exists is illustrated by the case of a woman who had lost all ability to create self-conscious memories as a result of brain damage. Every time her doctor saw her, he had to reintroduce himself. One day, however, he put a pin in his hand before the introduction. When the woman grasped his hand, she recoiled in pain as the pin punctured her skin. The doctor then left the room and after a while came back. Once more he offered his hand in introduction. Though the woman did not recognize him, she refused to shake his hand. She could not say why; she just wouldn't do it. The doctor "was no longer just a man . . . but had become a stimulus with a specific emotional meaning. Although the patient did not have a conscious memory of the situation, subconsciously she learned that shaking [the doctor's] hand could cause her harm, and her brain used the stored information, this memory, to prevent the unpleasantness from occurring again" (LeDoux 1996:181).

The brain is highly lateralized. In most people the left side is devoted to analytic, logical, verbal thinking, and the right to emotional processing. Whereas the left side is discrete and linear in its processing of information, the right side is more holistic and grounded. That is, the left neocortex is used for rational thought, whereas the right amygdala is employed for emotional processing. It is remarkable that each eye receives and transmits information to both sides of the brain at once:

The right side of both eyes sends information to the right side of the brain, and the left side of both eyes sends information to the left side of the brain.

Brain researchers have developed special contact lenses that refract incoming light to one side of the retina or the other, so that quite literally the left half of the brain does not know what the right side sees and vice versa. In one experiment, LeDoux, Wilson, and Gazzaniga (1977) showed disturbing images of people being thrown into flames to subjects wearing right-refracted lenses, thereby channeling the information to the emotional but not the rational brain. Afterward the subjects had no declarative memory of what they had seen—they could only describe a vague awareness of light and flashing—yet they felt quite upset and disturbed. Although they could not say why, they no longer liked the experimenter or felt comfortable in his presence.

Such unconscious learning reflects a very basic but very powerful psychological process identified long ago by the Russian physiologist Ivan Pavlov. In his regime of *classical conditioning*, an unconditioned stimulus (in the above example, a pin prick) is paired with a conditioned stimulus (the doctor's hand) to generate an unconditioned response (withdrawing from the pin prick). As a result of the pairing, the conditioned stimulus (the doctor's hand) becomes associated with the newly conditioned response (withdrawing from the pin prick) in the subject's memory. Because the memory is stored in the amygdala, however, it is not conscious, representing what LeDoux (1996) calls an "implicit memory."

Implicit memories can also be created through operant conditioning, whereby certain thoughts or behaviors are repeatedly paired with an emotional reinforcer. The creation of implicit memories through operant conditioning provides the basis for much human social learning. For example, Japanese women are taught from an early age to cover their mouths with their hand when they laugh. When they first laughed as young girls (stimulus), their mothers told them to cover their mouths and praised them for doing so, which made them feel good (an emotional reinforcer or reward). If they forgot, they were scolded, generating negative feelings (another reinforcer). Covering the mouth (the response) during laughter (the stimulus) came to be associated with the positive emotions engendered by maternal praise, whereas failure to do so was associated with the negative emotions associated with maternal displeasure. Over time, the behavior became automatic and no longer required the mother to administer the reinforcement regime.

Failure to cover the mouth during laughter will make a well-bred Japanese woman feel very uneasy (yielding an implicit memory of being scolded by her mother), whereas covering the mouth will feel right (drawing on the implicit memory of her mother's praise). Behaviors linked to implicit memories that have been conditioned through systematic pairing with specific emotions are difficult to extinguish. Even after many years of living in the West, for example, where covering the mouth during laughter is not culturally expected, women brought up in Japan persist in this distinctive behavior. When asked about it, they generally reply that it doesn't "feel right" to laugh without covering their mouth, even though they "know" they do not have to do so in the West. Because of such conditioned emotional responses, people who for the first time enter a new cultural milieu often report feeling uneasy and disoriented, for inevitably some of the social behavior they see will violate culturally expected norms that are imbued with implicitly conditioned emotional memories.

Implicit emotional memories exist independently of and apart from explicit verbal recollections, and they contribute an underlying valence to the facts and concepts that the neocortex stores and the thoughts that it processes. It is a fundamental feature of human cognition that all perceptions and memories have both an implicit and an explicit content. Explicit content is laid down in conscious memory by the hippocampus and stored in the cerebral cortex, whereas implicit content is filtered by the thalamus and stored unconsciously in the amygdala.

Conditioning was first studied by using an appetite—hunger—in which Pavlov's dogs learned to salivate in response to a bell that sounded just before food was given. In the past few years, scientists have identified a variety of neural structures, pathways, and transmitters associated with basic appetites such as hunger, thirst, tiredness, lust, playfulness, and curiosity (Carter 1998; LeDoux 1996; Panksepp 1998). They have also identified neural assemblies associated with fundamental human emotions such as fear, anger, disgust, nurturing, and liking (Panksepp 1998). Although some of the neurological mechanisms (such as fear) are better worked out than others (such as nurturing), all appear to be mediated through structures within the limbic system, thereby creating the neurological potential for conditioning by systematic pairing with emotions, generating implicit memories stored in the amygdala that may be activated without conscious awareness. Unconscious memories created through conditioning provide the emotional foundations for social behavior and social structure, telling us whom to approach, whom to avoid, and how we feel about different patterns of behavior.

*The Rational Brain*

It is only because our objective perceptions of people and objects carry emotional valences that we are able to use rationality to discriminate between them (Turner 2000). Without implicit memories stored in the limbic system to tell us what we like and don't like, we would not be able to act purposively and deliberately on stimuli from the real world that surrounds us. In the language of contemporary economics, each person's "utility" is created by a process of emotional conditioning that embodies implicit memories stored within the limbic system. This conditioning may be deliberate (through training given by parents, teachers, and other authority figures) or haphazard (through repeated pairings of stimuli that recur naturally in the empirical world), but it is always powerful and always plays a central role in human cognition. Without the emotional brain, rationality becomes superfluous because we do not have any idea of what we want to optimize.

Not only is decision making by the rational brain compromised without the benefit of input from the emotional brain, but the rationality of the neocortex is itself quite imperfect: It does not follow strict rules of logic, probability, or deduction. In contrast to the software and hardware of a digital computer, which work together to make decisions using a strict Boolean logic, the "wetware" of the human brain is messy, inconsistent, and often quite illogical in a deductive sense (Dawes and Hastie 2001; Kahneman and Tversky 2000). Indeed, human rationality has been shaped by evolution to depart in characteristic ways from strict adherence to the principles of logic and probability that are assumed by most rational choice models (Dawes 1998).

Given that the human brain uses a disproportionate amount of energy compared with other organs in the human body, it is not surprising that in the course of our evolution we developed certain inherited mental shortcuts designed to conserve cognitive resources. Operating with deductive rigor to consider all possible combinations, permutations, and contingencies before making a decision is possible for a powerful electronic computer solving a single problem; but if the brain were to adopt such an approach to decide the myriad of choices that human beings face in daily life, we would waste a lot of scarce energy pondering routine situations and everyday behaviors that have little effect on survival. Most of the decisions we make are not perfect or optimal in any absolute sense; they are just good enough for us to get by and live another day.

For this reason, human beings have evolved to function mentally as "cognitive misers." We take a variety of characteristic mental shortcuts and use simple rules-of-thumb and shorthands to make everyday judgments (Fiske and Taylor 1991:13). As organisms, we tend to satisfice (do the minimum needed to get by) rather than optimize (Newell and Simon 1972). We are wired cognitively to construct general categories about the world and then to draw on these categories in classifying and evaluating the stimuli encountered in daily life.

These conceptual categories are known as *schemas*; they represent cognitive structures that list the attributes of stimuli and the relationships between them (Fiske 2003). Unlike today's computers, whose working memories may be expanded indefinitely through the addition of more silicon chips, the working memory of humans is finite and not readily expandable. Indeed, the number of bits of information that can be held in short-term memory at any point in time is quite small. Experimental research has shown that human beings can hold no more than seven items (such as an unfamiliar phone number) in short-term memory at once, and that it takes 5 to 10 seconds of additional processing to fix information in longer-term memory (Miller 1956; Simon 1981).

Because the number of items is not expandable, in order to remember more pieces of information the brain combines, or "chunks," bits of information into larger conceptual categories (schemata) that use common properties to classify a much larger number of individual people or objects into a small number of readily identifiable groups for easier recall. For example, people can remember a familiar area code while rehearsing an unfamiliar phone number. Ultimately, schemas are nothing more than well-established neural pathways created through the repeated firing of particular constellations of synapses, leading to the formation of an integrated assembly of neurons that function together according to a specific sequence along specific routes to produce a consistent mental representation (LeDoux 2002).

People use schemas to evaluate themselves and the social roles, social groups, and social events they perceive around them (Fiske 2003). The categories into which we divide up the world may change over time and evolve with experience, but among mature human beings they always exist; and we always fall back on them when we interpret objects, events, people, and situations around us (Fiske 2003). Like all mental representations, moreover, they are stored in both explicit and implicit memory; the latter, being rooted in the limbic system, yields emotional valences that are largely automatic and unconscious.

Feelings lodged in the limbic system may be positive or negative, but when they are associated with particular classes of people or objects they contribute to *prejudice*, which is a predetermined emotional orientation toward certain individuals or objects. Prejudicial orientations may contain both conscious and unconscious components (Devine 1989; Dovidio and Gaetne 1986; Bargh 1996, 1997). For example, a person may be a principled racist who consciously believes African Americans to be inferior and thus rationally seeks to subordinate them; but another person may sincerely believe in equal opportunity and racial equality and yet harbor anti–African American sentiments that are unconscious and unintended, created through some earlier process of conditioning (e.g., the repeated visual pairing of violent crime scenes with black perpetrators on television). All human beings, whether they think of themselves as prejudiced or not, hold mental schemata that classify people on the basis of age, gender, race, and ethnicity. They cannot help it. It is part of the human condition; these schemata generally include implicit memories that yield subconscious dispositions toward people and objects (Fiske 1998).

In one experiment, for example, words associated with stereotypes about elderly people were flashed before the participants for around four thousandths of a second. This rate of exposure is too fast to be processed by the complex and lengthy neural pathways going through the neocortex (Cooper and

Cooper 2002), so the image was not registered categorically in conscious memory. Participants had no idea they had been subliminally primed with stereotypical words about elderly people; they were aware of only a bright but indistinct flash. Nonetheless, the 4-millisecond exposure was not too fast to be perceived and registered by the shorter and more primitive route of the limbic system, which retained an implicit emotional memory. After viewing words giving subliminal stereotypes about the elderly, participants were observed to walk more slowly and cautiously to the elevator than did the control participants, who were not subliminally primed (Bargh, Chen, and Burrows, 1996). Seeing words associated with stereotypes had primed the former group subconsciously to act more stereotypically "old" themselves.

In general, people are more likely to rely on stereotypes in making judgments when they are mentally challenged, facing uncertainty, or overloaded with stimuli (Bodenhausen and Wyer 1985; Bodenhausen and Lichtenstein 1987). When people have to make judgments under conditions of uncertainty, they draw upon schemata in characteristic ways, falling back on a small number of identifiable *heuristics*—simplified strategies of information processing and inference based on pre-existing mental short cuts (Kahneman and Tversky 1973, Tversky and Kahneman 1974).

People use the *representativeness heuristic* whenever they place a person or object into a conceptual category after observing certain traits that are representative of that particular category. If, for example, I pass someone on the street wearing a miniskirt, pink blouse, a gold necklace, and high heels, I quickly classify the person as female and treat her accordingly. Under most circumstances I will make this attribution quickly and not consider other possibilities because the skirt, blouse, necklace, and high heels are representative of the category of human beings known as females. And unless the person is an exceptionally well-turned-out drag queen, in Western societies I will be correct in making the inference.

Likewise, humans employ the *availability heuristic* when they estimate the likelihood of something occurring in the world on the basis of how readily examples of it come to mind. If people are asked to estimate the divorce rate in the United States, for example, they tend to offer a higher rate of marital dissolution if many of their acquaintances have recently been divorced, compared with people who have few divorced friends or relatives. If examples of divorce are relatively frequent in the person's social network, the idea of divorce will be cognitively available and its frequency of occurrence in the real world will be over-estimated. Likewise, African Americans from inner cities generally overestimate the proportion of blacks in the U.S. population because nearly everyone in their immediate world is black (Fiske 1993).

In contrast, the *simulation heuristic* comes into play when whenever a hypothetical scenario can be imagined to apply to an event or situation. Suppose, for example, one is late arriving at the airport and not expecting to make a flight, only to discover upon arriving that the flight itself was also delayed but that it had left just a few moments earlier. Logically, the amount of one's anger and frustration should be the same whether or not the flight was delayed, since in either event one has missed the plane. But anger and frustration are greater when the plane was delayed because one can readily imagine an alternate scenario: arriving just a few minutes earlier and making the delayed flight. Because one was easily able to imagine the alternative, one's subjective experience of missing the plane is different from the experience of missing it if the plane had left at its scheduled time.

Finally, human beings employ an *anchoring and adjustment heuristic* whenever they compare novel circumstances to an initial, fixed starting value. Professors, for example, are concerned about scholarly productivity; but what does it mean to be productive? Many faculty members use an anchoring heuristic by noting their own rate of publication and comparing it to that of their colleagues, considering who has published more or fewer articles in scholarly journals. The anchoring point of one's own scholarly productivity serves as a basis for deciding what constitutes "high" and "low" in the social environment of academia. The stereotypical American motivation to "keep up with the Joneses" is a popular expression of the anchoring and adjustment heuristic, as is the economic theory of relative deprivation whereby people feel deprived and work harder not because their income is low in some absolute sense, but because it is lower than that of their friends and neighbors (Runciman 1966).

One of the more important social judgments that human beings make is attributing motives to other actors in the social environment. In doing so, people appear—universally—to behave in pre-programmed ways that are not grounded in the rules of logic. First, people pay less attention to consensus information—knowledge about what everyone else does or believes—and tend to view each actor's behavior as distinct and unique (Kassin 1979). Second, people are inclined to see others' behavior as reflecting personal dispositions rather than circumstances (Jones 1990); and third, people consistently underestimate the importance of environmental factors in explaining others' behavior (Ross 1977). Together, these proclivities lead to a characteristic judgmental phenomenon known as the *fundamental attribution error*: "the general tendency to overestimate the importance of personal or dispositional factors relative to environmental influences" (Ross 1977: 184). An interesting point is that people suffer the opposite bias in making attributions about themselves, tending instead to attribute behavior to the particulars of the situation rather than to their own disposition, a proclivity known as the *actor-observer effect* (Jones and Nisbett 1972). This effect helps to preserve the illusion of flexibility and choice.

Another departure from strict rationality derives from a line of thinking in psychology known as *prospect theory* (Kahneman and Tversky 1979). Work has shown that human beings subjectively give the prospect of loss considerably more emotional weight than the prospect of an equal-sized gain, a phenomenon known as *loss aversion*. Thus, people anticipate far more displeasure at the prospect of losing $200 than pleasure from gaining $200 (Tversky and Kahneman 1986). The end result is that human beings work harder to avoid a loss than to achieve an equivalent gain, which is logically inconsistent but which makes sense from an evolutionary point of view: Avoiding losses will likely ensure survival, but risking gain will often lead to death. Although a proclivity toward loss aversion is a human universal, individuals nonetheless vary considerably in the strength of their aversion or risk-taking propensity (Thaler 1994).

## THE NATURE OF HUMAN SOCIALITY

The distinctive neural anatomy and cognitive organization of human beings are associated not only with a characteristic psychology but also with an identifiable human sociality. Our ancestors evolved in small, structured social communities grounded in emotion long before they developed rational faculties and innovated much in the way of macrosocial organization. The ability to evaluate potential costs and benefits of certain actions and to use these evaluations in planning for the future—the essence of what most theoretical models mean by "rationality"—emerged very late in the human career. Emotionality therefore remains a strong and independent force in human affairs, influencing perceptions, coloring memories, binding people together through attraction, keeping them apart through aversion, and regulating behavior through guilt, shame, and pride. As a result, human social behavior is driven by a limited number of core social motives that provide the impetus for most social action (Fiske 2003).

### *Core Motives*

As biological organisms, Homo sapiens evinces the same fundamental drives to attain food, water, warmth, sex, and environmental exploration that are common to all mammals. In addition, as sentient social beings, humans are guided by a set of social motives that determine their behavior toward others. These core motives underlie human social cognition, "the process by which people think about and make sense of other people, themselves, and social situations" (Fiske 2003:122). The core social motives encompass "fundamental, underlying psychological processes that impel people's thinking, feeling, and behaving in situations involving other people" (Fiske 2003:14).

The first of the core motives is *belonging*: People are strongly motivated to form social bonds with other people and to fit into groups. Indeed, belonging to a social group helps people to survive and thrive socially, psychologically, and physically. Individuals who are not well connected socially to others are less happy (Baumeister 1991; Williams, Cheung, and Choi 2000; Easterlin 2004) and less healthy (House, Landis, and Umberson 1988; Stansfeld et al. 1998), and at any given moment those who are less well connected are more likely to die (Rogers, Hummer, and Nam 2000).

The second of the core motives is *understanding*: People perceive and gather information about others in order to interact with them in practical terms (Fiske 1992, 1993). Understanding what another person does, feels, wants, and intends is important for survival in a social group; because the social group is the individual's main interface with the environment, survival in the group translates directly into physical survival itself. Being programmed cognitively to want to understand other people, individuals seek to develop meanings that are shared with others in their social environment. As people collaborate in constructing understandings about the world, they share their views in order to reach a consensus, or socially shared understanding (Moscovici 1988; Zajonc and Adelmann 1987).

The third core motive is *controlling*: By understanding and predicting other people's behavior, an individual acquires some measure of mastery over his or her social world (Fiske 2003). If, for example, I learn that my friend gets angry whenever the subject of George W. Bush is brought up, I can use this information to control my friend's behavior, bringing up the subject if I want to make my friend angry or avoiding it to smooth out our interpersonal relations. The goal of the control motive is to establish predictable contingencies between behavior and outcomes, and thereby to acquire a sense of competence and mastery over social situations. The need for control and the desire to be effective are expressed even in very young infants (White 1959).

A fourth core motive is *self-enhancement*, the need to maintain self-esteem and to achieve self-improvement: People are motivated strongly to feel good about themselves and to feel good when they receive positive feedback from other social actors (Taylor and Brown 1988; Swann et al. 1990). People thus strive to earn the esteem of others, yielding an intangible but very powerful social resource known as prestige, being liked and respected. Human beings also work to advance themselves materially, seeking to acquire money and possessions. The goals that we seek to achieve for self-enhancement have both objective and subjective utility, once again combining emotionality and rationality in cognition. In market societies, for example, people seek income not only because it improves material well-being but also because it confers prestige.

The final core motive is *trusting*: human beings have a positivity bias; we are programmed to see the world as a benevolent place and to assume that other people we encounter are likely to be competent, nice, honest, and trustworthy—in other words, good (Matlin and Stang 1978; Sears 1983; de Waal 1996). This predisposition facilitates social behavior by making cooperation and collective action more likely, benefitting both the individual and the group. When people's basic sense of the world as a benevolent place is disrupted by dramatic events (e.g., war, criminal victimization, or personal abuse), severe psychological trauma usually results (Janoff-Bulman 1985; Rothschild 2000; Schiraldi 2000).

Of course, all people are not equally trustworthy and not equally predisposed to trusting others. People high in trust tend to cooperate and expect others to do the same, which leaves them vulnerable to exploitation by those lacking or low in this predisposition. As a result, evolution has given human beings an innate mental module that renders them unusually sensitive to untrustworthy behavior, thereby conferring upon them an ability to quickly detect cheaters and free riders (Cosmides and Tooby 1989, 1992). Human beings tend to respond to violations of trust in kind, yielding a tit-for-tat pattern of behavior that over time either brings cheaters into conformity with collective norms or leaves them isolated from the social group, where they are unlikely to do social harm (Axelrod 1985).

### *Kinds of Relationships*

Just as human beings possess a limited set of social motivations that drive interpersonal behavior, they also have a relatively restricted repertoire of social relationships. Across all cultures and societies, there are just four kinds of social relationships (Fiske 1991). These elementary relational structures combine in different ways to describe the enormous variety of roles and interactions characteristic of all human societies. All four kinds of relationships exist to some degree in all cultures, but the prevalence of the different relational forms varies greatly across time and space.

First, people may relate to one another according to a principle of *communal sharing*, which is a relationship of interpersonal equivalence wherein the boundaries among individuals become indistinct and secondary to the identity of the collective (Fiske 1991:13). In a communal sharing relationship people pay attention to group membership, have a common sense of identity, and express weak individuality. Participants in such relationships often conceive of themselves as possessing a shared nature deriving from common descent, real or fictive. Communal sharing produces feelings of kindness, warmth, and generosity toward people perceived to be in-group members. Resources garnered by any member of the group are given over to the collective and distributed equally on the basis of need. Food sharing within kin-based households is the most durable example of a communal sharing relationship in human societies. The communal sharing of food within families stretches in an unbroken line from the earliest foraging hominids to people living in contemporary post-industrial societies.

A second kind of egalitarian relationship is *equality matching*, which occurs among peers who are recognized as equals but who are seen as distinct individuals worthy of separate consideration (Fiske 1991:14–15). Over time, the contribution of each person to collective resources is matched on a one-to-one basis so that inputs and outputs are balanced among participants. Equality matching may be expressed in the form of turn taking, whereby each person performs the same act or makes the same contribution in temporal sequence. Another form of this relationship involves in-kind reciprocity, whereby people take quantities of collective resources in amounts that are socially construed to be equivalent.

Equality matching provides a mechanism for distributive justice (the division and redistribution of resources according to equal shares) and a form of conflict resolution (eye-for-an-eye vengeance and tit-for-tat matching). Rotating credit associations, which are found in a variety of human cultures, represent a form of equality matching whereby members regularly contribute equal amounts of money to a common pot and then sequentially take turns withdrawing the accumulated proceeds at fixed points in the cycle.

Whereas communal sharing and equality matching are egalitarian relationships, *authority ranking* is an asymmetrical relationship of inequality based on hierarchy (Fiske 1991:14). In any hierarchy of three or more levels, authority ranking is transitive, such that if Person 1 is higher than Person 2 who is higher than Person 3, then Person 1 must also be higher than Person 3. The relationship of authority ranking is one of progressive hierarchical inclusion, so that as one moves upward in the hierarchy each successive rank dominates a larger number of subordinates.

Authority ranking does not necessarily derive from coercive power, wherein people at one rank dominate others at a lower rank by threat of force or harm. Although force may be brought to bear to enforce hierarchy at critical junctures, on a day-to-day basis the characteristic feature of most authority-ranking systems is that people lower in the hierarchy believe their subordination is legitimate and defer to those above them in the ranked structure as a matter of habit. The military constitutes the clearest example of an authority-ranking system:

Each person occupies a position in a graded hierarchy and must obey commands issued by those at a higher level while exercising dominion over those below them in the command structure.

The last kind of relationship is *market pricing*, a very different kind of social relationship wherein value is determined by competition between those who supply a good or service and those who seek it (Fiske 1991:15–16). Relationships in a market system are designated by a universal metric—price—that people use to compare each other and the goods or services they seek to exchange, no matter how dissimilar they might otherwise be. Price represents the exchange ratio in monetary terms of one item against all competing items within a defined market. People who interact through market pricing value each others' actions, services, and products according to the rates at which they can be exchanged. The relationship is defined by the structure and process of the market, not by any particular outcome (satisfaction, utility, or perceived value). People participating in a market may or may not maximize gains, and they may or may not be satisfied with a transaction.

All interpersonal relations in all societies take one of these four fundamental forms. As social beings growing up in a particular cultural milieu, we learn which form pertains to which relationship. In all societies one can find examples of each kind of relationship; but as the size and scale of human societies have increased over time, the prevalence of the four relational forms has shifted dramatically. In foraging societies, which prevailed everywhere until around 10,000 years ago, the predominant social forms were communal sharing and turn taking, with some authority ranking in larger and more sedentary communities (those forager societies wherein favorable ecological conditions permitted greater population densities, as among the Northwest Coast Indians and many Pacific Islanders).

Before agriculture, market pricing was close to nonexistent. With the invention of agriculture, however, new macro-level social organizations were developed that evolved into social hierarchies that produced new forms of stratification. As a result, the prevalence of relationships grounded in authority ranking increased dramatically under agrarian urbanism. Finally, although the existence of markets in a limited sense can be traced back thousands of years, market pricing did not constitute an important or prevalent social relationship in any society until quite recently, being attendant upon the arrival of industrialism in the nineteenth century.

## GENDER AND THE HUMAN CONDITION

The social and psychological predispositions discussed in this chapter are common to all human beings. Naturally, there is interpersonal variance with respect to any particular tendency, but to a greater or lesser degree all people possess emotional and rational brains that operate in parallel; they seek to interact with others in one of four characteristic ways, and they do so to satisfy one of five core motives. In making sense of the world around them, they draw upon both rational and emotional mental faculties, and the rational faculties are typified by a set of limitations and shortcuts that depart from strict principles of Boolean logic.

Many of the attitudes, behaviors, and expectations commonly associated with gender—the roles assigned to males and females within any culture—are socially constructed and malleable (Deaux and LaFrance 1998). There is no systematic evidence, for example, that females are less analytic than males, or that they are less achievement oriented, more social, or more suggestible. Whereas rigorous experiments do indicate that compared with males, females show slightly greater tactile sensitivity, verbal ability, timidity, and social compliance, and slightly less quantitative and spatial ability, these modest average differences are overshadowed by the extensive overlap of distributions for males and females on any particular trait (Macoby and Jacklin 1987).

The grounding of males and females in a common humanity stems from the fact that the human fetus develops ontologically as a female, which is then masculinized by the presence of testosterone and other male androgens under the control of genes located on the Y chromosome that circulate during fetal development (Konner 2002). Females possess two X chromosomes, one of which is redundant and rendered inactive after fertilization. In contrast, males possess one X and one Y chromosome, and the active genetic codes on the single X chromosome are shaped in their expression by steroids directed genetically from the Y chromosome.

Whereas most gender differences are subtle and strongly influenced in their ultimate expression by the social environment, there are clear and unambiguous differences with respect to genitalia, physical size, and propensity toward aggression. Gender differences with respect to the organs of sexual reproduction are obvious and require no elaboration. Although sexual dimorphism was substantially reduced in the course of human evolution, it did not disappear, and human males remain approximately 15% larger than their female counterparts, on average. As always, however, the expression of height and weight is conditioned on environmental influences, and within any population male and female distributions substantially overlap; thus, a significant share of women are taller than a significant share of men. Given current distributions in the United States, for example, 5% of all women will be taller than 25% of all men (Web site for Halls, MD: www.hallsmd/).

More dramatic are physical differences with respect to upper body strength and the use of that strength for physical aggression. Although females' capacities with respect to lower body strength, stamina, and endurance generally equal or exceed those of males, the musculature of the chest, neck, and arms is strongly influenced by testosterone (hence the extensive use of androgens by body-builders) and is consequently much better developed and stronger among males than females.

High levels of testosterone are very clearly associated with high rates of aggression across a variety of psychological and behavioral measures (Harris 1999; Simpson 2001). Testosterone affects behavior directly as it migrates from blood to brain, but the transfer is selective rather than uniform, concentrating in certain cerebral regions and not others—mainly the limbic system and particularly the hypothalamus. At puberty, testosterone levels rise by a factor of around 18 among boys but only of 2 among girls, and frequently pubescent boys experience a ten-fold increase within a single year. The effects on aggressive behavior are quite sudden and dramatic (Halpern et al. 1994).

In every known culture at least some homicide has been documented, and in every ethnographically documented case males are primarily responsible for murders. At the same time, males constitute the overwhelming majority of warriors across pre-industrial societies (Low 2000). In 67 studies of gender difference reviewed by Macoby and Jacklin (1987), males displayed significantly higher rates of aggression than females in 52 cases; the order was reversed in just 5 cases. Likewise, in their in-depth comparative analysis of 6 cultural systems, Whiting and Edwards (1988) found that boys consistently showed either greater egoism or greater aggression, and usually both.

The obvious conclusion, according to Konner (2002:96), is that "under natural conditions, boys are more aggressive and less nurturing than girls." These genetically controlled tendencies are reinforced in most human cultures. Out of 33 cultures surveyed by Whiting and Edwards (1988), 82% encouraged more nurturing from girls than boys, but none attempted the reverse; and out of 82 cultures surveyed, 85% offered boys more training in self-reliance than girls, whereas none attempted the opposite.

Despite the fact that males appear to be universally more aggressive than females, the size of the gender differential varies substantially across cultures. In general, the more time that males and females spend together, both as children and as adults, the smaller the gender differential becomes with respect to aggression, the less rigid are gender stereotypes, and the more egalitarian are gender roles (Sanday 1981; Macoby 1998). In other words, when social institutions and cultural expectations put males and females together with high frequency and force them to interact and cooperate, both sexes are pulled away from extreme expressions of gender-typical behavior and become more similar.

Among foraging societies, therefore, a critical variable is the amount of time that men spend away from the main group hunting on their own (Sanday 1981). When they spend large amounts of time away on a hunt in the company of other men, male-typical attitudes and behaviors are reinforced through a process of peer socialization and support, leading them to view women as subservient, sex as threatening, and menstrual blood as unclean and dangerous. This tendency is most pronounced in hostile, resource-constricted environments, like those that characterize many herding societies (Hayden et al. 1986). Likewise, in sedentary horticultural or agrarian societies, the greater the amount of time that fathers spend away from wives and children, the more boys develop pejorative attitudes toward women, the more aggressive and competitive they become toward each other, and the less attention the fathers pay to their offspring (Draper and Hardpending 1982). A similar pattern of behavior has recently been observed among male chimpanzees in the wild (Gibbons 2004).

In contemporary societies as well, Macoby (1998) found that from the earliest ages boys are more physically aggressive and more likely to seek out rough-and-tumble play, leading to a natural tendency toward gender segregation in play and friendship by age 3 that is so pronounced that it can only be forestalled by adult control. Sex-specific playgroups become more separate throughout childhood, and separate gender identities are formed as boys reinforce one another's masculinity and girls reinforce one another's femininity. By the time boys and girls reunite as adolescents seeking romantic liaisons, they have come to evince very different cultures that are moderated over time only through greater contact and cooperation in late adolescence and adulthood.

## THE WAY WE WERE AND ARE

Human beings evolved in small groups of less than 200 persons and retain a neural anatomy, social cognition, and structure of role relationships adapted to this background, which accounts for more than 97% of evolutionary time within the hominid line. Whereas human-like creatures have walked upright for some 6 million years, populations in excess of a few hundred individuals are entirely a product of the last 10,000 years. The dramatic changes in human society since the agricultural revolution cannot possibly have affected the inherited features of human nature. Indeed, all evidence suggests that genetic adaption to the environment ceased among humans with the advent of culture between 100,000 and 200,000 years ago.

Biologically, psychologically, and socially, therefore, not only are we who we are now; we are also who we were when the first "mitochondrial Eve" gave birth to the species in Africa more than 100 millennia ago. We possess a remarkable capacity to create mental categories and use them to process information and impose a coherent order on the universe. This ability, however, departs in important ways from strict adherence to the laws of deductive logic. Rather than evaluating the world according to strict principles of Boolean logic, people use a set of characteristic mental shortcuts in making judgments and decisions, relying on a few heuristics grounded in conceptual schemata that have been constructed through prior social learning. In practice, people function as cognitive misers, using categories to extend working memory and to conserve mental energy by making judgments that are "good enough" rather than maximal. As a result, human beings are satisficers (seeking to do the minimum to get by) rather than optimizers.

In addition, whatever the limitations on human rationality may be, the conscious processing of stimuli carried out in the cerebral cortex is accompanied by a parallel and unconscious emotionality grounded in the limbic system—a set of phylogenetically older, interconnected brain organs clustered around the amygdala and including the thalamus, hypothalamus, hippocampus, and cingulate cortex. Although the emotional and rational centers of the brain are interconnected, information processing is faster in the limbic system than in the neocortex, and the number of neural connections running from the limbic area to the cortex is much greater than that of the connections running in the opposite direction. Therefore, the emotional brain is more likely to affect the rational brain than vice versa, meaning that emotion constitutes a critical part of human cognition in addition to rationality.

The emotional brain embodied in the limbic system contains implicit memories that color explicit recollections of people, objects, events, and circumstances that are registered in the neocortex. As a result, the conscious, quasi-rational processing of information that human beings undertake in the neomammalian brain rests on powerful unconscious, automatic, and implicit sentiments that well up from the emotional centers of the paleo-mammalian limbic system. If either of these brain systems is compromised, then what we recognize as human cognition becomes impossible. Absent emotional valences for conscious mental representations, the brain does not know what it does or doesn't like and therefore cannot decide what to approach, what to avoid, or what sort of events or situations to maximize for satisfaction. Without guidance and control by the prefrontal cortex, human beings are unable to anticipate, plan, or defer gratification to achieve the outcomes they desire.

This distinctive neural anatomy and resulting cognitive style are associated with characteristic patterns of human psychology and sociality. Psychologically, humans possess a set of core social motives that complement the basic biological drives present in all mammals. These core motives cause human beings to seek the company of other people within social groups, to make attributions about the motivations and intentions of social actors they encounter, and through such attributions to acquire a measure of control over their social environment. In doing so, human beings are predisposed toward trusting—seeing the social world as benevolent and other people as generous—but at the same time they possess an innate ability to detect and act upon cheating, responding to defections from collective goals by using tit-for-tat strategies of reward and punishment that bring cheaters and free riders into conformity or isolation. Finally, human beings are motivated toward self-enhancement, both materially in terms of income, goods, and wealth, and socially by earning the esteem and acceptance of others in the social environment, thereby leading to the accumulation of prestige and warmth.

These core social motivations are fulfilled by interacting with other human beings in one of four elementary kinds of human relations: communal sharing, equality matching, authority ranking, and market pricing. In relationships of communal sharing, people such as family members contribute to collective resources on the basis of ability and withdraw on the basis of need. Under equality matching, people such as members of a rotating credit association contribute to and withdraw equal amounts from collective resources according to a socially defined schedule. Authority ranking is an asymmetric relationship that characterizes people interacting across levels of a hierarchy, such that people at higher levels wield more control over resources and power than those at lower levels. Finally, under market pricing people exchange resources by using a socially constructed institution known as the market, whereby values going into the exchanged service or good are determined by a price established through competition between multiple buyers and sellers.

These fundamental features of human psychology and sociality are exhibited across all cultures and societies and are generally shared by males and females. With respect to most social and psychological traits, gender differentials are nonexistent or quite small. Even with respect to size, the average male-female differential is only on the order of 15%, and the population distributions substantially overlap. The most important differences occur with respect to aggression. With the sole exception of females defending their offspring, violence is almost entirely confined to males: Across all cultures, males are overwhelmingly responsible for murder, assault, robbery, fighting, and militarism.

What changes across time and place are the number of social actors present and the social institutions that organize their behavior. As discussed in Chapter One, most of the history of human social change involved an interplay between elements of the environmental cluster and the structure of micro-level interpersonal relationships. Among foraging peoples and cultures, most interpersonal relationships follow a communal sharing form supplemented with some equality matching. Authority ranking is weak, and market pricing is virtually nonexistent. Relationships are generally egalitarian, with the few differences in access to resources and conflicts being diffused through mobility (i.e., leaving and joining another foraging band) rather than violence. Any stratification that exists in foraging groups occurs along the lines of age and gender, with inequality between men and women being determined mainly by the degree to which men form gender-specific hunting parties and spend time away from their wives and children.

Increases in the size and scale of societies, however, bring about changes in macrosocial structure that begin to exert significant independent effects on both the environment and microsocial relations. Although quasi-sedentary populations in the 1,000–2,000 range were possible under certain very favorable ecological circumstances before the advent of agriculture, and whereas foraging cultures in these niches did develop larger social structures such as clans and tribes along with new social relations such as chiefs and headmen, a fuller expansion of macrosocial structures awaited the emergence of the larger and more permanent human communities, which became possible only with the invention of agriculture and animal husbandry around 10,000 years ago.

# Chapter Four
# AGRARIAN URBANISM

THE SIGNATURE CHARACTERISTIC of foraging societies is that except for the very young and the very old, everyone produces food: Each day, all able-bodied people move about the environment hunting and gathering to ensure a caloric intake sufficient to survive another day. Until quite recently, human societies had no specialists devoted to tasks other than food production and certainly none devoted to full-time cognition. The leisure time necessary to think broadly and deeply became available only between 12,000 and 10,000 years ago with the emergence of the first sedentary villages, a social configuration rendered feasible by the invention of agriculture and the domestication of animals. For the first time in human experience, farming created a food surplus; the resulting accumulation of calories above one day's needs prompted a dramatic acceleration of human population growth, higher population densities, and the emergence of a new—albeit small—class of people who did not have to produce food for their own survival (Sjoberg 1960; Coale 1974; Livi-Bacci 1992).

## THE BIRTH OF CITIES

Agriculture, herding, and cities emerged at different times in different places according to the local availability of plants and animals amenable to domestication (Diamond 1997). Cities first materialized in a geographic arc (the "Fertile Crescent") extending from the eastern Mediterranean upward through Anatolia and down into the region of the Tigris and Euphrates rivers, centering on present-day Iraq. Here the ancient ancestors of modern cereal crops and herd animals were found in foothills adjacent to flat alluvial plains whose soil was annually replenished and watered by seasonal flooding, yielding a perfect environment for the emergence of intensive agriculture. Wheat, barley, and peas were domesticated in Mesopotamia by 10,000 BP, along with sheep and goats; by 6000 BP, several fruit-bearing trees and bushes had been tamed in the eastern Mediterranean (notably olives and grapes). Agriculture was independently invented in China, Mesoamerica, and perhaps India; but agrarianism spread to other world regions mainly through diffusion (Chant and Goodman 1999; Diamond 1997).

The domestication of plants and animals set the stage for a new kind of human society based in permanent settlements. The first cities emerged in the alluvial lowlands of Mesopotamia around 10,000 years ago, with populations in the range of 5,000 to 25,000 inhabitants (Sjoberg 1960; Chant and Goodman 1999). Given a pre-industrial technology, the amount of food that could be grown per hectare was quite limited, and the total size of the surplus was meager. Although intensive agriculture permitted cities to exist, they could not be very numerous and most people could not live in them. Prior to the industrial revolution just 200 years ago, no more than 5% of human society lived in cities, and the total population of a single city never exceeded 1 million (Chandler and Fox 1974; United Nations 1980).

With yields per hectare fixed by a limited and slowly changing technology, the only way for cities to become larger was for their inhabitants to gain control of more land and thereby commandeer a larger total surplus. The larger the empire controlled by a city, the larger the urban population it could sustain. The variegated topology of Mesopotamia lent itself to political fragmentation, however, and the size of its cities was limited by internecine rivalries and conflict. It was not until the pharaohs consolidated political control over the Nile River valley around 5,000 years ago that cities began to expand significantly in population. The first settlement to exceed 100,000 inhabitants was Thebes, in Egypt, around 3,400 years ago. It was succeeded a thousand years later by Babylon, which surpassed 200,000, and finally by Rome, which during the reign of Caesar Augustus (63 BC–AD 14) became the first city to surpass 500,000 (Chandler and Fox 1974).

Wherever it occurred, agrarianism displaced foraging as a way of life through direct conquest, demographic absorption, or ecological marginalization. The victory of agrarians over foragers occurred not because agriculture offered people progress in the form of less work, better nutrition, and longer lives. On the contrary, the sedentary residents of early agrarian societies worked longer hours, consumed fewer calories, evinced poorer health, and within cities died in much larger numbers (McNeill 1976; Diamond 1997). What gave agrarian societies their decided advantage in confrontations with hunter-gatherers was their demographic size, which enabled them to develop and sustain a more advanced technology, to train specialized fighters, and to inadvertently breed much deadlier germs.

With the advent of agriculture as a way of life, the Stone

Age gave way to the Bronze and Iron Ages, and metals replaced flint as the basis for more effective tools and more lethal weapons. Urban dwellers and the empires they built exhibited new instrumental needs and gave rise to a class of leisured specialists who dreamed up new tools to satisfy these needs. Traders and merchants obtained the raw materials; artisans made the tools; a political elite controlled their distribution; and a religious elite justified their deployment (Sjoberg 1960). As a result, in any encounter with a hunter-gatherer society, urban agrarian civilizations were able to wield weapons and technologies far superior to anything that the foragers could muster.

Agrarian societies also had more people spared from the necessity of food production to wield the new and improved weapons, leading to the emergence of professional soldiers and the first standing militaries. In any competition over land or resources, populations that numbered in the tens of thousands held a decided advantage over small bands numbering in the dozens or hundreds, especially when the former could field an army of well-equipped, well-fed, and well-trained professional soldiers.

Finally, the density of pre-industrial cities, along with their lack of sewage facilities, a limited understanding of the mechanisms of contagion, and the close association of humans with animals, gave one final advantage to agrarian societies: germs (Diamond 1997). Until the nineteenth century, in fact, health conditions in cities were so bad that infectious diseases were endemic and life expectancies were short, much shorter than among peasants in the countryside (McNeill 1976). Were it not for continuous rural in-migration, pre-industrial cities could not have sustained themselves demographically (Preston and Haines 1991).

Although death rates were high and life expectancies short, the urban dwellers who did manage to survive acquired an immunity to bacteria, viruses, and other microbes that hunter-gatherers could never attain. Given their low densities, foraging peoples could not achieve the critical mass of population sufficient to provide a permanent reserve for infectious agents. As a result, foraging peoples never evolved immunological defenses against microbes that became endemic to sedentary populations. Throughout history, therefore, the initial contact between a hunting-and-gathering people and an urban-based civilization has invariably led to the former's decimation through sudden exposure to diseases for which they had no natural immunity (McNeill 1976; Diamond 1997; Tierney 2000).

From the rise of the first city-states around 8000 BC to about AD 1800, agrarianism was the dominant form of human society, occupying ever larger portions of the world's geography with ever larger populations. The rough trajectory of world population growth is indicated in Figure 4.1, which graphs the estimated size of the human population from 500 BC to AD 1800. At the end of the Paleolithic period, the world's population stood at around 8 million; but over the next 8,000 years it grew to reach about 252 million in the year zero. Under the Pax Romana (27 BC to 180 AD) population growth reached a plateau, and with the collapse of the Roman Empire (476 AD), it declined to around 200 million before beginning to rebound slowly after the year 600. Somewhere around AD 1000, a variety of technological and social innovations coincided to unleash a demographic boom in Europe, which proceeded apace until the Black Death (bubonic plague) struck in the middle 1300s (Levine 2001). As the foundations for a global economic order based on large-scale production, trade, and investment were established after 1600 (Wallerstein 1974; Braudel 1982), the human population entered an era of sustained growth that accelerated up to the dawn of the nineteenth century, when the world's population stood at around 954 million (Livi-Bacci 1992).

**Figure 4.1**

**World Population, 500 BC to AD 1800**

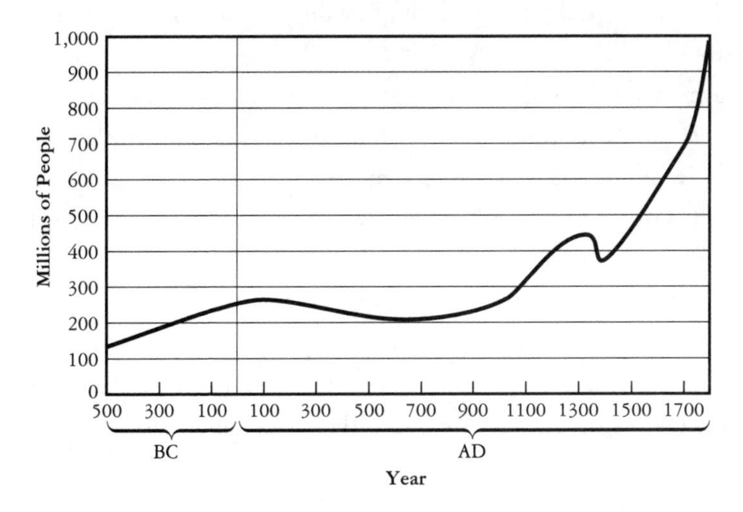


Across the 500 generations immediately preceding 1800, the proportion of human beings living in urban areas never exceeded 5% (United Nations 1980), and before that date only 65 cities in the entire history of the world achieved populations of over 100,000 (Chandler and Fox 1974). With the domestication of plants and animals, however, the economic foundations of human society broadened substantially, moving away from a singular reliance on hunting and gathering to include three new strategies of subsistence: herding, horticulture, and peasant agriculture.

*Herding economies* were based on the grazing of animals such as cattle, sheep, or reindeer, which grazed slowly across extensive grassland environments accompanied by a mobile community of humans who used the animals and their by-products to meet most of their material needs. *Horticultural economies*, in contrast, combined hunting and gathering with a simple form of cultivation known as swidden agriculture, which involved clearing a patch of vegetation, burning it, and then planting a stable crop on the ash-enriched land. The cleared patch was farmed for several seasons until the productivity of the land gave out, whereupon the community abandoned the plot and migrated to a new territory that was, in turn, slashed, burned, and farmed for several seasons before it was itself abandoned, thus beginning the cycle once again.

The size and density of communities associated with herding and horticultural economies were limited by the need to keep moving in search of new resources. Both herding and swidden agriculture exhausted the carrying capacity of the local ecology and required regular mobility across a large environment to remain sustainable. The resulting economies functioned largely at the subsistence level, yielding an unreliable food surplus and little potential for population growth. Herding and horticultural peoples tended to live together in relatively small communities, yielding a social world that was not very different in size and scale from that of foraging societies. Like hunters and gatherers, herding and horticultural peoples occupied small groups defined by kinship and friendship, with the content of social relations being established through repeated face-to-face encounters.

Given their limited margin for survival in relatively meager ecologies, however, horticultural and pastoral societies evolved distinctive cultural patterns that set them apart from their foraging predecessors. Because foragers make their living by roaming a particular territory and simply finding the plants and animals they need to survive, they have few possessions and no real concept of personal property. No one invests personal effort in cultivating any particular food resource or caring for any parcel of land. In contrast, among both horticultural and pastoral societies, socially defined groups of people (families, households, clans) invest considerable time and effort in cultivating a particular resource (crops or animals).

Herding and horticulture are thus characterized by heavy fixed investments in particular products for subsistence. The shift from hunting and gathering to the deliberate cultivation of plants and animals created a need for new social mechanisms to deter free riders from appropriating food resources to which they had not contributed time and effort in producing. The result was the emergence of a distinctive cultural style—a so-called culture of honor—in which males were socialized to build and maintain reputations for violence, aggression, and a quick temper as a deterrent to poachers (Nisbett and Cohen 1996). By building such a reputation, male family heads discouraged potential free riders from poaching, making them think twice before stealing crops or animals.

In herding and horticultural societies, sensitivity to insult and the willingness to use violence in the defense of personal or family interests are encapsulated in the concept of honor. By word and deed, men are called upon to project a reputation for courage and a willingness to use violence in defense of symbolic, emotional, and material resources. As a result, honor-based societies are characterized by high rates of interpersonal violence and a high degree of gender inequality (women simply become another resource that men defend in the name of honor).

In order to maintain sociability and prevent the frequent dissolution of social relations into violence, honor-based societies tend to evolve intricate codes of honor whereby males interact on a daily basis using elaborate rituals of respect and courtesy to acknowledge the reputation and worth of others. As long as these rituals are observed, social harmony prevails and interpersonal exchanges occur smoothly; but any perceived violation of courtesy or any seeming affront to a man's reputation is met by immediate and forceful action. Failure to do so would bring a loss of honor, and without honor or respect neither a man nor his family could expect to survive for long.

Cultures of honor have been observed throughout the world among herding and horticultural peoples who inhabit marginal habitats, including Europe (Cumliffe 1979; Fitzpatrick 1989), southern Asia (Mandelbaum 1988; Rosaldo 1980), Africa (Galaty and Bonte 1991), the Mediterranean (Peristiany 1966; Black-Michaud 1975; Fisek 1983), South America (Chagnon 1968), and the southern United States (McWhiney 1988). In these honor-based societies, relations within families are dominated by communal sharing, whereas relations among families are characterized by equality matching according to the philosophy of "an eye for an eye and a tooth for a tooth." Both relational styles may be supplemented by some degree of authority ranking within families and between clans. Relations governed by the mechanism of market pricing are minimal.

Men socialized into a culture of honor evolve a distinct neurophysiology and endocrinology characterized by a low threshold for activation of the "fight or flight" response. Any perceived lack of courtesy or respect quickly triggers the rage circuit in the brain's limbic system to set in motion the allostatic response described in Chapter Three. Compared with men reared in other cultures, those raised in cultures of honor evince significantly higher levels of the stress hormone cortisol in their blood after a perceived social affront, no matter how slight (Nisbett and Cohen 1996). The same social behavior, therefore, produces quite different physiological responses among men who were reared in and outside of a culture of honor.

## AGRARIAN URBANISM AS A WAY OF LIFE

Although changes in social life associated with the shift from foraging to herding and horticulture were modest, the micro- and macrosocial structures associated with the third political economy enabled by the domestication of plants and animals—*peasant agriculture*—were truly revolutionary. In this economic system, land is mapped cognitively and allocated socially to particular families, which cluster together residentially in sedentary villages (Chayanov 1966). Systems of land tenure vary from society to society, but in general village-based families are granted social rights of usufruct to specified farmlands, which are controlled by a separate class of landowners, usually hereditary, whose power and authority are rooted in cities. The vast majority of people inhabiting the so-called civilized agrarian societies of the past were, in fact, not cultured urban dwellers but illiterate peasants who lived in small villages and isolated hamlets that were not much bigger than the hunting-and-gathering communities of the Paleolithic period.

Within these communities, work was governed by the rhythms of the seasons. Most people lived and died within a few kilometers of where they were born, spending all their lives within a community of friends and relatives whom they knew personally (Laslett 1971). In this sense, the coming of agrarian urbanism posed few social challenges for the vast majority of human beings. Although peasants might periodically exchange goods and services at weekly markets or annual fairs held in particular towns or villages, most interpersonal behavior involved communal sharing within families and equality matching within networks of kinship and acquaintance. These social relations were supplemented by a relatively thin layer of authority-ranked relationships to city-based political authorities and their local representatives. Culturally, illiterate peasant villagers retained a mythic culture grounded in the spoken word that yielded a metaphoric understanding of the universe.

### *The Emergence of Stratification*

In contrast, for the small minority of people who were able to live in cities because of the food surplus created by intensive agriculture, aspects of social, economic, and cultural life were radically transformed. City dwellers are, by definition, people who do not have to produce the food they eat. Instead, food is produced by peasant farmers in the countryside and appropriated for consumption by urban workers who engage in other occupations. These new occupational specialties are defined by a macrosocial structure composed of people who work collectively to achieve ends that are, in social terms, quite different from those that prevailed before the agricultural revolution (Sjoberg 1960).

The existence of a food surplus made possible the first significant occupational specialization. Rather than finding food for themselves, urban workers labored to capture the food produced by others, to gather and store it in central locations, to consolidate and wield the political power that made this confiscation possible, to perpetuate an ideology justifying the appropriation as legitimate, and to undertake a variety of other practical activities necessary for the urban system to function. With the advent of cities as an institutional configuration in human affairs, new forms of categorical differentiation were therefore added to the long-standing division of people based on age, gender, and kinship (Sjoberg 1960). New distinctions were made on the basis of material well-being (rich versus poor), power (elite versus masses), holiness (priests versus laity), knowledge (literate versus illiterate), residence (urban versus rural), and occupation (non-manual versus manual).

Cities consist of large numbers of people concentrated at one place at one time, and the larger the number of people, the more ways they can be divided into meaningful social categories (Blau 1977). The resulting social differentiation in human society increased the potential for both heterogeneity (unranked differences among people on the basis of nominal classifications) and inequality (ordered classifications on the basis of hierarchically ranked categories). Agrarian urbanism thus brought about the first systematic stratification of human beings into classes defined by their differential access to material, emotional, and symbolic resources. For the first time, large, cohesive groups of people had conflicting material interests.

Given socially stratified categories of people, inequality is generated and perpetuated by two fundamental mechanisms: exploitation and opportunity hoarding (Tilly 1998). *Exploitation* occurs whenever people in one social group expropriate a resource produced by members of another group and prevent them from realizing the full value of their effort in producing it. *Opportunity hoarding* occurs whenever one social group restricts another's access to a scarce resource, either by outright exclusion or by exercising monopoly control that requires the out-group to pay a rent in return for access. By definition, city dwellers engage in exploitation when they confiscate a portion of the peasantry's agricultural production, and they likewise engage in opportunity hoarding when they define symbolic and material resources—money, power, holiness, wealth, prestige—and restrict access to a socially defined subset of people.

These two general mechanisms are reinforced by two additional social processes that function over time to institutionalize the categorical distinctions and lock them into place (Tilly 1998). The first of these processes is *emulation*, whereby one group of people copies a set of social distinctions and interrelationships from another group, or transfers the distinctions and interrelationships from one social setting to another. The second is *adaptation*, whereby social relations and day-to-day behaviors at the microsocial level become oriented toward ranked categories, so that decisions about whom to befriend, whom to help, whom to share with, whom to live near, whom to court, and whom to marry are made in ways that assume the existence and importance of asymmetric social categories. In the words of Tilly (1998:10), "exploitation and opportunity hoarding favor the installation of categorical inequality, while emulation and adaptation generalize its influence."

These four mechanisms operate within all urban-based societies. They are ultimately social in origin and follow from pursuit of the core motives defined by Fiske (2003)—belonging, understanding, controlling, self-enhancing, and trusting. The only difference between urbanites and foragers is that these motivations are now expressed within a new, differentiated social structure that divides a much larger population of people into many more social categories that are characterized by unequal access to material, emotional, and symbolic resources, thereby producing stratification. Among the inhabitants of early pre-industrial cities, therefore, relationships of authority ranking proliferated in comparison with hunter-gatherer societies. Whereas the latter tended to be egalitarian (most interpersonal relations were based on communal sharing or equality matching), city dwellers are always stratified (exhibiting a multitude of interpersonal relations based on relations of authority ranking).

### *The Invention of Markets*

In both ontological and historical terms, the social stratification of human society preceded the division of people on the basis of unequal access to income. Cities existed for thousands of years before an entity known as "money" was invented to make possible something called "income." Before these concepts were even imaginable, a new and very different kind of social institution—the market—had to be conceived and implemented, and this took considerable time. At first, the macrosocial behavior of cities was ordered primarily according to the principles of authority ranking, with goods and services being produced and distributed mainly through a variety of command mechanisms. For millennia, the agricultural surplus of peasants was expropriated by coercive rulers who were backed up militarily by an army and ideologically by a priesthood. Using conquest along with social institutions such as indenture, tithing, and slavery, rulers commandeered not only food but also labor and other resources to build palaces, temples, bridges, roads, and other public projects.

These new institutional forms were administered by a centralized bureaucracy of officials who derived authority from the rulers and their religious agents. To be sure, early cities also developed mechanisms that allowed for the exchange of goods and services through bartering. A quarter linked with public exchange—a bazaar—is found in the archeological ruins of most early cities (Chant and Goodman 1999). But for a very long time there was no market pricing in the contemporary sense of the term, for the simple reason that there was no money.

Over the millennia, however, as cities grew in size and scale and the volume of goods, services, and commodities to be exchanged rose, bartering proved to have serious practical drawbacks. First, it is time consuming. Each transaction must be negotiated face-to-face, which requires that humans spend time traveling to a site where they can meet and then argue over terms. Second, each exchange must be negotiated independently. In effect, each transaction requires setting a new and unique price. Third, the terms of the exchange are not transparent and are difficult to observe and compare with others. Finally, bartering entails excessive costs of shipping and transportation. Not only does a person have to show up at an agreed-upon location to bargain, but he or she must also carry all the goods or commodities to be offered for immediate exchange on the spot.

The lack of a socially agreed-upon medium of exchange tended to inflate transaction costs and discourage trade. Although the costs associated with bartering may have been trivial in small foraging societies and small in peasant villages, they grew progressively larger as the size and scale of cities increased. The first recognizable effort to create money occurred around 4,000 years ago when the Cappadocian Greek kings smelted silver ingots and guaranteed their weight and purity to ensure their acceptance as a standardized form of payment. The first coins were minted by a people in Asia Minor known as the Lydians between 700 and 600 BC. The idea of coinage spread to Greece in the following century, was adopted throughout the Hellenistic world shortly thereafter, and was taken over by the Romans shortly before the common era (Davies 2002).

Although a crude form of market pricing could occur among people interacting in a barter economy, the full expression of this social relationship awaited the invention of money and its application across a wide range of social settings. Only then could pricing mechanisms emerge as a means for adjudicating supply and demand. The use of market pricing as a basis for human interrelations probably did not occur on any significant scale until the time of the Roman Empire, when the imperial treasury began to mint and circulate a large quantity of gold and silver coins for public use. The existence of a common currency, a well-developed network of cities, and well-established routes of transportation and communication prompted a surge of trade and investment and the first sustained expansion of markets.

For the first time, in other words, the Pax Romana made possible the significant use of market pricing as a basis for human interaction. Even though market pricing became firmly established in the integrated system of cities and provinces known as the Roman Empire, it only applied to a narrow range of human relationships, and most interpersonal exchanges continued to take place outside of markets (Garnsey and Saller 1987). Although urbanites may have at times purchased property, acquired goods, sold labor, and exchanged services on monetized markets, most social interactions were still governed by the older mechanisms of communal sharing, equality matching, and authority ranking.

Slavery and other forms of coerced labor remained common throughout the Roman Empire, and families continued to pool resources within extended kinship networks. Moreover, most inhabitants of Roman provinces were peasants living in tiny, self-sufficient villages. Even within Roman cities, property changed hands more through inheritance or confiscation than through sales or purchase. Indeed, the most common means of accumulating wealth was not investment or participation in markets, but conquest. From the flowering of the first cities until just a few hundred years ago, most human interactions transpired outside of markets, and market pricing accounted for a small share of all interpersonal relationships.

*The Emergence of Writing*

Not only did the advent of markets bring about the invention of money and the commercialization of human behavior, but markets had a more profound effect on the structure and organization of society by leading directly to the invention of writing. The origins of the alphabet lay in the need of Sumerian traders for an accounting system to keep track of sales and shipments. As early as 10,000 years ago, urban traders began using a stylus to mark clay tokens of different shapes to indicate the quantity and nature of goods being shipped or stored (Harris 1986; Lawler 2001). Over the millennia, these clay tokens expanded into tablets and the markings were systematized and elaborated, until around 5,000 years ago, when they developed into a syllabic script for the Sumerian language, known as cuneiform. About 4,000 years ago, the Phoenicians borrowed the concept of writing and invented the first phonetic alphabet, which was later adopted and modified by the Greeks, only to be taken up by the Romans, who bequeathed to us the system that we in the West essentially use today (Diamond 1997).

The advent of writing brought into existence the first external memory devices: tablets, scrolls, and stone monuments. These devices dramatically reduced demands on biological memory and freed up human cognition for other tasks, leading to an unprecedented burst of innovation and technological progress (Goody 1986). Whereas biological memory is inherently limited by a fixed neural capacity, writing offered an external system of data storage that was potentially unlimited in size (Goody 1977). Moreover, by facilitating communication and interaction among individual brains, dense urban environments dramatically increased human computing power

(Wright 2000). In a very real way, early cities functioned as macrosocial "computers" that contained thousands of parallel processors organized socially to work together on common problems using common concepts and rules of behavior.

The efficiency of information processing was greatly enhanced by the mere contiguity of people within cities; but the invention of writing further raised the amount of data that could be processed by increasing the capacity of human beings to store, retrieve, and apply information to diverse tasks (Goody 1986; Diamond 1997). The invention of writing thus created the foundations for a new and very different kind of *theoretic culture*, a logical system of thought grounded in experience and reason and capable of making relatively accurate predictions about events in the natural and social worlds (Donald 1991).

Almost by definition, access to such a culture was limited to the small minority of urban dwellers who were literate and freed from the burdens of daily food production. Moreover, even among those who could read and write there were always two competing modes of thought (Snow 1959; Bruner 1986). Narrative thought, which is centered on the right side of the brain and infused with emotion grounded in the limbic system, is basically a written extension of oral culture expressed as literature in the form of plays, poems, stories, novels, operas, and the like. In contrast, analytic thought, which is centered on the left side of the brain and located in the outer cortex, plays host to the newer, rationally grounded theoretic culture.

Although theoretic culture gained adherents and increased its influence in human affairs across the millennia, it remained a small part of total human experience until industrialization, given the small number of people who were literate. For city dwellers, however, adaptation to an urban way of life implied a shift of mental operations from the right to the left side of the brain, suggesting a reconfiguration of neurophysiology. Using a series of instruments to measure cognition on the left versus the right side of the brain, TenHouten and colleagues have shown that rural dwellers display greater right dominance compared with urban dwellers and that the brains of literate city dwellers are structurally and chemically distinct from those of illiterate foraging or village-based peoples (TenHouten, Thompson, and Walter 1976; TenHouten 1980, 1985, 1986).

*New Forms of Separation*

Because inequality under agrarian urbanism stemmed mainly from categorical distinctions grounded in hierarchical social organization rather than pricing mechanisms emanating from markets, a great deal of attention in pre-industrial cities was devoted to the definition and maintenance of social boundaries (Sjoberg 1960). Although elite status was ultimately determined by networks of blood, marriage, and friendship, the processes of exploitation and opportunity hoarding are greatly facilitated by the existence of readily perceived status markers. In order to set themselves apart from the masses, therefore, members of the pre-industrial urban elite generally adopted distinctive modes of dress, special rules of etiquette, characteristic patterns of speech, and a particular bearing and comportment that were difficult for the masses to learn or imitate (Sjoberg 1960).

The ruling class who also confined education and learning

to a narrow franchise and privileged certain forms of symbolic knowledge as essential to elite status, creating an intangible yet important entity that sociologists call "cultural capital" (Bordieu 1986). In contrast to human capital, which is the knowledge, skills, and abilities that make people directly productive as individuals, cultural capital consists of knowledge that does not make individuals more productive in and of themselves, but permits them to be more effective actors within a particular social context.

Because members of the urban elite have gone to the same schools, read the same classics, learned the same stylized manners, developed the same accents and speech patterns, and acquired a common set of socially defined markers that designate what is considered to be good taste, they are instantly recognizable to one another and to the masses. The possession of cultural capital makes an individual more productive not because he or she can perform a given operation better or faster, but because he or she can navigate structures of power with ease, feel relaxed and comfortable in the social settings they define, and interact with other persons of influence to get things done. In short, pre-industrial elites evolved cultural capital as a symbolic resource they could manipulate through opportunity hoarding, enabling exploitation and trade through closed kinship networks.

As a result, the social structure of pre-industrial cities was rigid and hierarchical, with limited possibilities for social advancement. The evolution of mechanisms to promote social exclusion was inevitable given the fixed size of the pre-industrial food surplus and the limited number of so-called civilized people it could support. If markets were allowed free reign under a pre-industrial technology, then social mobility would quickly overwhelm the meager food surplus. The full development of markets and the emergence of fully capitalist societies awaited the arrival of industrialism, which made it possible for 95% of the population to engage in something other than agriculture. Although markets may have been invented under agrarian urbanism, therefore, their role in pre-industrial cities was limited, and relatively few human interactions were grounded in market pricing.

In addition to making possible new categorical distinctions among growing classes of people, cities also made possible new spatial distinctions among social groups. Because cities consist of dense concentrations of people who compete to make the best use of a limited amount of space, urban landscapes tend to become socially segmented and symbolically organized, even in the absence of functioning real estate markets. As with social stratification, therefore, residential segregation among social groups precedes the emergence of the market as an institution. Neither inequality nor social segregation can be blamed on the so-called evils of capitalism. Rather, they result from urban living itself.

Foraging communities display relatively little differentiation in the social use of space. Dwellings are impermanent and clustered along lines of kinship, usually following patriarchal rules, with male offspring generally living near their parents (Kelly 1995). Within households, nuclear family members typically sleep together in a common area and arrange themselves in a circle or semi-circle around a central hearth (Gamble 1999). Given limited social stratification and low population densities, foragers lack identifiable neighborhoods, and except for a few dense, sedentary communities located in unusually rich habitats (such as the Northwest Coast Indians), there is little variation in the size or construction of dwellings.

Since most foraging groups had to remain mobile, dwellings tended to be simple, impermanent, and built on top of bare dirt using perishable materials. Internal living space was generally not divided into separate functional areas for cooking, sleeping, socializing, or other social activities. Although stones may have demarcated hearths and, along with postholes, traced the outline of the dwellings themselves, shelters were generally not differentiated internally and most social life took place in the outdoors among people interacting publicly on a face-to-face basis. Animals and objects rather than specific places or locations were imbued with symbolic and spiritual significance.

The concentration of a large number of people in space—the demographic essence of a city—changed this settlement pattern entirely. At the household level, dwellings began to diverge in terms of size, construction, and material comfort. Homes also became more internally segmented, as dwellings were subdivided into different functional spaces—rooms—devoted to different social functions. Outside the household, distinct neighborhoods or quarters began to be discernable on the basis of factors such as prestige, wealth, power, and function. Typically the various socially defined residential quarters were arrayed around a well-defined central place, and a wall or rampart at the city's edge provided protection from invasion as well as internal security. By delineating a clear boundary between city and countryside, the city wall also symbolically defined membership in the urban community and distinguished insiders (urbanites) from outsiders (hicks, bumpkins, peasants—see Sjoberg 1960).

Before the industrial era, overland transportation was slow and costly, and communication required the physical presence of the communicating parties themselves, or a surrogate such as a messenger delivering a note, letter, or oral recitation. Cities emerged as a way to overcome the barriers of space and time—to solve the problems of temporality and territoriality—using a pre-industrial technology. Cities were an institutional mechanism that brought together a large number of human beings in close proximity so that they could interact regularly to coordinate actions, share information, and develop new ideas. In order to maximize communication while achieving greatest access to the rest of society, the ruling classes clustered residentially at the city center (Sjoberg 1960); because transportation was largely on foot, members of the ruling classes, like other urban dwellers, had to live near their places of work, meaning that palaces, temples, and monumental structures were also located at the urban center.

In essence, cities emerged as a way of providing rulers and their minions with a valuable social resource: propinquity. By segregating themselves at the city center—living and working in close proximity to one another at the point of greatest access to outlying districts—the ruling classes were able to maintain themselves socially, politically, and demographically as a coherent social group. Although some residential segregation may be an inevitable by-product of urban living, the *degree* of segregation in pre-industrial cities was limited by technological constraints. Because everyone had to live within walking distance of their places of employment and service consumption, spatial separation could not be extreme. Servants had to live near their masters, artisans near their patrons, soldiers near their rulers, and outcasts near the waste they were required daily to eliminate—hence the great emphasis on categorical distinctions and social markers of class in pre-industrial societies (Sjoberg 1960).

Indeed, since the advent of urban civilization, human societies have evinced a direct trade-off between social and physical separation as mechanisms of social differentiation and stratification. When the possibilities for physical separation are limited by technology, social distinctions loom large and a great deal of time and effort is put into the definition and maintenance of social boundaries. As improvements in technology allow a separation of work from residence and the segmentation of urban functions into discrete districts, categorical social distinctions decline in importance and are replaced by physical separation as a mechanism for perpetuating inequality (Massey and Denton 1993).

Pre-industrial cities were probably characterized by greater functional than class segregation, owing to the logic of agglomeration economies. An agglomeration economy occurs whenever a social actor's costs of producing some good or service are lower when carried out in close promixity to other actors producing the same product. By locating a single block of one street, for example, shoemakers could reduce their costs of transport by allowing suppliers to bring all necessary inputs to one central location rather than sending them to scattered locations throughout the city. Shoemakers clustering together also enjoy greater access to customers because potential clients could come to a single place to shop rather than search through the entire urban landscape. Once a "cobblers' row" had been established, it was foolhardy for a shoemaker to locate anywhere else, as urban dwellers would naturally go to that central location whenever they needed shoes. For this reason, preindustrial cities generally included functional streets, districts, or quarters dominated by specific crafts, guilds, and trades, a fact often indicated by street names that survive to the present (e.g., Baker Street in London, or Rue des Bouchers in Brussels).

In addition to enabling social and spatial segmentation on the basis of hierarchical and functional distinctions, early cities allowed the segmentation of people on the basis of ethnicity, a poorly developed social category in most foraging cultures, which typically invoke a binary distinction between insiders and outsiders, people and strangers. Foraging peoples are typically scattered widely across relatively large expanses of territory, with the precise density depending on the carrying capacity of the local ecology. Although foragers do evolve understandings of territory and acknowledge social rights to forage within particular ranges, the ranges themselves are loosely defined and overlap considerably along the edges.

Moreover, for any particular foraging band, the people they encounter in neighboring territories generally speak the same language and share a common mythic culture. Individual bands are generally considerably smaller than the sum total of individuals who constitute the "people" in question. The cultural unit actually corresponds to a larger population of individuals who gather together seasonally for social interaction, ritual ceremonies, cooperative endeavors, and most important, mate exchanges.

In the ancestral environment, therefore, foragers rarely came into contact with people speaking a different language, holding a different set of mythic beliefs, and possessing a radically different culture. The intergroup encounters that did occur were likely characterized by wariness that assumed the worst intent until members of the other group could communicate their benign intent through gesture and symbolic offerings (Mauss 1967). The most common approach to encountering other cultural groups was suspicion and avoidance. The outsider status of "stranger" was assigned to unknown peoples by default and then had to be negotiated away socially during the course of an interaction (Colson 1978).

In contrast, the existence of pre-industrial cities required control over large agricultural hinterlands, and agrarian empires therefore tended to rule over a diverse array of cultural groups that possessed different languages and different mythic understandings of the social and natural world. Through a variety of social and political mechanisms (slavery, trade, pilgrimage) as well natural disasters (flight from flood, fire, famine), diverse peoples were displaced from their native communities and came to settle in cities, bringing about a new differentiation of human beings on the basis of ethnicity.

Social boundaries that had remained latent and unacknowledged within home regions of the empire (because cultural groups were geographically isolated and largely unknown to one another) suddenly became salient and explicit (as the groups encountered one another and interacted within the city). The contact and competition arising from the juxtaposition of distinct peoples within a single urban landscape sharpened intergroup differences and highlighted social boundaries (Blau 1977; Fischer 1975). As a result, ethnic categories became more salient as schemata in social cognition; ethnicity became an important categorical distinction used to perpetuate inequality using mechanisms of exploitation and opportunity hoarding; and ethnic segregation emerged as a geographic means to allocate emotional, material, and symbolic resources differentially toward or away from specific groups (Sjoberg 1960).

Residential segregation makes stratification on the basis of ethnicity easy and efficient, for once a group is segregated within a specific geographic area, it is possible to disinvest in the people simply by disinvesting in the place (Blau 1977; Massey and Denton 1993). By channeling resources away from a segregated ethnic enclave, actors in the broader society can deprive the out-group of resources, thereby subordinating it most effectively. In contrast, when an ethnic group is well integrated in an urban environment, processes of ethnic subordination become more difficult and inefficient because disinvestment in the out-group must occur on a person-by-person, family-by-family basis. Throughout history, whenever the powerful have sought to stigmatize and subordinate a particular ethnic group, they have endeavored to confine its members to specific neighborhoods by law, edict, or practice (Wirth 1928).

In addition to creating new categorical distinctions and permitting their systematic social and spatial manipulation to increase stratification, agrarian urbanism exacerbated the degree of separation along a more traditional cleavage: gender. The transition from foraging to sedentary living strongly affected the degree of sex segregation in human life (Kelly 1995). As people began to form settled communities, they initially combined agriculture with hunting and gathering. Foraging from a permanent base, however, quickly exhausted the ecological resources on adjacent and nearby lands. The longer and more densely a site was occupied, the greater the distance that people had to go to secure fresh resources.

As settlement proceeded and populations grew, therefore, men had to travel farther to hunt game and thus spent more time by themselves in gender-segregated groups. At the same time, women separately had to move farther afield to gather resources and cultivate crops. With women devoted to local food processing and men away hunting, the care of children was given over to peers, enabling young boys to self-select friendships to form homogenous all-male play groups. These were typically supervised by older girls, who were thus socialized into specialized care-giving (Macoby 1998).

As the two gender groups separated from one another, males interacted more intensively to reinforce masculine behavior and cognitive tendencies while females interacted more intensively to reinforce feminine behavior and cognitive tendencies. Instead of balancing and moderating one another's physiologically based and neurologically controlled proclivities, the segregation of men from women caused members of each sex to exaggerate gender-specific tendencies: Women became more caring, nurturing, and accommodating, whereas men became more independent, aggressive, and domineering (Sanday 1981). The net result was an increase in gender inequality in pre-industrial cities.

By supporting city populations in the tens of thousands, agrarian urbanism vastly increased the scope for gender differentiation and stratification. In shifting first from foraging to herding and horticulture, then to sedentary agriculture, and finally to full-time urban living, women were removed further and further from involvement in economic production outside the home while men came to specialize more and more in productive work and public action away from the family. Although all cultures display some level of occupational segregation by gender, the degree of such segregation generally increases with the size and scale of society (Sanday 1981; Scott 1994).

Among foragers, men predominantly hunt and women predominantly gather. However, even within societies where hunting is defined as "male," women are usually observed to hunt small game in the course of gathering, whereas men are observed to gather while they hunt (Kelly 1995). The larger size and scale of agrarian cities not only allowed new occupational differentiation in general, but it also permitted more task specialization by gender. Among agrarian urban societies, certain tasks (e.g., soldiering, hard physical labor) became defined as the exclusive domain of men, while other tasks (e.g., political leadership, bureaucracy, the priesthood, many skilled crafts) grew to be dominated by men even if women were known to participate from time to time. Other functional roles in society—specifically child bearing, child care, food preparation, clothes washing, house cleaning—became the exclusive preserve of women.

The growing differentiation of gender roles in pre-industrial cities was encouraged, if not mandated, by an entirely new demography. Given the very high rates of death that prevailed in pre-industrial cities, perpetuating a family and preventing population decline required that women devote much more time and energy to the bearing and raising of children, thereby reifying their specialization in "caring labor" (Folbre 2001). Pre-industrial cities, in essence, created demographic conditions that favored the social definition of home and hearth as the preserve of women and the public sphere of action and work as the realm of men (Saller 1996). In the absence of antibiotics, sanitation, potable water, and a clear understanding of the principles of contagion, pre-industrial cities evinced a distinctive demography characterized by high mortality and high fertility—much higher than the levels that typically prevail in foraging societies.

According to Saller's (1996) review, the expectation of life at birth in cities of the Roman Empire was on the order 25 years. At this level of mortality, roughly one third of all births would not reach their first birthday and roughly half would not live to age 5 (see Coale and Demeny 1966). Given this level of mortality, each woman had to give birth to at least six children simply to avoid population decline (compared with just three children among the typical foraging society, where life expectancies were on the order of 35 years). The brutal demographic logic of agrarian urbanism—and for sedentary communities in agrarian societies generally—was that women had to maximize child bearing and, to the greatest extent possible, invest in child care to balance out the inevitable toll taken by infectious diseases during infancy and childhood. The resulting urban demographic structure is depicted in Figure 4.2, which shows the age pyramid for a stationary population of 100,000 inhabitants associated with a life expectancy at birth of 25 years and a total fertility rate of around 6.0 (Coale and Demeny 1966, West Model, Level 3). Although a city of 100,000 is probably larger than the average that prevailed before industrialization, it is considerably smaller than the maximum. It would be the size of a capital city of a modestly sized empire (such as ancient Egypt) or an important provincial city in an expansive empire (such as Imperial Rome).

**Figure 4.2**

**Population Pyramid of a Typical Pre-Industrial City**

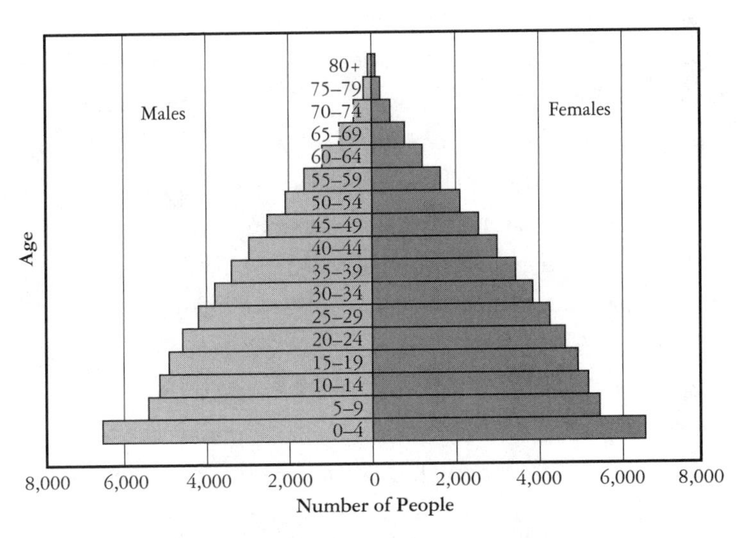


Coale and Demeny 1966, West Model, Level 3.

Although both the urban and the foraging populations are pyramidal in shape, the urban pyramid has a wider base that constricts more sharply between age intervals 0–4 and 5–9, reflecting the much higher rates of infant and childhood mortality that prevailed in pre-industrial cities. Thereafter, the share of persons in each interval is reduced systematically with rising age, gradually at first but more sharply as age increases, yielding a more gradual step-shape than in the forager population (compare Figure 2.2).

The most obvious difference between the two populations lies not in shape of their age pyramid, but in their size and scale. The community population of 159 shown for hunter-gatherers, which lies near the upper limits of foraging societies, has given way to a community of 100,000 people, which is not even close to the upper limit of size for agrarian cities. The increase in the absolute size of the population carries important implications for the organization of society and the nature of sociality. First, in a population of 100,000 people it is impossible to know everyone personally and directly through face-to-face interaction. Frequent encounters with strangers, something that rarely occurs in foraging societies, becomes commonplace in cities, and new social mechanisms governing interaction among strangers have to be worked out.

Second, the death of a young child has become a universal experience for parents living in pre-industrial cities, and serial bereavement would be the norm. This condition, moreover, probably did not vary much by social class, as the elite's understanding of the principles of contagion and its access to sanitary conditions were nearly as limited as among the masses. Children themselves could expect to lose the lion's share of their age mates as they moved from infancy to adolescence. Of 4,000 infants born in any year, just 2,180 would reach age 5; 2,048 would reach age 10; and 1,949 would reach age 15.

Death was thus a constant companion of urban dwellers in the best of times, and during periods of famine, plague, or social breakdown it would strike all ages at the same time, touching all families simultaneously. It is no surprise, therefore, that pre-industrial urban civilizations tended to develop religious beliefs centered on capricious, vengeful gods who required constant sacrifices and worship to be placated (Sjoberg 1960). Cults of death depicting skulls, skeletons, and other images of mortality were common to pre-industrial urban cultures. It is perhaps no coincidence that the world's three great monotheistic religions, all of which developed the image of God as an all-powerful but nonetheless merciful father figure, emerged in herding rather than urban societies; and all three religions—Judaism, Christianity, and Islam—contain numerous references to cities as places of iniquity and evil.

Third, although the absolute size of the urban population may have been quite large, the number of peers dropped rapidly and steadily as urban dwellers aged. In our hypothetical population of 100,000, for example, there were 13,000 people age 0–4, but there were only 7,000 people age 35–39. Thus, face-to-face interaction and relationships based on personal knowledge became more feasible as people aged, especially if one assumes that close interpersonal relations were confined to people of the same class. Adult members of the ruling class probably did know one another personally through years of face-to-face interaction.

Finally, despite the progressive reduction of numbers with rising age, the increased size and scale of cities means that for the first time in history a human society contained a significant density of old people. As never before, a society could benefit from more than a handful of people who had accumulated a long lifetime's worth of experience and knowledge. An urban population of 100,000 would be expected to have 3,000 people over the age of 65. These people were uniquely qualified to compare experiences, reflect on past events, share their wisdom, and then write it down for succeeding generations. In this hypothetical urban population we would expect to observe 560 people over the age of 80 and 160 over the age of 85. Given these small numbers, it is almost certain that within any given social class, elders would know one another well and share a long history of interaction. As scarce resources, the elderly would occupy a revered status in the social hierarchy of cities.

The population depicted in Figure 4.2 assumes that, in the long run, births balance out deaths, but many if not most pre-industrial cities probably would not even have achieved stasis were it not for ongoing in-migration from the countryside and the coerced importation of indentured workers through conquest and enslavement. As in-migration is highly selective of people in the age range 15–30 years, it would have caused a distinctive bulge in the pyramid within these age ranges. This modified shape most likely defined the social world of the pre-industrial city.

## The Limits of Agrarian Urbanism

The emergence of cities around 10,000 years ago brought about a quantum transformation of human social structure, shifting the dynamic origins of social change from the environmental and microsocial clusters to the macrosocial cluster, thus rendering Pathways 3 and 5 in Figure 1.1 increasingly important as avenues of societal evolution. The concentration of human cognitive power within a confined space enabled more efficient communication and coordination among minds and created new possibilities for parallel information processing. Once cities emerged, the pace of technological change and innovation accelerated markedly to promote further increases in population and more social differentiation, which in turn stimulated additional innovation and discovery, yielding a powerful and self-reinforcing macrosocial cycle that fed back on microsocial relations and the environment.

From around 8000 BC to around AD 1800, many important ideas and technologies were developed. The invention of writing and money in the course of constructing the first markets was followed by a string of remarkable innovations, including the sickle (2800 BC), windmills (1700 BC), gunpowder (700 BC), the iron plow (200 BC), paper (100 BC), the stirrup (AD 300), block printing (AD 700), the clock (AD 1300), movable type (AD 1400), the rifle and explosive bombs (AD 1500), the thermometer (AD 1593), the telescope (AD 1605), the barometer (AD 1643), and the bicycle (AD 1690). Each of these inventions had important effects on the size and structure of cities and the nature of social relations within them, so that there is no single or uniform "type" for a pre-industrial city (Chant and Goodman 1999).

Yet none of these innovations fundamentally altered urban living or the relative prevalence of cities in human society. Prior to industrialization, very few humans beings were able to live in cities: The meager surplus created under a system of peasant agriculture could sustain an overall rate of urbanization of only around 5% (Preston 1979); individual city size was constrained by high morality and endemic disease (Preston and Haines 1991); density was limited by an inability to build higher than four stories using brick-and-mortar (Sjoberg 1960); and physical sprawl was limited by a reliance on human- and animal-power for all transportation and communication (Hershberg et al. 1981). As a result, the vast majority of humans continued to live in small towns and agricultural villages, the number of urban settlements remained small, few ever reached a population of 100,000, and none exceeded a million inhabitants.

Although stratification within cities could be quite rigid and social mobility was limited, the absolute need for people to live near jobs, shops, and services limited the potential for spatial separation by class, occupation, or ethnicity. In many ways, therefore, social life continued to be dominated by face-to-face interactions on streets of low-density pedestrian traffic or within small open spaces situated in neighborhoods that were not much larger than villages. Within a particular quarter, people generally knew one another either directly from personal contact or indirectly through position in an identifiable social network. Of all forms of stratification, perhaps the one between men and women was greatest, with the public sphere of work and politics given increasingly over to men and the private sphere of home and family reserved for women.

Although the pace of life in cities may have been rapid in comparison with that of foraging societies, it was slow by contemporary standards. For roughly 10,000 years the size, density, and heterogeneity of cities were determined more by the fate of the external empires than by internal characteristics or processes, which remained broadly similar and relatively stable across space and time. What changed everything was a series of inventions and discoveries that led to another revolution in technology, population, and social organization. This revolution was to have even more far-reaching consequences than the agricultural revolution: a complex of dramatic social and economic changes that came to be known as industrialization.

# Chapter Five
# INDUSTRIAL URBANISM

FOR MOST OF HUMAN EXISTENCE, social change was powered by the environmental cluster, with microsocial relations and macrosocial structures being determined mainly by temporal and geographic variation in temperature, terrain, and the availability and form of water. The creation of the first cities heightened the importance of macrosocial factors—population, technology, and social organization—as agents of social change, bringing about significant feedback effects on both environment and human interactions at the micro level. However, the potential for these feedbacks to set off a cycle of self-reinforcing societal evolution was ultimately constrained by the limits of pre-industrial technology.

All in all, agrarian urbanism proved to be a relatively stable and durable social system. Although numerous empires came and went in the nine thousand years from approximately 8000 BC to AD 1000, the basic contours of urban society remained largely unchanged. Throughout the period, city size was limited by the area of the agrarian hinterland; the rate of urbanization was limited by low productivity in agriculture; communication required physical travel by human beings; the fastest transport was by sail over water, and overland travel was slow, costly, and dependent on animal power; goods were manufactured by skilled artisans fabricating one item at a time within a single workshop; stratification was rigid and social mobility limited; few markets existed; and social interactions continued to be dominated by relations of communal sharing and equality matching, overlaid with a veneer of authority ranking imposed by urban elites (Sjoberg 1960).

Empires persisted for hundreds and even thousands of years without altering their basic structure, organization, or culture. Somewhere around a thousand years ago, however, the world began to change in important ways. Innovations in political organization and technology gave birth to a material revolution that vastly increased human productivity and released cities from technical limits on their size, density, and number. The resulting wave of urbanization transformed human social and economic life and shifted the impetus for social change decisively away from the environment and placed it firmly in the macrosocial cluster.

## EMERGENCE OF THE INDUSTRIAL ORDER

The collapse of the Roman Empire in 476 brought about a marked decline in urbanism throughout western Europe as cities, markets, and trade routes withered and gradually fell away (Pirenne 1925). Although large swaths of the former Roman Empire were absorbed into the successor agrarian states of Byzantium, the Islamic caliphates, and for a time the Carolingian empire, after 1000 most of western Europe languished outside of any centralized polity and was divided into a series of small, independent kingdoms that competed with one another in a shifting patchwork of alliances known as feudalism. Although, like agrarian urbanism, feudalism rested on an agricultural base, its politics were quite different compared with those of the agrarian empires that had gone before.

Whereas agrarian states imposed political order from above by using military force and administrative power, a new technology of warfare changed the calculus of political domination in feudal Europe (Levine 2001). With the adoption of the stirrup, mounted horsemen in heavy armor acquired a decisive battlefield advantage over infantry, bowmen, and regular cavalry. Maintaining a knight in the field, however, required a rather large capital investment that was beyond the capacity of a single lord. Feudalism emerged as a means of financing this new man-of-war. Vassals were granted suzerainty over a territory and its people, from which they were expected to support themselves as knights. The knights—basically the armored tanks of their day—were then expected to remain on call as soldiers to defend the king's interests.

Under feudalism, an all-powerful sovereign did not issue imperial orders from above, but contracted with semi-autonomous lords who offered arms in return for socially defined privileges. These lords in turn negotiated a social compact with peasants, who in turn surrendered their labor and agricultural produce to support their squire's knightly enterprise in exchange for other rights and privileges. Although feudal relationships may have been decidedly asymmetrical and unequal, they were nonetheless *negotiated* and therefore fundamentally different from the politics of empire that had transpired before.

Cities also came to acquire semi-autonomous power in the feudal order (Pirenne 1925). Urban merchants began to rebuild the trade routes and markets that had shriveled with the demise of Rome, and they extended new trade routes into northern and eastern Europe and the Islamic empires of northern Africa, the Middle East, and Spain. The revival of trade brought about a resurgence of markets, the reintroduction of currencies, and a new burst of capital accumulation. As a result, urban merchants offered kings and nobles an attractive source of tax revenue to support their knightly ambitions.

In return for granting merchants the freedom to pursue commercial interests, make investments, and reap profits, the royals and the landed gentry imposed tolerable rates of taxation. Urban merchants and feudal lords shared a common interest in local autonomy and commercial freedom. With limited rights of self-government being granted to cities, more wealth was produced by merchants to provide more tax revenues for the knightly enterprise (Pirenne 1925; Levine 2001).

The Roman Catholic Church, meanwhile, provided a multilateral framework that held the whole system together. The expansion of papal power, in particular, provided a semblance of international stability and global governance (Levine 2001). At about the same time, Gregorian reformers inserted themselves into medieval social life, forcing celibacy on a reluctant priesthood, restricting sex to marriage, and making primogeniture (the right of the eldest son to inherit all property) the basic rule of inheritance. This ecclesiastical revolution created a new family system characterized by late marriage, widespread spinsterhood, and inheritance of property by the eldest male, providing both monasteries and commerce with a ready source of recruits from among the younger sons of landed families (Hajnal 1982; Coale and Watkins 1986; Levine 2001).

The new family system slowed population growth by reducing the number of married women and thus the number exposed to the risk of childbearing. Primogeniture, meanwhile, limited the fragmentation of landholding. These social changes occurred in tandem with technological innovations that raised agricultural productivity—namely, the introduction of the iron plow, new methods of crop rotation, the substitution of horses for oxen, and the application of wind and water power for the milling of grain (Levine 2001). As a result of these and other changes, the food supply increased, peasant households reproduced, and European population densities rose in both town and countryside.

By around 1340, even the most marginal lands were in production and feudalism was on the verge of sinking into a low-level equilibrium trap where population growth overwhelmed land resources to create chronic food shortages (Levine 2001). The event that prevented this cycle of economic decline from setting in was the arrival in 1348 of the Black Death, a flea-borne plague that killed rich and poor alike, city dweller as well as rural villager, and within a few years cut western Europe's population by one third (McNeill 1976). This massive wave of mortality transformed the social order in several important ways (Levine 2001).

First, by opening vacancies at the top of the social hierarchy, it created new possibilities for social mobility from below. Second, by reducing the number of workers, it enhanced the bargaining power of labor and enabled workers to renegotiate the terms of their social contracts, leading to a rise in wages and the creation of nascent labor markets. Third, rural population loss led to farm abandonment and the emergence of the first land markets. Fourth, because the plague killed people but left capital untouched, it dramatically increased capital:labor ratios, yielding a sudden, if perverse, surge in capital formation. Finally, the experience of massive mortality reoriented the outlook of those who survived, prompting them to focus more on the fruits of this world rather than on promised rewards in the next.

Once the plague had run its course, the stage was set for the emergence of the modern world. All that was needed was a set of new technologies that could increase productivity enough to support a large non-agrarian population. The invention of the blast furnace in 1621 made possible the mass production of steel and offered a cheap metal that was strong enough to contain boiling water under pressure, leading in 1698 to the invention of the steam engine. Although the original engine was inefficient and of little practical use, its design was improved in successive steps until 1765, when James Watt of Scotland added a separate condenser connected to a cylinder by means of a valve, thereby enabling the condenser to remain cool while the cylinder was hot (McClellan and Dorn 1999).

Watt's patented design yielded a steam engine that efficiently converted heat from burning coal into mechanical power that could be applied to a wide variety of practical tasks. The productive potential of the steam engine was fully realized when it was combined with a social reorganization of manufacturing that broke production down into a series of discrete but interconnected steps. Rather than occurring in small workshops where one or a few artisans worked on one item from start to finish, production was reconfigured to occur in a cooperative *division of labor* that involved a large number of people applying machine power independently in coordinated fashion across a series of discrete steps that were linked together to form an integrated productive process.

When this revolution in social organization was combined with steam technology, it enabled human beings to fabricate a very large number of standardized items at very low cost. The end result was a revolutionary increase in human productivity: the ability to produce a vast array of goods with relatively modest inputs of human labor. The Industrial Revolution emerged in England as steam power was applied to transform the cotton and woollen industries. After the invention of spinning frames and mechanized looms in the late 1760s, textile mills were established along rivers; but after 1780 Watt's steam engine was substituted for water power and mechanized plants began to spring up throughout the English Midlands. Between 1780 and 1840 the production of British textiles increased by a factor of 50, creating vast new fortunes among the entrepreneurial factory owners.

In the 1770s factory methods were first applied to agriculture; and the introduction of the steel plow in 1837 dramatically increased farm production to overcome the historical imbalance between population growth and food supply, which up to then had held population growth in check (Malthus 1798). After 1820 British entrepreneurs and engineers applied steam power successively to a growing array of manufacturing processes to create a plethora of new products that were sold to paid laborers, who in turn spent their resulting earnings to buy the manufactured products on expanding urban consumer markets.

In 1787 steam power was harnessed to a propeller and used to drive ships through water, and by 1807 the first commercial steamship line had been established; these developments provided a quick, reliable, and inexpensive means of transoceanic and riverine travel. Steam power and factory organization soon spread across the English Channel to Germany and the Netherlands and then moved steadily southward and eastward to reach Russia by 1851, Italy by 1854, and Spain by 1859 (Massey 1988). By 1870 it had jumped across the Atlantic to launch industrialization in the Americas, notably in Argentina, Canada, Brazil, and the United States (Thomas 1973).

In 1800 the first steel suspension bridge was built and in 1804 the first steam locomotive was constructed, finally liberating human beings from their dependence on animate power for overland movement. With the advent of railroads, cost-effective transportation for the first time could be supplied to human settlements regardless of location or terrain (McClellan and Dorn 1999). The telegraph was invented in 1837, and railroad beds were put into service as clear corridors for cables to create an integrated network of transportation and communication linking the new industrial cities. The first transatlantic telegraph cable became operational in 1857. With the advent of the telegraph, for the first time in human experience a person did not have to travel physically through space to transmit information from one place to another. The functions of transportation and communication began to separate.

All of these technological changes brought about the massive societal transformation known today as the Industrial Revolution. The revolutionary nature of the change in the economy is indicated in Figure 5.1, which shows gross world product (GWP)—the total value of goods and services produced by human beings throughout the globe—from the dawn of modernity in 1000 to the apogee of industrialism in 1950. At the beginning of this period, GWP was estimated to have been around $102 trillion (see Maddison 2001). Seven hundred years later it reached $370 trillion, for an average growth rate of just 0.2% per year between 1000 and 1700.

As small as this rate of growth was, it was still much larger than that prevailing over the prior nine millennia. After 1700, however, the pace of economic production accelerated dramatically, and it surged after 1850 to reach exponential levels. Between 1850 and 1950, GWP increased from $939 trillion to $5,336 trillion, for an average annual growth rate of 2.1%—a tenfold increase over the period 1000–1700 and a quantum leap over the rates of economic growth that had prevailed under agrarianism (Maddison 2001).

**Figure 5.1**

**Gross World Product (GWP), 1000–1950**

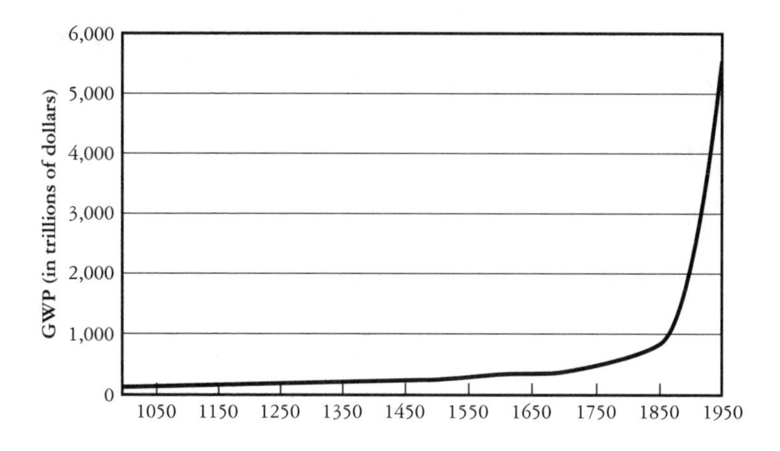


Adapted from *The World Economy: Historical Statistics*, by Angus Maddison, 2004. Paris: Organization for Economic Cooperation and Development, Table B-18.

The Industrial Revolution likewise promoted a sustained increase in population after 1600. As shown in Figure 5.2, the number of human beings on earth accelerated and population growth also reached exponential levels after 1700 (see the dashed line). Most of the new people were absorbed by urban areas, and in 1800 the share of human beings residing in cities finally pierced the 5% cap that had constrained human societies since the invention of agriculture. As the solid line shows, after nearly 10,000 years of low-level stasis, the level of global urbanization grew rapidly from 5% to 28% in just 150 years, from 1800 to 1950 (United Nations 1980).

**Figure 5.2**

**World Population and Percentage Urban, 1000–1950**

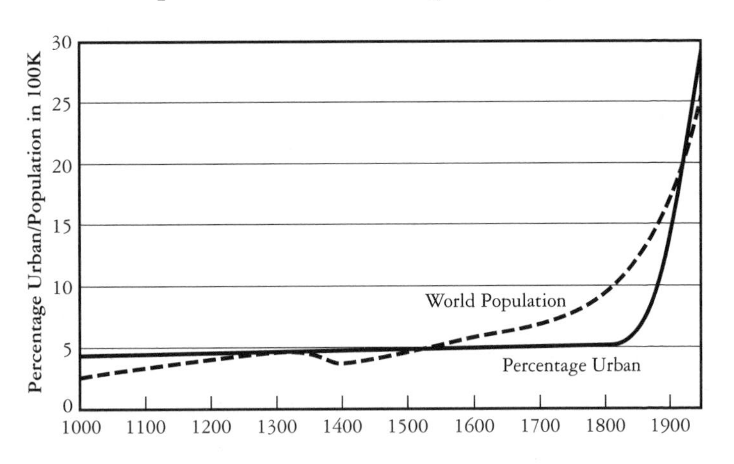


Adapted from ***A Concise History of World Population***, by Massimo Livi-Bacci, 1992. Oxford: Oxford University Press, Table 1.3; and *Patterns of Urban and Rural Population Growth*, United Nations, 1980. New York: United Nations, Tables 2 and 3.

Impressive as this gain in urbanization may seem, however, it fails to convey the full scale of the transformation that was occurring in the world's industrializing societies, for most of the world had not yet achieved the prerequisites of industrial takeoff. Figure 5.3 shows trends in urbanization separately for nations that were classified as more and less developed as of 1950. Urbanization in less developed nations only began to rise around 1900 and in 1950 stood at just 17%. In contrast, urbanization in developed nations began a century earlier and by 1950 had reached 53%. For the first time in recorded history, an absolute majority of a society's members were able to live in cities rather than in the countryside. Remarkably, in western Europe and

**Figure 5.3**
**Urbanization in More and Less Developed Nations, 1800–1950**

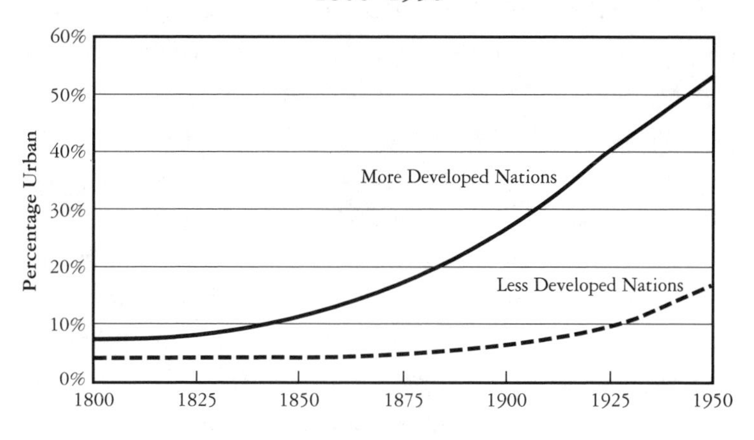


Adapted from *Patterns of Urban and Rural Population Growth*, United Nations, 1980. New York: United Nations, Table 3.

North America almost two thirds (64%) had become city dwellers by the mid-twentieth century (United Nations 1980).

Although the interconnected revolutions in food production, manufacturing, transportation, and communication enabled the number, population, and geographic range of cities to increase, until late in the nineteenth century urban densities were still constrained by two obstinate technical limits. The first was medicinal: As long as infectious diseases remained outside of human control, urban mortality continued at high rates to create a permanent structural imbalance between births and deaths that offset the positive effect of in-migration to inhibit urbanization. Although the first successful vaccination occurred in 1796, it was not until 1881 that Louis Pasteur proved the germ theory of contagion to provide public officials with the scientific knowledge they needed to bring urban mortality under control. Municipal investments in water purification, sewage treatment, and housing in the late nineteenth and early twentieth centuries caused urban death rates to plummet and reversed the historical rural-urban mortality differential (Preston and Haines 1991). It soon became safer to live in cities served by efficient water and sewage systems and near hospitals and clinics than in the countryside.

The second limitation on density was mechanical: the inability to build very far upward. In theory, the availability of milled steel might have permitted humans to construct metal-framed structures as early as the eighteenth century, but heights were still constrained by the reluctance of people to walk up more than four flights of stairs on a regular basis. Density was also limited by the inability to heat, light, and ventilate large multistory buildings without suffocating, freezing, or overheating the inhabitants. These technical constraints were overcome with the adoption of electricity as a means of transmitting and distributing power.

The first electric generator was built in 1831 by Michael Faraday. After 1870 the first coal-fired generators were placed into service, followed in the 1880s by the first hydroelectric dams. Elisha Otis invented the elevator in 1852; once electric power became widely available, he began installing elevators in tall buildings throughout the developed world. Suddenly people could travel up and down dozens of floors effortlessly and the four-story height ceiling was permanently breached: The era of the skyscraper had arrived. At the same time, the invention of the incandescent light bulb (1879) and the electric fan (1882) provided solutions to the long-standing problems of heating, lighting, and ventilating interior spaces; and the invention of the telephone in 1876 enabled instantaneous communication between floors, not to mention across town.

With the last of the technical constraints having been lifted, urban population densities exploded in the nineteenth and early twentieth centuries. The rise in urban density is illustrated by Figure 5.4, which shows population density for Manhattan from 1790 to 1920. Being an island, the total amount of land is fixed, creating a natural barrier to population growth. As long as the constraint of building height prevailed, density was ultimately limited by the availability of land. Once the island was fully built out at around four stories, a point more or less reached around 1860, further increases in density were not possible because the only room for expansion was upward. Al-

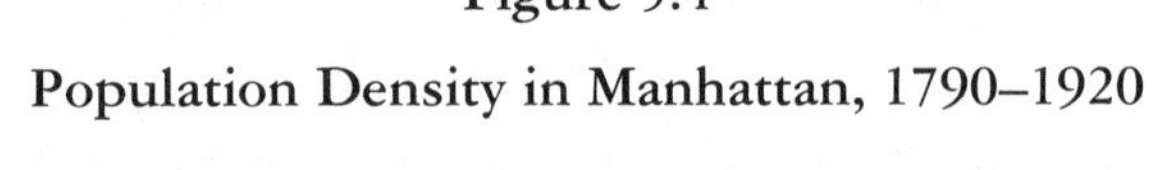

**Figure 5.4**

**Population Density in Manhattan, 1790–1920**

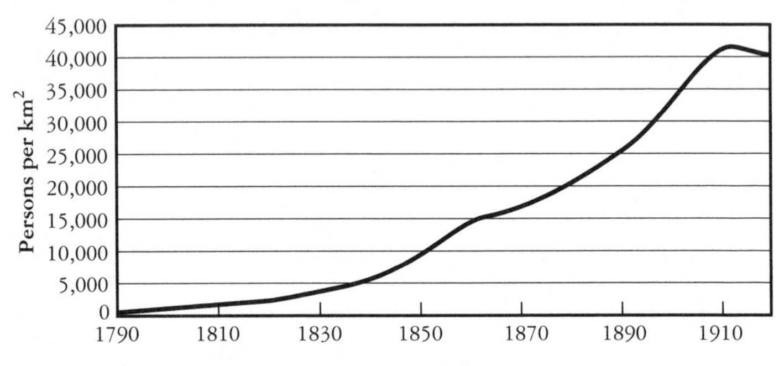


Adapted from Web site of *Demographia*: www.demographia.com/dbx-nyc.htm.

though Manhattan's density rose by a remarkable yearly average of 4.6% between 1790 and 1860, in the decade after 1860 it stalled and fell to just 1.5% per year.

With the technical constraints on building height lifted after 1870, however, population growth resumed and density increased at a rate of 2.3% per year until 1910, when it peaked at around 41,000 persons per km$^2$. At that date, an astounding 160,000 persons per km$^2$ lived in Manhattan's most densely settled neighborhoods, and the total number of New Yorkers soared to 5.6 million within a larger urbanized region of 7 million people (Gibson 1998). No human settlement that large had ever before existed, and an utterly new social form had come into existence.

## The Industrial City

The social sciences emerged in tandem with the Industrial Revolution, and in many ways they represented an attempt by contemporary observers to make sense of the new social order. It is clear that social scientists working in the late nineteenth and early twentieth centuries realized that something extraordinary was afoot, that a significant milestone in human history had been reached. The belief that a Rubicon had been crossed is reflected in the prevalence of contrast theories, conceptual models that posited diametrically opposed kinds of societies: "traditional" versus "modern." Thus, Tönnies (1940 [1887]) spoke of Gemeinschaft versus Gesellschaft, Durkheim (1933 [1893]) of mechanical versus organic solidarity, Weber (1968 [1914]) of traditional versus charismatic or bureaucratic authority, and Redfield (1934) of the folk-urban continuum. Regardless of the words they used, social scientists around 1900 were clearly fascinated by the new social order and how it differed from social orders of the past.

### *A New Scale of Society*

Perhaps the most obvious effect of the Industrial Revolution was to increase the absolute size of human agglomerations and thus raise the sheer scale of human societies (Shevky and Bell 1955). As late as 1800, no human settlement contained more than a million inhabitants and only six exceeded 500,000. By 1925, however, 44 cities contained at least half a million inhabitants and 35 held more than a million. In 1950, the number of cities with more than a million inhabitants reached 77 and an additional 99 cities contained more than 500,000 residents. By mid-century, the New York metropolitan area alone contained 12.3 million people and metropolitan London had 10.4 million residents (Chandler and Fox 1974). In just 150 years, the number of people living in cities of 1 million or more went from 0 to 187 million and the total number of people living in cities over half a million reached 255 million, constituting more than one third of all urban dwellers and one tenth of all human beings on earth (United Nations 1980).

Societies of this scale were unprecedented in human experience. Never had so many people occupied such small amounts of space at the same point in time. In the course of daily life, a typical resident of New York, Chicago, London, or Berlin could expect to come into contact with thousands of people. In the densest neighborhoods, a person would be surrounded by tens of thousands of "neighbors," and a single factory might regularly bring together as many as 60,000 workers or more. At its peak in the 1930s, for example, the Ford Motor Company's Rouge River plant in Dearborn, Michigan, employed some 100,000 people (Stepan-Norris and Zeitlin 1995).

*New Social Structures*

The increasing size of cities and the growing scale of society were accompanied by a marked increase in the extent of social differentiation (Shevky and Bell 1955). The invention of the steam engine may have made the Industrial Revolution possible, but it was the division of labor that enabled the new machines to be used efficiently. The reconfiguration of manufacturing into constituent tasks entailed occupational specialization. As noted earlier, in the new division of labor, workers were trained for specific, narrowly defined tasks that were organized sequentially into a larger, interconnected set of operations. Workers no longer made an object from start to finish using hand tools, but applied customized machines to carry out specific tasks in a longer chain of transformative operations that produced a finished product.

Not only were urban workers allocated to different tasks as part of a coordinated chain of production; other workers were employed in ancillary roles to design the machines, manufacture them, and keep them working. Still other workers were required to plan, manage, and supervise the factory's coordinated operations, maintain its accounts, ship its products, and sell its goods; and even more workers were needed to train people in the skills and abilities necessary to undertake these activities. The money earned by these various laborers created new demands for personal and professional services that were met by still more workers. To manage growing urban populations, city governments formed police departments, fire departments, health departments, sanitation commissions, libraries, transportation authorities, and a host of other agencies, leading to the rapid growth of municipal bureaucracies (Hershberg et al. 1981).

The generation and spending of income by factory, service, managerial, and professional workers had strong multiplier effects, producing an upward cycle of investment, hiring, production, consumption, and, ultimately, occupational differentiation. The resulting diversification of the occupational structure is illustrated by Figure 5.5, which plots variation in the distribution of U.S. workers across occupational categories from 1850 to 1950, using data from the Integrated Public Use Microdata Sample Web site (http://ipums.edu). To ensure continuity over time, occupations in each year are classified according to the 1950 occupational coding scheme. Changes in

Figure 5.5
Occupational Differentiation in the
United States, 1850–1950

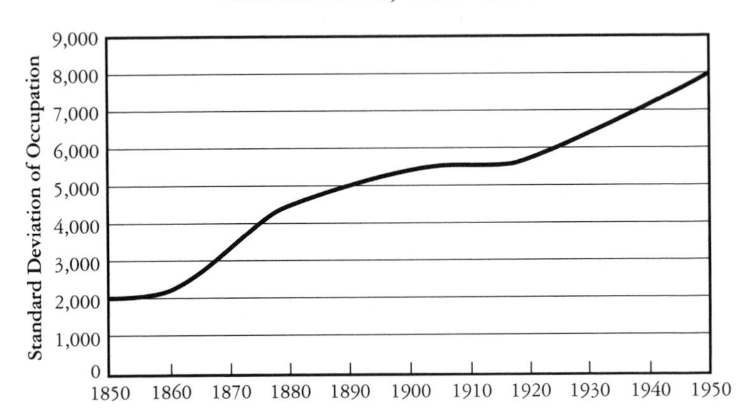


Adapted from data downloaded from the Web site of the Integrated Public Use Microdata Samples: http://ipums.edu.

occupational diversity therefore reflect the growing differentiation of workers across a fixed set of categories rather than shifts in the number of categories themselves.

As the figure shows, on the eve of the American Industrial Revolution in 1850, variability in the distribution of workers across occupational categories stood at around 2000. It thereafter increased rapidly from 1860 to 1890, slowed down briefly, and then resumed rapid growth after 1920, reaching a figure of 8,000 in 1950. Over the course of a century, in other words, the degree of occupational differentiation in the United States increased by a factor of four. More people were distinguished from one another in more ways across more categorical boundaries than ever before. Social heterogeneity grew at an unprecedented rate.

Occupational diversification not only implied nominal or qualitative differences among people; it also entailed differentiation on the basis of skill, control, power, and value-added. Workers in different occupations were paid at different rates by entrepreneurs and employers, whose own interests lay in keeping wages and salaries as low as possible to maximize profits. Occupational differentiation thus led directly to increased inequality on the basis of income and wealth, as indicated by Figure 5.6. The solid line shows the largest personal fortune in the United States at various times between 1790 and 1940, and the dashed line depicts the ratio of this fortune to the median U.S. income (from Phillips 2002).

In 1790, the United States was still a pre-industrial agrarian economy and the distance from the top to the bottom of the

**Figure 5.6**

**Income Inequality in the United States, 1790–1940**

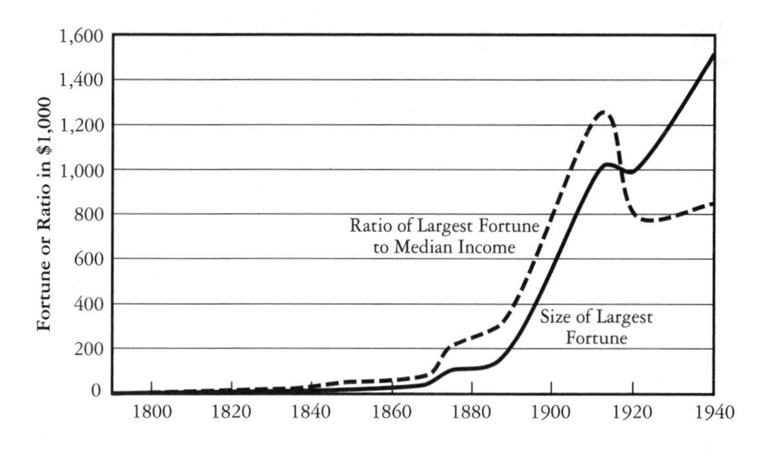


Adapted from *Wealth and Democracy: A Political History of the American* ***Rich***, by Kevin Phillips, 2002. New York: Broadway Books, p. 38.

wealth distribution was around $1 million. The ratio of this fortune to the median income was on the order of 4,000:1. Not much changed in the United States until the Civil War, when the U.S. economy experienced its structural transformation to industrialism (Thomas 1973). After 1870, both indicators shot dramatically upward as material inequality increased at an exponential rate. Between 1870 and 1910, the distance from the top to the bottom of the wealth distribution rose to $1 billion (a tenfold increase) and the ratio of the largest fortune to median income grew from 4,000:1 to 12,000:1 (a threefold increase). After 1920, the wealth-to-income ratio moderated as median incomes rose faster than the size of the largest fortune; but the absolute distance from the top to the bottom of the wealth distribution continued to widen, reaching $1.5 billion by 1940.

This new stratification arose from pricing mechanisms that were quite different from the categorical mechanisms of inequality that had prevailed beforehand. To be sure, social boundaries between haves and have-nots continued to be defined and reified during the industrial era, thereby enabling the concomitant operation of the age-old stratification processes of exploitation and opportunity hoarding; but in quantitative terms, the stratification of income and wealth produced between 1850 and 1950 stemmed more from pricing mechanisms associated with the rise of markets than from the operation of traditional mechanisms of categorical exclusion.

As industrialization proceeded, the receipt of wages and salaries by ever larger numbers of workers led to the rise of markets as the primary means by which goods and services were produced and distributed. As a result, the relations of market pricing extended into more and wider circles of social interaction and eventually came to dominate those of communal sharing and equality matching. In addition to small, localized commodity markets that had long been housed in cities, mass markets for the sale of labor, capital, insurance, credit, and consumer goods arose within and among the new urban areas.

The consolidation and expansion of markets, in turn, required currencies that were convertible, weights and measures that were standardized, and contracts that were enforceable within in a common legal system. With industrialization, barriers to trade and exchange became barriers to economic progress and were gradually eliminated, though not without struggle, mostly by the formation and consolidation of nation-states. With bourgeois intellectuals and urban merchants leading the way, the plethora of kingdoms and principalities inherited from the feudal era (as well as the multitude of colonies they established in the Americas) were welded together to form unified states that supported a common legal and monetary order backed up by authorities who claimed a monopoly on the legitimate use of force.

At first, national unification occurred under the auspices of powerful monarchs; but as markets and commercial relations increased in importance, the prerogatives and privileges of the nobility were curtailed and power was ultimately transferred to elected assemblies, sometimes gradually (as in Britain) and sometimes suddenly and violently (as in France). Over time, the voting franchise progressively expanded to incorporate ever-widening segments of society, beginning with male landowners and then extending to adult male merchants, professionals, workers, nonworkers, and eventually in most Western industrial societies, women.

Markets did not spring into existence as forces of nature, however. Rather, they were gradually created by specific human actions and decisions, sometimes deliberate and sometimes coincident with other developments (Swedberg 2003; Massey 2005). Whatever their specific character and origins, markets remained socially embedded in the societies that created them (Granovetter 1985). Although the history of modern society coincides with the rise of markets and their insertion into ever-widening spheres of human behavior, there was no single path to the market. Rather, the world produced a set of "divergent capitalisms" (Whitley 1999) composed of a range of different "varieties" (Hall and Soskice 2001) built on varying economic "architectures" (Fligstein 2001).

The macrosocial differentiation that accompanied the industrialization and urbanization of society brought about profound changes in sociality at the micro level, notably in the family life cycle (Shevky and Bell 1955; Bogin 2001). The economic logic of family life changed dramatically in the course of shifting from peasant agriculture to industrial manufacturing. Within peasant economies, children expanded production by contributing more labor as they grew older. Young people married as soon as they could and lived with or near parents to help them farm and thereby diversify the costs and risks of production. Within rural agrarian economies, farm production rose in tandem with growing families and children constituted an economic asset rather than a liability (Chayanov 1966). The more children, the greater the amount of food produced for consumption or sale, the greater the accumulation of household resources, and the greater the likelihood that parents would be supported in old age. In rural agrarian societies, wealth tends to flow from children to parents, yielding high rates of fertility and large families living together in multigenerational households or compounds (Caldwell 1982).

Within industrial cities, in contrast, children came to represent liabilities rather than assets. The need for better-educated, more skilled, and more mature workers brought about the expansion of public education, the imposition of mandatory schooling, and the passage of child labor laws. Within industrial societies, the period of childhood was lengthened and a new stage of prolonged adolescence was created. Rather than bringing economic resources and wealth to the family as they grew older, children constituted an ongoing drain on resources because they consumed much and produced little, at least until they were young adults and about to leave the household. As a result, fertility rates fell, family sizes dropped, and women increasingly worked to supplement family income.

Families in industrial societies, in other words, were increasingly differentiated from one another by stage in the life cycle (Mayer and Shoepflin 1989). Rather than constituting a homogenous population of multigenerational households, urban society became a diverse composite of nuclear families located at different stages of the life course. The earliest stage consisted of a young, recently married couple with no children, followed in sequence by couples with young children, couples with older children, couples with no children, and a widowed parent living alone or with one of their children. As household structure became increasingly heterogeneous, the process of human aging was played out across a series of discrete households rather than within the confines of a single extended family.

Although the emergence of mass markets occurred first within the new nation-states, soon the trade in goods, services, raw materials, and capital expanded to transcend national boundaries, leading to the emergence of a vigorous international economy and an expanding regime of global trade and commerce that flourished from 1800 to 1914 and persisted in a weakened state until 1929 (Kenwood and Lougheed 1999; O'Rourke and Williamson 1999; James 2001). This global trading regime was characterized by a remarkable and sustained increase in international factor mobility (Hatton and Williamson 1998).

In general, capital flowed outward from core European nations such as Britain, the Netherlands, and Germany and was invested in the emerging markets of eastern Europe, the Mediterranean, Oceania, and especially the Americas. Periods of capital investment in developing economies were followed by surges of construction and factory production that attracted emigrants from Europe (Thomas 1973). When growth slowed in the emerging economies, investment was redirected back to cities in core nations to bring about an expansion of economic activity there that promoted rural-urban migration to the exclusion of international movement (Thomas 1941; Lowell 1987).

The end result was the urbanization of Europe and the emigration of millions of peasants to emerging industrial cities overseas. Between 1800 and 1929 some 54 million people left Europe, with 60% going to the United States and the rest divided among Canada, Argentina, Brazil, Australia, and New Zealand, thereby fueling the growth and urbanization of these nations (Ferenczi 1929). The mass emigration of Europeans between 1800 and 1929 far surpassed the earlier transfer of 12 to 14 million slaves from Africa to the Americas between 1500 and 1800 (H. S. Klein 1999).

The movement of millions of immigrants of diverse origins across international boundaries brought about a new differentiation of urban society on the basis of ethnicity. Within the course of a few decades, industrial cities emerged and were transformed into mosaics of people who spoke different languages, practiced different religions, and held widely divergent cultural values and beliefs. Although these people may have been differentiated by class and religion in their home countries, for the most part nationality constituted a latent dimension of social identity prior to their arrival in industrial cities. For example, if everyone at home spoke the same dialect of Italian and was baptized, married, and dispatched in the same parish while consuming the same food, music, and literature, then labeling one's self "Italian" was not particularly meaningful. Only after migrating to a foreign metropolis along with thousands of other people from the same region and then working in factories and sharing neighborhoods alongside many thousands of other immigrants speaking Polish, Yiddish, Russian, Slovak, Lithuanian, Czech, German, and Spanish did the identity "Italian" become salient as a meaningful social category (Alba and Nee 2003). Ethnicity was an emergent phenomenon that was created and re-created through countless social encounters within industrial cities (Yancey, Ericksen, and Juliani 1976).

Within industrial cities, social boundaries among people of different national origins were sharpened by ongoing processes of conflict and competition (Park 1925; Olzak 1992), leading to a new differentiation of urban populations on the basis of ethnicity. The quintessential city of the age was Chicago, as its social structure and spatial organization were entirely a product of the industrial era. As of 1830 it was a sleepy hamlet of 100 people located on the grassy banks of the Chicago River near Lake Michigan. A century later it had a population of 3.4 million inhabitants, around 25% of whom were foreign born and another 40% the children of immigrants.

Figure 5.7 presents the distribution of Chicagoans by race and ethnicity for 1930, just after the end of mass immigration from Europe. As can be seen, native whites of native parentage—those widely considered at the time to be "real" Americans—constituted a distinct minority within the city of Chicago: just 28% of the population. Around 7% of Chicagoans were African American, and the remaining 65% were divided among 40 other national origin groups, none of which constituted more than 13% of the city population. The largest ethnic group was Poles at 12%, followed by Germans at 11%, Irish at 6%, Russians and Italians at 5%, Czechoslovakians and Swedes at 4%, and the British (those from England, Scotland, and Wales) at 3%. Although pre-industrial cities may have contained one or two religious or national minorities, ethnic diversity on this scale had never before existed within a single human settlement.

### *A New Urban Ecology*

The rise to prominence of industrialism after 1800 brought a dramatic increase in the size and scale of markets. Although markets had existed for thousands of years under agrarian ur-

## Figure 5.7
## Ethnic-Racial Composition of Chicago, 1930

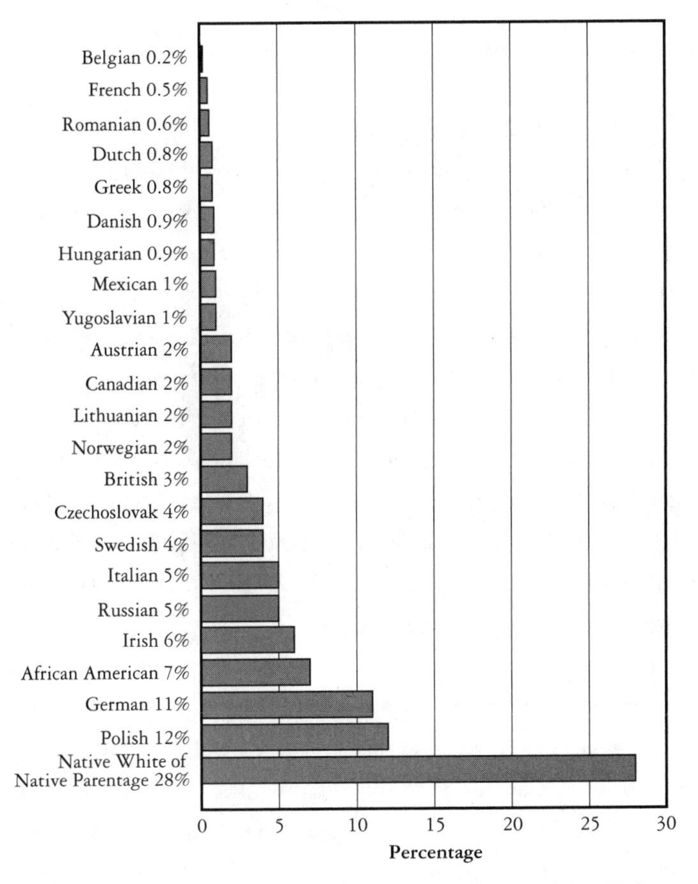


Adapted from *Fifteenth Census of the United States, Population*, Volume III, Part 1. Washington, DC: U.S. Bureau of the Census. Tables 59, 60, 67.

banism, in the industrial era they became the preeminent mechanism for interpersonal exchange and human interaction. The end result comprised a new commercialization of human behavior, a monetization of interpersonal relationships, and a growing reliance on market mechanisms for the satisfaction of most human desires: for goods and services, of course, but also for capital, credit, futures, insurance, labor, housing, and land. The material, symbolic, and emotional resources that until then had been exchanged through microsocial networks were increasingly traded on macrosocial markets.

Given the emergence of real estate markets as the principal means for determining land use and allocating people to dwellings, it was perhaps inevitable that the growing differentiation of urban society with respect to class, life cycle stage, and ethnicity would be expressed spatially. Functionally, industrialism segmented the urban landscape into zones given over to work or residence. Places of work were themselves divided according to the nature of the goods and services they produced, leading to identifiable districts devoted to heavy industry, light manufacturing, warehousing, wholesale distribution, retail sales, office and clerical work, entertainment, transportation, communication, and so on.

The separation of work from residence was enabled by the advent of efficient urban transportation, as foot and carriage traffic gave way to trolleys, streetcars, elevated trains, and subways. If workers sought to live within, say, 30 to 40 minutes of where they worked, the coming of mechanized transport extended the commuting radius from under 1 mile to 10 miles and beyond, greatly expanding the geographic area potentially open to urban settlement (Hawley 1950). Urbanization spread more rapidly along transportation axes running outward from the center, giving early industrial cities a star-shaped settlement pattern (Hurd 1903).

Efficient transportation also permitted the construction of huge factories on large tracts of land devoted exclusively to industrial functions (Hawley 1950). Factory districts within large cities routinely employed tens of thousands who labored collectively in coordinated fashion to produce a range of manufactured products. The agglomeration economies evident in pre-industrial cities were even more apparent in the industrial landscape. Heavy industry gravitated to districts well served by rail and water transport so that the high costs of transporting bulk inputs could be minimized through the use of shared infrastructure.

Industrial production also created strong *negative externalities*—conditions that adversely affected people and institutions located nearby. Steel mills, for instance, generated large amounts of heat, dust, soot, smoke, and noise, thereby providing disincentives for certain functions to locate nearby, pushing offices, stores, theaters, restaurants, and residences to locate in other specialized districts of their own.

Work-related districts sorted themselves spatially by their ability to pay the costs of land. The price of land rose in proportion to a location's accessibility within the urban system, which was greatest at the city center. The reliance on fixed-route transportation technologies during the industrial era favored a hub-and-spoke configuration wherein rail lines extended outward from a central terminal. In the archetypical industrial city, long-distance and commuter trains discharged passengers from a central station at the city core, and intra-urban rail lines—trolleys, subways, streetcars, elevated trains—converged at this or a nearby point to create a large transportation hub, such as Penn and Grand Central Stations in New York, the Chicago Loop, and 30th Street Station and Suburban Station in Philadelphia.

Given a hub-and-spoke transportation network, it was at the city center that the greatest number of people could be assembled in the smallest amount of space in the least time at the lowest cost, making it by definition the point of greatest accessibility. Rents and land values were thus highest at the city center and declined as one moved outward toward the periphery (Hawley 1950; Alonso 1964; Mills 1972).

The high cost of land encouraged more intensive use of space at the urban center, which after 1870 was achieved through upward expansion. In the United States especially, skyscrapers became the defining characteristic of the central business district. Small parcels of land were purchased at high unit cost and then put to intensive use by concentrating people and activities in tall structures. After taking into account the daytime population of workers, commuters, and shoppers along with nighttime residents, population densities within central business districts were found to reach astronomical heights (Breese 1949).

The central business district thus came to house activities that required great accessibility, used relatively little space, and could afford high rents, such as white-collar services, high-end retail shops, department stores, luxury apartments, and expensive entertainment venues such as theaters, clubs, and fancy restaurants. Because warehousing and wholesaling needed relatively large amounts of space but still had to remain accessible, they tended to locate on the fringes of the central business district in neighborhoods undergoing transition from residential to commercial land use. Heavy industrial firms also required access but consumed considerable space and produced serious externalities, leading them to locate in outlying districts along major axes of transportation, frequently at "break-in-bulk points" where arriving inputs would have to be unloaded and transferred to another transport system (Haggett 1977).

In addition to being differentiated according to function, industrial cities were also subdivided residentially. Lots and dwellings exchanged through markets were differentiated on the basis of price, leading neighborhoods to become differentiated on the basis of wealth and income. The spatial differentiation of people according to socioeconomic status was expressed residentially in terms of class segregation. Figure 5.8 shows the degree of segregation among occupational groups in Chicago at the height of the industrial era around 1950 (from Duncan and Duncan 1955).

Segregation is measured using the index of dissimilarity (Massey and Denton 1988), which varies from 0 (complete integration wherein occupational groups are distributed evenly across neighborhoods) to 100 (total segregation wherein members of different occupational groups share no neighborhood in common). Values below 30 are generally considered "low"; those from 30 to 60 are labeled "moderate"; and those over 60 are interpreted as "high" (Kantrowitz 1973). Major occupational categories are arrayed along the x-axis in order of status or prestige, moving from the lowest rank (unskilled laborer) to the highest (professional).

As shown in the figure, occupational segregation in the industrial city was generally in the low to moderate range, with index values ranging from 10 to 55 and averaging around 30.

## Figure 5.8

### Occupational Segregation in Chicago, 1950

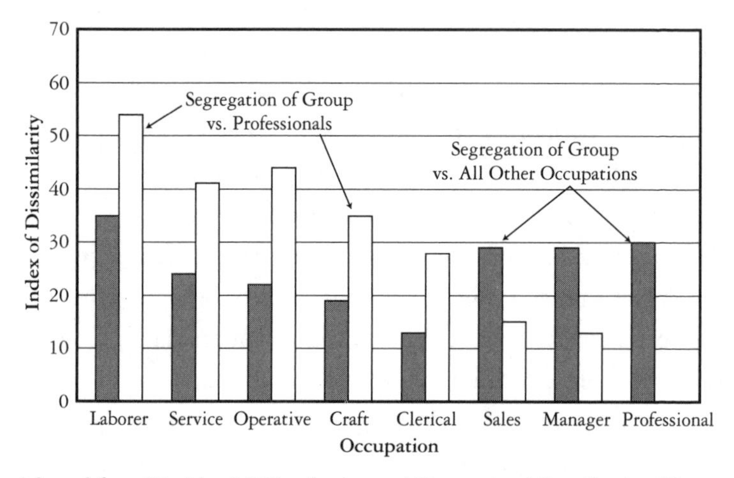


Adapted from "Residential Distribution and Occupational Stratification," by Otis D. Duncan and Beverly Duncan, 1955. *American Journal of Sociology* 60:493–503, Tables 2 and 3.

The shaded bars show the segregation of the group in question compared to incumbents of all other occupations. This series shows higher levels of segregation at the two extremes of the distribution. In other words, people with high and low occupational statuses tend to be more isolated spatially from the rest of society (with indices in the range of 30–35) compared with those in the middle of the distribution (indices of 13–24).

A general principle of industrial societies is that segregation reflects social distance: The farther apart two groups are on a social dimension, the greater their spatial separation in the urban landscape (Park 1926). The clear bars in the figure confirm this principle by showing segregation scores computed between professionals and each of the other occupational groups.

As is evident, professionals are most segregated from workers at the bottom of the occupational distribution, displaying indices of 55 relative to laborers and 41 relative to service workers. In contrast, levels of segregation between professionals and white-collar workers adjacent to them in the status distribution are much smaller, with indices of just 13 with respect to managers and 15 with sales workers.

Households with greater wealth and income naturally select housing in the most desirable residential areas. Those putting a premium on accessibility rent or buy small but expensive apartments in the city center, whereas those seeking larger houses and more land gravitate toward the periphery. Affluent households tend to settle on high ground; away from industrial districts; along favored transportation lines; near parks, lakes, or other exemplars of natural beauty; and upstream from sources of air, water, or noise pollution (Hoyt 1939). For their part, middle-class households attempt to locate as close to the wealthy as they can, and working-class households settle in districts that provide easy access to factory employment. The poor live wherever they can, most often in areas undergoing transition from one kind of land use to another.

In general, class segregation is not characterized by abrupt transitions between neighborhoods of high and low status. Rather, rich and poor neighborhoods are typically buffered by intervening neighborhoods inhabited by the middle and working classes and by non-residential land uses. No matter what their wealth or income, however, households in industrial society evinced different needs for space at different stages in the life cycle, leading to residential sorting of people on the basis of age and family type. Thus, single persons and young married couples tended to live in one part of the city; young families with children tended to locate someplace else; and those with grown children sought out other neighborhoods entirely.

The only historical study of life cycle segregation is that of Cowgill (1978), who computed dissimilarity indices to measure the degree of segregation between elderly (age 65 or older) and non-elderly (age 64 or younger) persons in U.S. metropolitan areas. His summary statistics are shown in Figure 5.9. Compared to segregation on the basis of occupation, age segregation is relatively low, at least between the elderly and the non-elderly. In 1950, average segregation between these two groups stood at just 16 across U.S. metropolitan areas, compared to values in the range of 20 to 50 for occupational segregation. There is a clear trend of rising age segregation over time, however. Between 1940 (still very much within the industrial era) and 1970 (as this era was drawing to a close), the degree of segregation between the elderly and non-elderly rose by 60%, going from an index value of 14 to one of 23.

Finally, neighborhoods of the industrial city also grew more differentiated with respect to ethnicity, as a result of international migration. Human migration invariably occurs through the use of social networks, with settled immigrants sponsoring the entry, employment, and housing of friends and relatives from the home country (Tilly and Brown 1967; MacDonald and MacDonald 1974; Massey et al. 1987). Processes of "chain migration" lead to the formation of ethnic enclaves and the clustering of people by national origin, which then serves to attract entrepreneurs who establish businesses that cater to ethnic-specific tastes (Massey 1985). The presence of group-specific amenities then encourages the arri-

Figure 5.9

Segregation between Elderly and Non-Elderly in U.S. Metropolitan Areas, 1940–1970

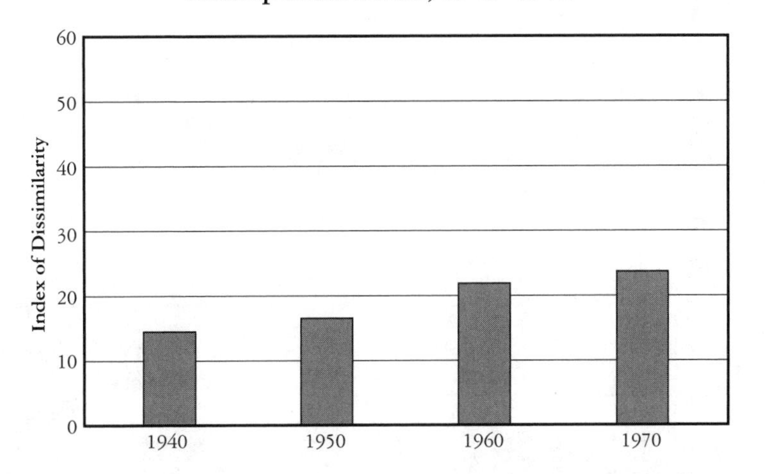


Adapted from "Residential Segregation by Age in American Metropolitan Areas," by Donald O. Cowgill, 1978. *Journal of Gerontology* 33:446–53, Table 3.

val and settlement of still others of the same national origin.

Within industrial cities, the emergence of residential clusters containing high densities of people of the same national origins produced segregation on the basis of ethnicity (Lieberson 1963). Figure 5.10 shows the segregation of different national origin groups from native whites of native parentage in Chicago during 1950 (taken from Duncan and Lieberson 1959). Most of the indices fall into the moderate range of 30 to 60. The lowest level of segregation is observed for Austrians (index value of 18), followed by the British (19), the Germans (27), the Irish (32), and Swedes (33). As can be seen, the degree of segregation from native whites is generally greater for more recently arrived European groups such as Italians (41), Russians (44), Poles (45), Czechs (49), and Lithuanians (52). In general, levels of ethnic segregation are higher among foreign-born immigrants than among their native-born children, and they decline with rising socioeconomic status (Lieberson 1961, 1963, 1980; Kantrowitz 1969, 1973; Bleda 1978, 1979).

**Figure 5.10**

**Ethnic Segregation from Native Whites of Native Parentage in Chicago, 1950**

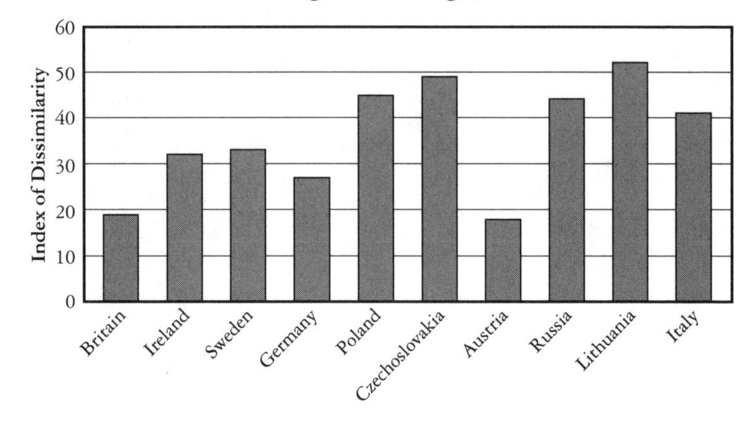


Adapted from "Ethnic Segregation and Assimilation," by Otis Dudley Duncan and Stanley Lieberson, 1959. *American Journal of Sociology* 64:364–374, Table 1.

The market-based expression of housing needs and residential preferences shaped by socioeconomic status, life cycle stage, and ethnicity generally produced low to moderate levels of segregation. Life cycle segregation was generally least, followed by socioeconomic segregation, and ethnic segregation was usually the highest, although levels varied considerably depending on the recency of the group's arrival and its socioeconomic composition. For some European ethnic groups in some cities, segregation spilled over into the "high" range with dissimilarity scores of 60 or above (Hershberg et al. 1981), suggesting the potential operation of categorical mechanisms of exclusion rather than the expression of preferences through markets.

Indeed, the 1920s were a time of great anti-foreign prejudice and intense nativism in the United States (Higham 1955), and many of the newer immigrant groups were widely perceived to be less than fully white, despite their European origins (Ignatiev 1995). Over time, however, as generational succession and socioeconomic mobility ensued, the children and grandchildren of European immigrants were gradually incorporated into the residential structure of American cities. Without a steady supply of new immigrants from abroad, the enclaves eventually withered to become skeletons of their former selves, yielding segregation indices that steadily fell across the decades (Alba and Nee 2003).

For most ethnic groups in the United States, therefore, moderate to high levels of segregation constituted a passing moment in a larger process of assimilation and resulted mainly from the interaction between markets and preferences. Although not absent, mechanisms of categorical exclusion diminished in importance as successive waves of immigrants were spatially assimilated into the fabric of American society (Massey 1985, 1988). There was, however, one great exception to the primacy of market over categorical exclusion in the industrial era: African Americans.

The social construction of race was entirely different from the social construction of ethnicity. Whereas ethnicity was socially defined *after* the arrival of heterogeneous European groups in the industrial city, race was defined *before* Africans were captured and forcibly transmited to the New World as chattel for exploitation in a pre-industrial plantation system (Frederickson 2002; Winant 2001). Indeed, the categorical definition of blacks as genetically inferior, unworthy of respect, and suited only to the meanest of labor served to justify their forced migration, enslavement, and subordination.

As late as 1870, the vast majority of African Americans lived in the rural South and remained outside the urban industrial system (Farley and Allen 1987), partcipating instead in a pre-industrial system of indentured labor regulated by a rigid racial hierarchy known as Jim Crow (Woodward 1955). The mechanization of southern agriculture and the ending of immigration from southern and eastern Europe, however, instigated a mass migration of African Americans from the rural South to the industrial North, dramatically altering the residential configuration of cities throughout the United States (Massey and Denton 1993).

At first, observers thought that African Americans might be incorporated into American cities in the manner of European immigrants (cf. Burgess 1928). It soon became apparent, however, that African Americans would be treated very differently and that the categorical mechanisms of exclusion and opportunity hoarding, not markets, would play the central role in creating and pepetuating racial inequality. Indeed, upon their arrival in industrial cities, African Americans were systematically excluded from markets and separated from other groups by a rigid color line, a phenomenon that is most clearly seen in the operation of industrial-era housing markets (Lieberson 1980).

As urban black populations grew through in-migration from the rural South, residential color lines were imposed in city after city. This occurred first by laws that demarcated "black" and "white" neighborhoods, and after this mechanism was declared unconstitutional in 1917, by institutionalized discrimination in the real estate, banking, and insurance industries, buttressed when necessary by targeted anti-black violence and the disciminatory application of government power (Massey and Denton 1993). The end result was a remarkably high degree of racial segregation that was in no way comparable to the moderate segregation experienced by European immigrant groups on the basis of ethnicity.

The unique severity of black residential segregation is documented in Figure 5.11, which shows dissimilarity indices measuring the segregation of blacks from native whites and 10 European immigrant-origin groups in Chicago during 1950. For purposes of comparison, lines are drawn to show the rough averages for segregation by ethnicity, occupation, and age that prevailed in that year. As is evident, segregation by age, occupation, and ethnicity is generally low to moderate; but black segregation is universally high. Black dissimilarity from native whites of native parentage stood at 80, and black dissimilarity scores were likewise in excess of 80 for Irish, Swedes, Germans, Poles, Czechs, Austrians, Russians, and Lithuanians. Only the British and the Italians displayed dissimilarities against blacks that were under this threshold, with values of 78 and 70, respectively.

Figure 5.11

Black Segregation in Chicago, 1950

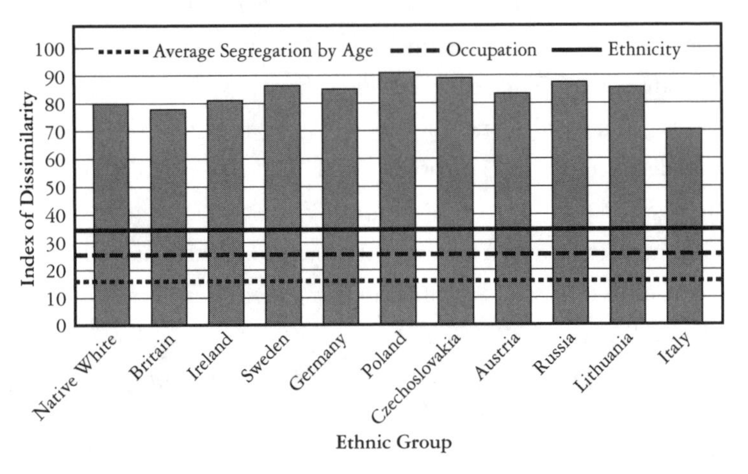


Adapted from "Ethnic Segregation and Assimilation," by Otis Dudley Duncan and Stanley Lieberson, 1959. *American Journal of Sociology* 64:364–74, Table 2.

*Urban Ecology and the Chicago School*

No other group in the industrial era within any city or in any country displayed segregation indices in excess of 80, and high levels of black segregation did not change over time, across the generations, or with rising socioeconomic status (Massey and Denton 1993). Nonetheless, the unique position of African Americans within the urban landscape was not appreciated during the 1920s when sociologists located at the University of Chicago were attempting to derive theories to describe the new urban reality (Philpott 1978). To them, black migrants from the South were just the most recently arrived in a long line of migrant groups (Taeuber and Taeuber 1964).

These sociologists—most notably Robert E. Park and

Ernest W. Burgess—appropriated ideas from classical social theory and combined them with new insights then emerging from evolutionary biology to specify a new model for spatial organization of urban society, which they tested empirically using the city of Chicago as a laboratory (Bulmer 1984). The resulting school of thought—the Chicago School of Urban Sociology—endeavored to bring conceptual order to the seeming chaos of the industrial city.

The basic precepts of the model were developed by Park (1926), who assumed that spatial structure emerged from an ongoing struggle between social groups and opposing land uses for advantage in urban space. He saw the contestation for space as being played out in a cycle of four distinct stages: competition, conflict, accommodation, and assimilation. He viewed *competition* as a kind of interpersonal jostling for spatial advantage that was constant and impersonal, occurring as a result of detached interactions among people participating in urban land and housing markets. Competition turned into *conflict* when the struggle for position became personal, involving face-to-face confrontations among identifiable members of specific social groups within the physical reality of urban space. Whereas competition determined a group's spatial location, conflict determined its social position. Hence, social and spatial positions were inextricably linked (Park 1925, 1926).

*Accommodation* occurred once conflict ceased and group members came to accept their position in the social and spatial order, going about their daily lives in ways that assumed the existence of a prevailing social ecology, thereby reifying the social and spatial structure of the city and leading to the formation of "mental maps" that divided urban space into discrete, socially defined segments (Suttles 1968; Hunter 1974). Once social and spatial relations were stabilized, *assimilation* began to occur as members of different groups interacted to share memories, sentiments, attitudes, and values over time, creating a common urban culture.

The cycle of competition, conflict, accommodation, and assimilation was expressed spatially in terms of a patterned transition process known as *ecological succession*, a concept that Park borrowed directly from the discipline of plant ecology. Ecological succession involved a three-stage shift from one functional land use to another (residential, commercial, industrial, etc.) or one social group to another (defined on the basis of class, life cycle stage, or ethnicity). The first stage of ecological succession was *invasion*, whereby a competing social group or land use encroached on other groups or land uses within a specific urban neighborhood. Encroachment was followed by *consolidation* as the new social group or land use steadily replaced the old to change the composition and character of the neighborhood. The *climax stage* occurred when the new social group or land use had fully displaced the original inhabitants to yield a new spatial equilibrium.

According to Park, ecological succession was the mechanism that caused urban space to be divided into identifiable *natural areas*, stable neighborhoods associated with particular social groups or land uses. In Park's view, cities were a patchwork of natural areas, ecological niches created by ongoing cycles of competition, conflict, accommodation, and assimilation expresssed through processes of ecological succession, yielding a series of discrete social worlds that "touched but did not overlap" (Park 1952: 198). Although Park described the mechanisms that generated urban ecological structure, he did not specifically describe the form that structure took. This task was taken up by his friend and close colleague at the University of Chicago, Ernest Burgess.

The ecological structure Burgess postulated is summarized in Figure 5.12. Burgess (1925) argued that industrial cities assumed a concentric structure composed of five distinct zones that radiated outward from a core area known as the Central Business District (CBD). The CBD was the focus of the city's social, economic, and cultural life and was created by competition at the point of greatest accessibility, which created a zone of high rents that were affordable only by specialized commercial and administrative interests. The CBD generally housed important financial institutions, corporate offices, premier department stores, civic and political organizations, large cinemas and theaters, expensive hotels, and exclusive apartments and condominiums.

Immediately outside the CBD was the Zone in Transition. Earlier in the history of the city, this zone was part of the suburban fringe and contained stately homes for the upper middle class. With the growth of the city, however, the CBD encroached on these former residences, leading to social downgrading and physical deterioration within the neighborhood. Land prices, however, were kept high by speculators anticipating the land's eventual incorporation into the CBD, even though the homes were no longer attractive to affluent families. To cover costs while waiting to cash in on the CBD's expansion, landlords subdivided formerly stately homes into cheap single-room apartments and boarding houses that were rented by newly arriving immigrants and members of other

Figure 5.12
The Burgess Concentric Zone Model of Urban Spatial Structure

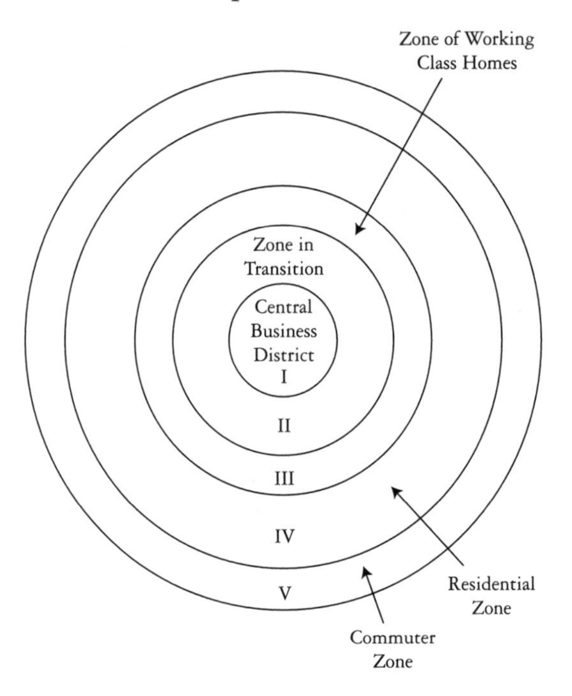


marginal social groups, such as artists, writers, gamblers, sex workers, the mentally ill, and criminal gangs. Neighborhoods of the Zone in Transition were thus transient and unstable, and contained few families with children. As soon as a couple prospered enough to have children, they moved outward to better circumstances.

The third in the series of concentric circles was the Zone of Working Class Homes, which contained families of factory workers and unskilled laborers who had prospered sufficiently to seek out better dwellings and neighborhoods. It consisted of bungalows, row houses, and tenement apartments interspersed with factories and petty retail districts. It housed members of the "respectable" working class, hard-working people who stressed traditional values and maintained strong family ties.

The Zone of Working Class Homes was followed by the Residential Zone, an area of substantial private houses and good apartments inhabited by members of the stable middle class. Burgess suggested that these individuals possessed values and orientations similar to those of small-town America, with women tending house while men traveled to work in the CBD on trolley lines, subways, or eleveated trains. Social life in this zone was matrifocal, managed by women who tended families, raised children, and socialized with one another in schools, churches, charities, and other voluntary organizations.

Finally, the most distant ring was the Commuter Zone, which was located 30 to 60 minutes from the CBD by train. It consisted of large single-family dwellings on spacious lots situated along wide, leafy streets (Ernest Hemingway referred to his native Oak Park, Illinois, just across the line from Chicago, as a place of "wide lawns and narrow minds"). This zone housed families of managerial and professional workers who staffed office towers in the Central Business District. As in the middle-class Residential Zone, social life in the Commuter Zone was matrifocal and characterized by sharp swings in the number, age, and gender of people by time of day. During working hours the Commuter Zone was inhabited primarily by women, children, and the elderly, but it achieved a more balanced age and sex distribution at night and on weekends. Of all the zones, Burgess saw the Commuter Zone as the most highly differentiated, segmented into a series of discrete communities that were separately incorporated with independent retail and civil districts that made them feel more like small villages than natural areas within a large urban area.

Burgess (1925) originally postulated this ecological structure as a framework to guide urban research. As empirical studies of cities accumulated, however, urban researchers came to question the validity of his zonal hypothesis as a universal pattern and proposed alternative ecological models. Hoyt (1939) undertook a detailed examination of the distribution of income classes, analyzing rents and housing characteristics across city blocks among 142 cities in 1900, 1915, and 1936. Whereas Burgess saw radial growth as the only process of urban expansion, Hoyt echoed Hurd's earlier observation and noted that urban growth proceeded axially as well as radially. He discovered that high-rent neighborhoods tended to move outward in sectoral fashion along established transportation lines, dividing the city ecologically into pie-shaped wedges differentiated from one another on the basis of socioeconomic status. Wealthy households tended to move outward because it was the path of least resistance, as expansion to either side usually required invading a competing natural area dominated by another social group or land use; and land was always cheaper on the periphery anyway.

A second alternative was proposed by Harris and Ullman (1945), who rejected the idea that cities were dominated by a single, all-powerful Central Business District. They postulated instead that cities were composed of many interdependent, subsidiary centers, each specializing in a particular kind of activity—retail, industrial, commercial, or residential. Their *multiple nuclei theory* argued that because different functional activities have different spatial needs, require specialized facilities, benefit from different agglomeration economies, create specific negative externalities, and differ in their ability to pay rent, they tend to cluster within identifiable areas of the city, yielding a variety of secondary centers in addition to the CBD: a financial district, a government district, a wholesale district, a manufacturing district, an industrial district, a medical district, and so on.

Shevky sought to unify the various ecological theories under the rubric of *social area analysis* (Shevky and Williams 1949; Shevky and Bell 1955). He argued that the increase in societal scale brought about by industrialization created social differentiation with respect to socioeconomic status, family status, and ethnic status, and that this heterogeneity was expressed spatially. Each group or individual could be viewed as occupying a position in a three-dimensional social space defined by these three axes of differentiation, and this social position mapped directly to a neighborhood within an ecological space defined by the same three dimensions: socioeconomic status, family status, and ethnic status.

To determine whether this three-dimensional structure indeed characterized the ecological structure of cities, Shevky and colleagues used the then-novel technique of factor analysis, a complex statistical algorithm designed to reduce a large number of empirical indicators down to a small set of underlying dimensions of common variation. They assembled indicators available from the U.S. census and factor analyzed patterns of covariation across census tracts in Los Angeles (Shevky and Williams 1949), and then refined the analysis and replicated it for the city of San Francisco (Shevky and Bell 1955).

Both studies uncovered an interpretable factor structure of three dimensions. The first and strongest factor was socioeconomic status, displaying high correlations with variables such as income, home value, rent, education, employment, and occupational status. The second ecological factor, which they called family status, was highly correlated with indicators of a tract's age composition, sex ratio, birth rate, and household structure. The third factor was correlated with indicators of mobility, such as the relative number of recent in-migrants, the relative number of foreign-born, and the relative number of people born in a different state. It was also correlated with measures of ethnic composition, such as the percentage of blacks, Italians, Poles, Russians, Latinos, or Asians present in the neighborhood. Thus, the researchers called this factor ethnic status.

Between 1955 and 1970, as computers and software improved to make factor analysis more accessible (it is computationally intense, laborious, and quite impractical without computers), factor analyses were carried out for a growing variety of urban areas, first in the United States, then in other developed countries, and finally throughout the developing world (Timms 1971). The ongoing search to identify the latent dimensions of urban spatial structure evident at different times and places came to be known as factorial ecology.

Taken together, these analyses suggest that pre-industrial cities are characterized by a relatively simple factor structure, with spatial differentiation occurring mainly on the dimension of socioeconomic status. Households in pre-industrial cities were segregated from one another on the basis of income, occupation, and wealth, but not on the basis of life cycle stage or ethnicity. The greater differentiation caused by industralization, however, brought about the progressive emergence of the second and third dimensions, leading to a segmentation of urban space on the basis of ethnicity and life cycle stage as well.

When Berry and Rees (1969) analyzed historical data from Calcutta, India, for example, they found the gradual evolution of the three characteristic dimensions of spatial variation. To see how the factors were distributed in space, however, Berry and Rees computed factor scores to represent a tract's position with respect to composite measures of socioeconomic status, family status, and ethnic status and plotted them on a map. They discovered that family status was distributed zonally, socioeconomic status was distributed in sectoral fashion, and ethnic groups were distributed in clusters. In a sense, therefore, Burgess, Hoyt, Harris, and Ullman were all correct in their identification of ecological structures: The zonal model applied to the distribution of families by life cycle stage; the sector theory applied to the distribution of social classes; and the multiple nuclei theory explained the clustering of ethnic groups in space.

As shown in Figure 5.13, therefore, human populations can universally be characterized by degree of social differentiation with respect to three fundamental axes of variation: socioeconomic status, family status, and ethnic status. Moreover, position in the resulting three-dimensional social space is linked in a one-to-one correspondence to position in the segmented space of an urban landscape defined by the same three dimensions, each distributed in characteristic fashion, yielding what Timms (1971) called "the urban mosaic." Neighborhoods of different social classes proceed outward from the center like wedges of a pie. These are cross-cut by concentric rings of neighborhoods distinguished by family status, and within neighborhoods defined by these two intersecting dimensions settle different ethnic groups, giving each of the segments a different "color."

**Figure 5.13**

**Translation of Position in Social Space into Spatial Location within the Ecological Structure of the City**

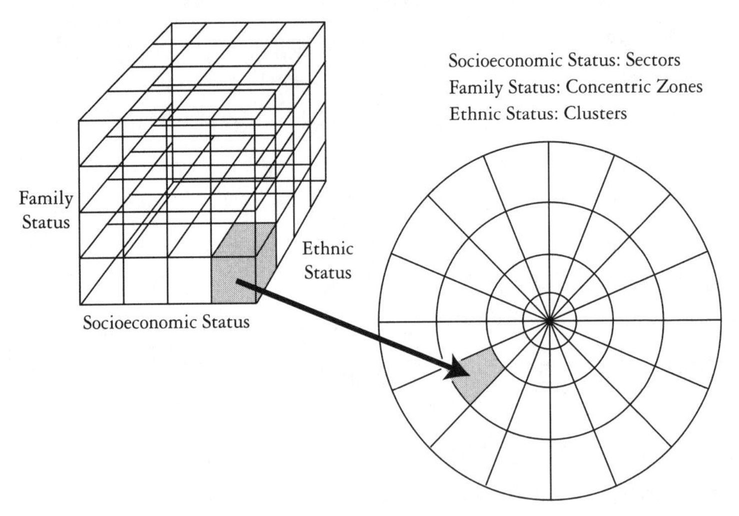


Perhaps Park (1926:18) put it best when he said that "it is because social relations are so frequently and so inevitably correlated with spatial relations; because physical distances so frequently are . . . indexes of social distances, that statistics have any significance whatsoever for sociology. And this is true, finally, because it is only as social . . . facts can be reduced to, or correlated with, spatial facts, that they can be measured at all." A close connection between social and spatial distance was thus a hallmark of industrial urbanism.

*A New Urban Culture*

The idea of theoretic culture was introduced in Chapter Four as a logical system of thought rationally grounded in experience and appropriate for making accurate predictions about events in the real world (Donald 1991). Although the foundations for this kind of culture were laid during the agrarian era with the invention of writing, technical constraints of pre-industrial agriculture limited the proportion of people who could live in cities and placed an upper limit on the diffusion of literacy. Almost by definition, full access to theoretic culture was limited for thousands of years to the small minority of people who were literate and freed from the burden of food production. Although theoretic culture gained influence in human affairs during the agrarian era, it remained a minor part of the total human experience, given the small number of people who could read and write.

The full flowering of a rational culture awaited the coming of mass literacy in the industrial era. Figure 5.14 shows trends in the literacy of adults from 1800 to 1950 in Europe, the United States, and the world using data from Cipolla (1969), Lestage (1982), Graff (1987), and Wagner (1993). In 1800, the vast majority of human beings would not have had much access to theoretic culture, as 85% of the world's population was illiterate. Even in Europe, only around 40% could read and write, owing largely to the persistence of mass illiteracy within czarist Russia. The United States fared better, with literacy rates approaching 60%. As Europe and North America industrialized in the nineteenth and early twentieth centuries, however, the degree of literacy rose dramatically in both regions, and by 1950 literacy rates had reached 90% or above in these developed countries. In the world as a whole, however, literacy was just barely over 50%, owing to slower progress in developing nations.

**Figure 5.14**

**Percentage Literate, 1800–1950**

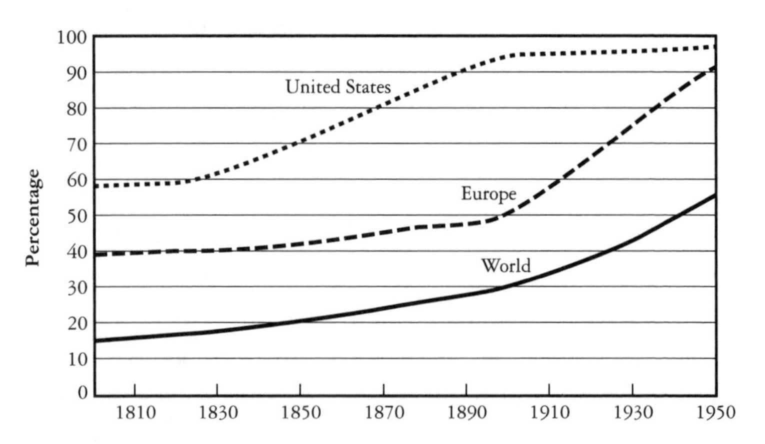


Adapted from data taken from *Literacy and Development in the West*, by Carlo Cipolla, 1969. Baltimore, MD: Penguin; *Legacies of Literacy: Continuities and Contradictions in Western Culture and Society*, by Harvey J. Graff, 1987. Bloomington, IN: University of Indiana Press; "Literacy and Illiteracy," by Andre Lestage, 1982. *Educational Studies and Documents*, No. 42. Paris: UNESCO; and "Literacy and Development: Rationales, Assessment, and Innovation," by Daniel A. Wagner, 1993. LRC/NCAL International Paper I93-1, National Center on Adult Literacy, University of Pennsylvania, Philadelphia, p. 6.

The mass diffusion of literacy (and numeracy) throughout populations in the industrialized world provided the foundations for an unprecedented extension of rational, theoretic culture. As markets expanded to distribute an ever larger share of the material, symbolic, and emotional resources, a cost-benefit, utility-maximizing mentality was adopted by larger segments of the population and applied in a growing array of settings. Decisions that before had been left to God, the family, parents, or the fates were increasingly included in the calculus of conscious choice and made by individuals acting in their own self-interest.

As a result, individualism became increasingly predominant in theory and practice, and informal social structures that had formerly been used for the exchange of material, symbolic, and emotional resources (guilds, lodges, clans, families) atrophied whereas formal organizations devoted to the rational exchange or distribution or resources (corporations, governments, universities, philanthropies) grew and eventually came to dominate society. Within industrial nations, more and more adult time was spent maximizing personal well-being using the tools of theoretic culture, and less time was spent embracing mythic culture and trading in emotional, symbolic, and material resources within a limited circle of family and friends. To a greater extent than in the past, urban dwellers began to think and behave like the autonomous, utility-maximizing free agents assumed by classic economic theory, and relationships of market pricing expanded rapidly while those based on communal sharing, equality matching, and authority ranking remained fairly static and shrank in relative importance.

*Urban Society and the Chicago School*

If people in industrial societies came to act more as rational, self-interested, utility-maximizing individuals, then what held society together and prevented people from destroying each other and the social groups they inhabited? This question preoccupied the classical social theorists who pondered the rise of industrialism, from Tonnies to Durkheim and from Simmel to Weber, and it became the particular obsession of one sociologist at the University of Chicago: Louis Wirth. His article "Urbanism as a Way of Life" (1938), one of the most influential sociological papers ever published, addressed head-on the issue of social solidarity in urban industrial society. He began by defining the urban community as "a relatively large, dense, and permanent settlement of socially heterogenous individuals" and then traced out the social, psychological, and behavioral implications of high levels of population size, density, and heterogeneity.

He argued that population size and high density increased the number of ways that people differed from one another and thus provided more bases for social organization and differentiation. In a large, densely populated city, Wirth maintained, the individual is likely to find more fellows who share a given interest, trait, or experience about which a meaningful social group can cohere. Large and dense populations also imply greater dependence on a wider range of people but less dependence on particular individuals, higher rates of interaction with more people but specific knowledge about fewer people, and greater association with more diverse groups but less allegiance to any single group.

As a result of these intrinsic urban conditions, Wirth argued, cities were characterized by a *predominance of secondary over primary role relationships*. Primary relationships are those that involve detailed personal knowledge of social actors gained through sustained close, personal interaction; secondary relationships are those that are superficial and fleeting, involving little or no personal knowledge. Because the number of people one can know well is ultimately limited, but the number with whom one can interact superficially is not, cities necessarily bred anonymity, opening up new possibilities for free expression and behavior that departed from the norms, standards, and desires of primary groups.

Within large cities, in other words, individuals achieved more personal freedom from control by friends and relatives. In the anonymity of a large population, people were much less constrained by mechanisms of social control inherited from foraging and peasant village societies, such as gossip, ridicule, and shame, which only operate when social actors are known to others and have reputations to protect.

According to Wirth, the effects of size and density were, in turn, augmented by the influence of social heterogeneity. In a large population that is diverse with respect to factors such as income, birthplace, ethnicity, race, religion, and language, interpersonal relations come to be dominated by symbols. Lacking common social, cultural, and even linguistic referents, visual symbols acquire particular importance in guiding human behavior within public settings. More than in small foraging groups or agrarian villages, where similarity prevails and everyone is known to everyone else, in the city visual cues become critical to interpreting situations and regulating behavior. Urban dwellers constantly make judgments about how to interact with others based on a quick appraisal of appearance, typically resorting to standard, superficial scripts in response to what they see.

Since the dawn of cities, clothing has always been important as a social marker, setting apart the elite from the masses, distinguishing guilds from one another, and readily identifying peasants visiting the city (Sjoberg 1960). In urban industrial societies, however, the symbolic value of clothing increased, for it worked not simply to denote class background but to label people according to function, leading to a proliferation of uniforms. Seeing the distinctive dress of a police officer, fire fighter, bus driver, janitor, mechanic, repair person, sales clerk, meter reader, doctor, or nurse, urban dwellers could make instant attributions about motivations and intentions and unconsciously invoke one of a range of standard scripts to guide the interaction that ensued. Given a uniform or some other stylized apparel (e.g., a business suit), no personal knowledge was required to sustain an effective social interaction. In the city, clothes assumed importance as communicators not only of function and class but also of race, ethnicity, and life cycle stage, telling other urban dwellers who the person is and how to behave toward him or her.

The social heterogeneity of the industrial city also increased the importance of money as a symbolic as well as an accounting device. If a society lacks common values, sentiments, religions, and beliefs, money acquires critical importance as a universal arbiter, the core measure of worth not just in a monetary sense but in a moral sense as well. Money alone simply and quickly defines the value of whatever material, symbolic, or emotional resource is being considered in a way that everyone can understand. One may not fully comprehend the symbolic value of a work of art, for example, but by knowing its price one gains a clear appreciation of its worth and the social deference to be accorded its owner. Immigrants from diverse nations may not have been able to speak the same language, but they could all appreciate the worth of something when it was expressed in dollars.

The aforementioned characteristics of urbanism—greater anonymity, less control by primary groups, a predominance of secondary over primary role relationships, a lack of common values, a diversity of social backgrounds, and the core importance of symbols—suggested one final consequence to Wirth: *the greater importance of formal rather than informal mechanisms of social control.* Moral codes that were implicit, shared, and passed from parents to children and spread informally among peers in small-scale communities had to be formalized as laws and official regulations in the industrial city. To function smoothly, efficiently, and effectively, markets required institutional stability, predictability, standardization, transparency, and the rule of law. In market societies, therefore, human behavior increasingly came to be guided by legislation and rules that were written down, sanctioned by political authority, and enforced by professionals. Urban dwellers were deterred from violating public morality more by the formalized threat of fines, incarceration, and the loss of privileges than by time-honored informal mechanisms such as gossip, ridicule, shame, and ostracism.

This line of reasoning led Wirth to a rather bleak conclusion about the nature and future of human sociality. He felt that the rise of anonymity, formality, impersonality, transience, and superficiality in human relationships led inevitably to anomie at the social level, alienation at the psychological level, and deviance at the behavioral level (Fischer 1972). He expected urban societies over time to become increasingly less consensual, less cohesive, and less integrated, leading to a vacuum of moral principles, a lack of shared social understandings (anomie), and a gnawing feeling of disconnection from others (alienation); and he argued that these pathological states would in turn cause urbanites to act out in destructive ways (deviance). According to Wirth, urbanism as a way of life led inexorably to "urban malaise."

In the decades following the publication of Wirth's celebrated essay, social scientists turned to cities and datasets from around the world to study the connection between urbanism and various indicators of malaise. Most of Wirth's hypothesized connections, however, failed to be confirmed (Fischer 1972). Studies of the effects of size and density did not find a clear relationship to social or psychological pathology (Choldin 1978). Studies of alienation likewise failed to find that urban dwellers were any more alienated, unhappy, or socially disconnected than rural dwellers (Fischer 1972, 1981); and successive generations of urban ethnographers who ventured into slum neighborhoods found poor urbanites who were anything but anomic, but instead enmeshed in a variety of close-knit, micro-level social structures (Whyte 1943; Gans 1962, 1967; Suttles 1968; Stack 1974; Anderson 1978).

The only prediction that seemed to be sustained with any reliability was that urban areas displayed higher rates and more tolerance for "deviant" behaviors of all sorts. It was, however, not entirely clear in what sense, or by whose standards, the behavior of urbanites could be considered deviant (Fischer 1972,

1975). As popular morality shifted after World War II, many of the behaviors labeled by Wirth and other Chicago School theorists as deviant came to be accepted as normal, even if unconventional by the standards of small-town, white, Protestant American society.

The intellectual problem, then, was how to explain the high rates of unconventional behavior that clearly prevailed in urban settings without resorting to a theoretical model that rooted them in pathological conditions such as anomie and alienation and described the behavior pejoratively as deviant. In addition to biases stemming from Wirth's own race- and class-specific moralities, which caused him to see elements of lower-class life and ethnic subculture as deviant, a more serious error was his conclusion that the forms of sociality associated with nonurban ways of life would somehow be lost within industrial cities. That is, the rise of secondary role relationships would come at the expense of primary relationships, and that over time deep emotional ties based on long histories of personal interaction would give way to shallow, superficial connections that could be discarded as necessary, like any other consumer product in a mass market consumer society.

This conclusion was mistaken, however, because it failed to distinguish between *the public and the private spheres of social life* (Lofland 1973; Fischer 1981). The public sphere consists of settings where anonymous strangers meet in passing with little or no prior personal contact or specific information to guide their interaction. In contrast, the private sphere consists of social contexts where people are familiar, feel emotionally connected, and have a prior history of association that structures current and future interactions. Although urbanization vastly expanded the number and range of structural contexts supporting the public sphere, it did not necessarily eliminate or even weaken other, older structural settings that supported the private sphere (Fischer 1981). Although people may interact superficially with one another by invoking socially learned scripts and cognitive schemata in response to visual cues, this impersonal behavior is situational and not built into the personal psychology of the urbanite.

Urban dwellers are essentially the same organisms that emerged on the savannahs of Africa 150 millennia ago and are capable of the full range of lasting, emotional attachments. They are still driven by the same set of core social motives (Fiske 2003). According to Fischer (1975, 1981), urbanites do not lose the capacity for lasting, emotionally rich primary relationships based on shared knowledge and experience. On the contrary, while retaining these abilities they simply gain new capacities for fleeting secondary relationships, and they acquire new abilities to discern the appropriate occasion for each of the two contrasting styles of behavior. Surveys that Fischer (1982) conducted in large and small communities of the United States found that urbanites and rural, small-town dwellers had the same sized personal networks and expressed the same degree of satisfaction with their social lives. The only real difference was that the social networks of city dwellers were relatively more likely than those of rural dwellers to be composed of friends rather than kin.

Turning to the issue of urban deviance, Fischer (1975) theorized that higher rates of unconventional attitudes and behavior within urban settings stem not from a lack of social integration among urbanites, but from their closer integration into urban subcultures. The larger and more heterogeneous a city, the greater the variety of subcultures it contains. Because large cities are associated with greater structural differentiation with respect to any social characteristic, and because they attract a larger and more diverse array of in-migrants, they are more likely to house a larger number and greater variety of subcultures.

If we assume that gay men and lesbians constitute no more than 10% of the total population, for example, then a town of 1,000 people will yield only 100 homosexuals scattered across the age range—not enough to sustain a bar, much less a full set of subcultural institutions. In contrast, a metropolitan area of 10 million can be expected to yield 1 million homosexuals, enabling a full array of specialized clubs, institutions, political action committees, lobbying groups, churches, and other voluntary associations. Moreover, the vibrancy of the city's subculture will selectively attract gay men and lesbians from smaller towns and cities who wish to find a setting where they can more easily fit in and interact with like-minded people.

Thus, the larger, denser, and more diverse the city, the more intense the subcultures it contains, yielding a prediction precisely opposite that derived by Wirth. Rather than being anomic, members of urban subcultures are more integrated and involved because they have access to a critical mass of like-minded people with whom to share the effort of sustaining a common culture and its supporting institutions. At the same time, competition and conflict are greater in large cities, strengthening boundaries among subcultures and producing stronger affirmations of group identity in response to outside challenges. The end result is a more supportive internal environment for group members.

The more urban the place, therefore, the greater the number and variety of subcultures; and the more people who are involved in subcultures, the greater the raw cultural and social material for other groups to borrow and exchange, thereby diffusing subcultural symbols, emotions, and materials to other groups, who in turn create new combinations and permutations that are re-expressed as hybrids to produce new subcultural variation (Crane 2000). The end result is that large cities evince much higher rates of unconventional attitudes and behaviors than small cities and towns, not because of anomie but because of integration around a greater number of poles of attraction.

Fischer's subcultural theory of urbanism is summarized in Figure 5.15. Basically, rising urbanism (greater size, density, and heterogeneity) produces a rising variety of more intense subcultures, whose material, symbolic, and material resources are then diffused to other groups and to the population at

**Figure 5.15**

**Fischer's Subcultural Theory of Urbanism**

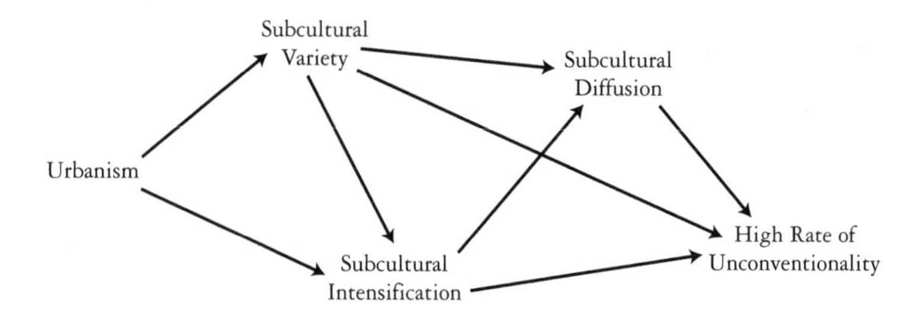

large, yielding a proliferation of unconventional behaviors, ideas, and social forms. These traits are deviant in the sense that they depart from typical practices in small towns or even urban society at large, but they are not at all deviant when viewed in light of the urban subcultures from which they emerge and within which they are rooted. Rather than reflecting anomie and alienation, apparent deviance in cities actually stems from greater integration within subcultures that would be difficult or impossible to sustain in smaller communities.

### INDUSTRIAL URBANISM AS A WAY OF LIFE

The size and demographic structure of the human communities that routinely came to exist under industrial urbanism are suggested in Figure 5.16, which presents a population pyramid for the city of Chicago in 1930. With the taming of mortality and massive in-migration from both rural areas of the United States and overseas, the classical pyramidal shape that had characterized human societies for millennia gave way to a modified pyramid characterized by relatively large absolute numbers of people in age cohorts 0–4 and 5–9, as larger numbers of births survived through childhood. Nonetheless, the base at age 0–4 is narrower than at the middle of the distribution because of a distinctive bulge in age intervals from 10–14 through 40–44 caused by the selective in-migration of able-bodied adults looking for work. The top of the distribution is characterized by very rapid tapering to small numbers above the age of 70. Whereas the infectious diseases of infancy and childhood had been brought under control by 1930, the degenerative diseases of old age—coronary heart disease and cancer—had not.

Such a population structure gives rise to a very low depen-

## Figure 5.16
## Population Pyramid for City of Chicago, 1930

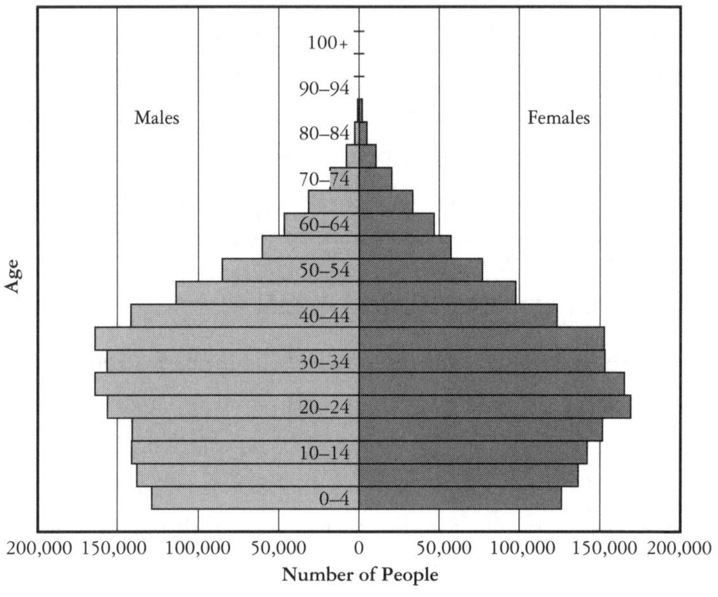


Adapted from *Fifteenth Census of the United States, Population*, Volume III, Part 1. Washington, D.C.: U.S. Bureau of the Census, Table 61.

dency burden, defined as the ratio of nonworkers to workers. This ratio is often approximated by dividing the sum of those age 0–14 (dependent children) and those age 65+ (retirees) by the number of persons age 15–64 (roughly those of working age). In Chicago in 1930, this dependency burden stood at 0.39, meaning there were roughly 0.4 people too old or too young to work for every person of working age, compared to a burden of 0.55 in the agrarian city shown in Figure 4.2. Moreover, given the relatively small number of people above the age of 65, most of the dependency that did exist in Chicago in

1930 was childhood rather than old-age dependency. Such a demographic structure could, through taxes on workers, finance a good public education system for those age 0–15 while simultaneously offering generous pensions to those above age 65, who at that point were few in number and modest in life expectancies (the average life expectancy at age 65 was about 12 years in 1930).

In addition to the shape of the age distribution, another important change was the number of people in each age interval. Whereas the number of people in age-sex cohorts from 0 to 44 in the pre-industrial city of Figure 4.2 ranged from around 3,000 to 6,500, the size of the same cohorts in Chicago ranged from 125,000 to 175,000. Such a huge increase in scale implies that most interactions were secondary role relationships based on market pricing or informal schemata, as these numbers vastly exceeded human capacities to know other social actors personally.

By causing a vast increase in the size and scale of human societies, industrialization dramatically altered the nature, number, and diversity of social contexts in which people could potentially interact. It did not change the fundamental nature of the people themselves, however. Urban-dwelling human beings continued to be governed by the same core social motives as their agrarian and foraging ancestors—belonging, understanding, controlling, self-enhancing, and trusting. As these basic motivations could not be satisfied in the anonymity of the public sphere or the impersonal superficiality of the market or public spaces, they had to be expressed within the new social settings created by industrial urbanism: households segmented by life cycle stage; age-graded classrooms and peer-dominated playgrounds; street corners and blocks within neighborhoods defined by class, ethnicity, and household structure; worksites divided according to occupational specialty and skill; and a host of voluntary organizations cohering around common interests such as churches, clubs, lodges, political committees, charities, and sports.

People continued to seek out primary role relationships and interact with other people over extended periods of time on a face-to-face basis; they continued to engage in relationships of communal sharing and equality matching; they continued to influence one another's behavior using gossip, ostracism, ridicule, praise, and esteem; and they continued to exchange emotional, symbolic, and material resources within microsocial networks.

Rather than occurring within a single small community of known individuals who went through life in one another's company and in constant close proximity, however, the core social motives and their ensuing social behaviors were played out in multiple social settings, each relatively self-contained spatially and defined socially in terms of fundamental axes of differentiation. These settings vary across time and space, shifting throughout life as people age, move geographically, and attain new socioeconomic characteristics. Although industrial cities may have been huge, dense, heterogeneous, and anonymous, most people still moved through life enmeshed within dense sets of microsocial networks within which emotional resources were exchanged to create durable connections to friends and relatives, and through them to the rest of industrial urban society.

# Chapter Six
# POST-INDUSTRIAL URBANISM

DATING THE END OF ONE ERA and the beginning of another is always an exercise in the arbitrary. Nonetheless, it is clear that sometime during the 1970s the reign of industrial urbanism came to an end. For a variety of reasons, the critical moment seems to have been around 1975. The mid-1970s coincided with a severe recession throughout the industrial world, the appearance of a new malady known as stagflation (high inflation combined with high unemployment), the end of a 30-year rise in median income, the bottoming out of the equally long decline in poverty rates, and a sharp turnaround from falling to rising income inequality (Danziger and Gottschalk 1995; Atkinson, Rainwater, and Smeeding 1995; Levy 1998; Phillips 2002).

Regardless of the precise date of the transformation, the industrial era proved to be of remarkably short duration. Compared with the 40,000 years of foraging and the 10,000 years of agrarianism, the 175 years of industrialism was short indeed. If human beings did not have sufficient time in 500 generations to evolve genetic adaptations to agrarian urbanism, they certainly could not do so in the eight generations that encompassed the rise, peak, and decline of the industrial order (Massey 2002). Just as human beings in pre-industrial and industrial cities were more adapted physiologically, psychologically, and socially to foraging as a way of life, so too are the inhabitants of today's post-industrial urban landscapes.

## EMERGENCE OF THE POST-INDUSTRIAL ORDER

Throughout the nineteenth and early twentieth centuries, wealth accumulated within industrial cities at an unprecedented rate. At the same time educational levels steadily rose, mortality rates fell, and the pace of technological innovation quickened. Although socioeconomic inequality increased as well, new social movements emerged to press for reform, and by the second decade of the twentieth century they had begun to achieve significant redistributions of power and wealth in a growing number of countries.

For intellectuals, politicians, and the public, the continued march of progress under the banner of industrialism seemed inevitable. Faith in the inexorability of human improvement died violently, however, with the outbreak of World War I in 1914. Known in its day as the Great War, its causes were complex and are still much debated (Martel 1996; Ferguson 1999; Mombaur 2002). Perhaps the simplest explanation is that global trade proceeded too fast and moved too far ahead of global governance (Massey and Taylor 2004). In 1914 the world lacked a set of multilateral political institutions capable of adjudicating disputes and diffusing the tensions that inevitably arose from a more intense interaction of nations within a globalizing economy.

Regardless of the precise causes of the war, the end result was four years of horrific blood-letting among the world's industrial powers. The wholesale destruction of land, labor, and capital during the Great War sowed the seeds for economic collapse in the era that followed. When the war finally ended in 1918, international political stability was gone. The regimes of most belligerent nations had been overthrown, and the nascent system of international economic institutions crafted in the late nineteenth century lay in tatters (Kenwood and Lougheed 1992; James 2001). World War I opened a Pandora's box of contradictory forces, and it would take most of the twentieth century to reconcile them: the intensification of the struggle between labor and capital, the polarization of political ideology between communism and fascism; a widespread retreat from liberal democracy among former trading nations, the fatal wounding of one hegemonic power and the reluctance of its successor to assume the mantle of responsibility.

Reflecting these paralyzing contradictions, the period from 1918 to 1945 witnessed the collapse of international trade, the rise of autarkic (i.e., self-sufficient) economic nationalism, and the widespread implementation of chauvinistic restrictions on trade, investment, and immigration (James 2001). Although the world economy hobbled along for a while on the strength of wealth accumulated in Oceania and the Americas during the Great War, the global system of trade and investment finally came crashing down in 1929. Laws passed by an isolationist U.S. Congress during that decade progressively choked off international flows of people, goods, ideas, and capital, ultimately producing an economic meltdown of unprecedented depth and duration.

During the years of the Great Depression, international trade, capital formation, and industrial expansion all but ceased, and technological progress slowed to a crawl (Massey and Taylor 2004). Following 10 years of social, economic, and political turmoil, the ideological contradictions unleashed in 1914 were partially resolved on the battlefield between 1939 and 1945, as a coalition of communist and liberal democratic states arose to defeat fascism in World War II. Hostilities ended in 1945 with much of the industrial world bombed into ruins and the world polarized into conflicting ideological camps.

Because of this unique history, the social and spatial forms associated with pre-1914 industrial urbanism were largely frozen in time through 1945 and changed slowly for three decades thereafter, especially in the United States, which never suffered physical damage during the years of violent warfare. Although telltale signs of the new, post-industrial order were evident in North America as early as the 1920s, the economic collapse of 1929 and the virtual absence of private investment through 1945 meant that the basic social, economic, and spatial infrastructure of industrial cities persisted more or less unchanged through 1950, when urban industrialism may be said to have reached its zenith. On or about that year, the population, wealth, employment, and influence of U.S. central cities peaked.

Over the next 25 years, economic growth continued under institutional arrangements developed largely during the 1930s in response to problems of the 1920s, a social compact among workers, owners, and professionals generally known as the *welfare state* (Trattner 1998; Pedersen 1995). Although its specific institutional manifestations varied from country to country (see Esping Anderson 1990), the welfare state generally attempted to maintain balanced economic growth by regulating markets, protecting citizens against market failures, providing universal retirement and health care systems, and extending popular access to education and housing. Beginning in the 1970s, however, the institutions of the welfare state came under increasing pressure as a result of two notable developments: a revival of global trade, and a return to rapid technological innovation (Esping Anderson 1996). Together, these two macrostructural transformations gave birth to the post-industrial order.

*The Revival of Trade*

As already noted, the end of World War II did not bring about a full resumption of global trade because of the armed standoff between liberal capitalist democracies and communist dictatorships. Billions of people lived outside of markets within command economies in China, the Soviet Union, and their satellite countries. Millions more lived under autarkic regimes that sought to promote economic development internally by applying tariffs, capital controls, exchange regulations, and import quotas to insulate themselves from the global economy. The attempt to promote national economic growth by insulating domestic markets from the global economic forces was known as *import substitution industrialization* (Clark 1970). The period 1945–1975 was generally one of state dominance in the political economy of both developing and developed nations.

Among Western industrial powers, the United States finally assumed the mantle of responsibility it by rights should have assumed after World War I and took the lead in rebuilding a transnational market economy while attempting to correct the mistakes of the past. It joined with other liberal democracies to create a new, more effective international system to ensure international security, liquidity, convertibility, investment, and trade through multilateral institutions such as the United Nations (UN), the North Atlantic Treaty Organization (NATO), the World Bank, the International Monetary Fund (IMF), the General Agreement on Tariffs and Trade (GATT), and ultimately the World Trade Organization (WTO) (Massey 2005). Through these and other institutions, the United States supported the economic reconstruction of Europe and Japan and worked to facilitate their integration into the reconstituted global trading system.

These policies led to a revival of trade, first among industrialized nations and then, as decolonization proceeded, between the developing and developed worlds. As the reconstruction of Europe and Japan drew to a close, agencies such as the UN, the IMF, and the World Bank shifted their agendas to promote economic growth in developing nations and worked to facilitate their entry into the global market (Stiglitz 2002). During the 1970s and 1980s, newly industrialized nations such as Korea, Taiwan, Singapore, and Malaysia developed economically by selling manufactured goods to overseas markets in developed countries, a strategy that became known as *export industrialization*. During the 1990s, this strategy became reified as the "Washington consensus" and was imposed by the bureaucrats at the World Bank and the IMF on countries throughout the world. Rather than insulating domestic economies from global economic forces, the new strategy sought to achieve fuller incorporation into the international trade regime by reducing tariffs, relaxing capital controls, eliminating import quotas, downsizing government, privatizing state industries, and cultivating export markets (Naim 2000; Kuczynski and Williamson 2003).

After 1975, flows of capital, goods, raw materials, and information increased and were accompanied by a revival of immigration, first among industrialized nations and then between developing and developed regions. The link between global trade and international migration is illustrated using U.S. data in Figure 6.1 (from Massey 2003). The clear bars show the number of immigrants to the United States (in millions) by decade during the twentieth century. The shaded bars show international trade as a percentage of the U.S. gross national product (GNP).

The statistical correlation between these two series is strong: 0.84. The figure shows that early in the century both trade and immigration ran at very high levels. During the period 1901–1910, for example, a record 8.8 million immigrants entered the United States, and trade constituted roughly 10% of total gross domestic product (GDP). World War I truncated immigration in the ensuing decade, even as it boosted trade, which rose to nearly 13% of GDP; but the effect of isolationist policies in the 1920s is clearly evident as immigration declined to 4.1 million and trade fell to 9% of GDP in that decade despite the "roaring" years of economic boom.

During the 1930s, international trade and immigration both reached a nadir. From 1931 to 1940, only 500,000 persons entered the United States and international trade accounted for a mere 6% of U.S. economic activity. The 1930s and the subsequent three decades constitute a kind of interregnum among global economic regimes. From 1950 to 1970, trade fluctuated at around 7% of GNP while immigration slowly increased, going from 1.0 million during the 1940s to 3.3 million in the 1960s, still only a fraction of the level

Figure 6.1

U.S. Immigration and Foreign Trade by Decade, 1901–2000

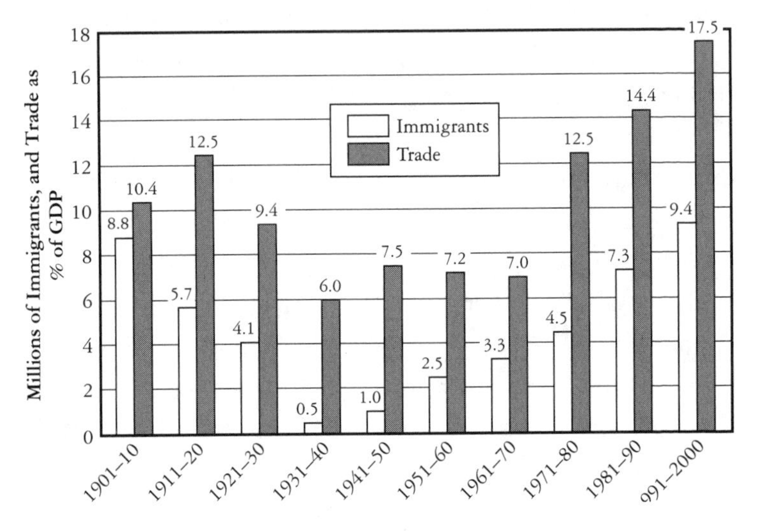


Adapted from "Mondialisation et Migrations: L'Exemple des Etats-Unis," by Douglas S. Massey, 2003. *Futuribles* 284:1–a, p. 2.

achieved during the first decade of the century and lower than that of any decade from 1870 through 1930.

The revival of trade and immigration became evident only in the 1970s. In that decade, trade increased sharply, finally equaling the share of GNP reached during the decade 1911–20 (12.5%). At the same time, in absolute terms immigration surpassed the level it had last achieved during the 1920s. Until the 1990s, however, the global economy could not flower fully because nearly one third of all human beings were isolated from it within rigid command economies. Only with the fall of the

Berlin Wall in 1989 were conditions ripe for a full return to international trade and the emergence of a truly global economy. With the collapse of the Soviet Union and the decisive shift of Chinese Communist leadership away from command and toward market mechanisms, the world finally returned to a stage of integrated economic development that it had last achieved in 1914.

Over the final two decades of the twentieth century, both international migration and trade expanded to new and unprecedented heights. During the 1990s, for example, immigration surged to 9.4 million persons while trade rose to almost 18% of GNP (Massey and Taylor 2004). At the dawn of the new century, therefore, the United States stood at the center of a new global economy characterized by the massive international movement of people, goods, capital, commodities, services, and information, reflecting a remarkable burst of economic growth and wealth creation.

*Technological Revolution*

Despite the aforementioned historical contingencies, the roots of the post-industrial revolution were ultimately technological. Industrial urbanism ended because its characteristic technologies were replaced by a new set of technical innovations that sparked a wholesale reorganization of human society. Electric motors replaced steam engines in manufacturing; gasoline engines replaced steam propulsion in transportation; satellite and cellular transmission replaced wire networks in communications; and digital processing using silicon chips and fiber optics replaced analog computation using mechanical switches and copper wires in information processing. These technical shifts led to a revolution in transportation, communication, computation, and production.

The accelerating pace of technological change during the post-industrial era is indicated in Figure 6.2, which depicts the annual number of patents filed in the United States from 1960 to 2000. During the 1960s and 1970s, the pace of technological innovation was relatively stable, with the number of applications fluctuating at around 100,000 per year. Suddenly in 1984, however, the rate of innovation shifted sharply upward, with the number of patent applications doubling by 1994 and tripling by 2000. In the last decade of the twentieth century, some 2.5 million patent applications were filed, compared with just 1 million during the 1970s.

**Figure 6.2**

**U.S. Patent Applications Filed 1960–2000**

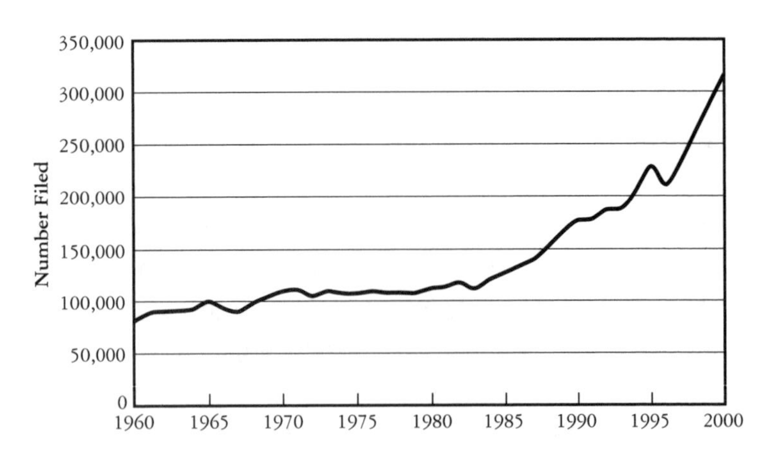


Adapted from "U.S. Patent Activity 1790–Present." Web site of U.S. Patent and Trademark Office: www.uspto.gov/.

Never before had human society witnessed technical change on such a scale. Decreases in the cost and increases in the rapidity of transportation, communications, and computation after 1970 turned the economic logic of the industrial order on its head. Whereas the material foundations of industrial society lay in the manufacture of standardized goods within large, stable institutions, the economic basis for post-industrialism was the production of symbols—ideas, knowledge, and information—within small, flexible institutional settings. The new post-industrial regime did not favor economies of agglomeration and scale, mass consumption, homogeneous markets, or large centralized cities managed by hierarchical bureaucracies; it favored dispersed production, segmented markets, and fragmented settlements linked by formal and informal networks managed by smaller and more compressed bureaucracies (Harvey 1989; Castells 1996, 1997, 1998; Clarke 2002).

## THE NATURE OF POST-INDUSTRIALISM

In many ways, post-industrialism simply involved a return to the steady, ongoing process of social and economic differentiation characteristic of the early industrial era. Whereas the period 1800–1914 was marked by a dramatic increase in diversity with respect to socioeconomic status, family structure, and ethnicity, the "freezing" in place of institutional arrangements during the 1930s through the 1970s was associated with a remarkable, but temporary, lessening of diversity along all three dimensions. During the 1930s and 1940s, the distribution of income and wages was severely compressed (Goldin and Margo 1992); and during the 1950s and 1960s, progressive taxation and social welfare legislation brought about a sustained decline in income inequality along with a steady rise in median income (Atkinson, Rainwater, and Smeeding 1995).

Given this economic climate, earlier generations of people who had postponed family formation during the years of economic depression and warfare made up for lost time just as new generations were marrying earlier and having children sooner than ever before. The end result was a "piling up" of births and marriages during the 1950s and 1960s and a homogenization of household structure (Campbell 1978). At the same time, ethnic diversity was mitigated by decades of minimal immigration and steady assimilation. As immigrants died off and were replaced by their children and grandchildren during the 1960s and 1970s, formerly disparate nationalities integrated spatially and socially, and through intermarriage they came to form an undifferentiated mass of European Americans (Alba and Nee 2003).

Thus, economic and demographic trends produced a remarkable homogenization of urban society during the period 1914–1975. Post-industrialism involved a reversal of this pattern of homogenization and a renewal of societal differentiation with a vengeance. As the twentieth century ended, individuals, families, nations, and the world were launched into a new "age of extremes" in which class divisions sharpened, categorical divisions among people reified, and social segregation increased (Massey 1996).

### *The Return of Inequality*

*Inequality* is another word for *diversity within a hierarchical structure of social categories:* the greater the inequality with respect to occupation or income, for example, the greater the differentiation of people with respect to material well-being. Inequality is measured using the Gini coefficient, which varies from 0 (complete equality of income) to 1.0 (complete inequality, where one person has all the income and everyone else has nothing). Figure 6.3 displays Gini coefficients for U.S. income inequality from 1950 to 2000.

**Figure 6.3**

**Gini Coefficient for Family Income Inequality in the United States, 1950–2000**

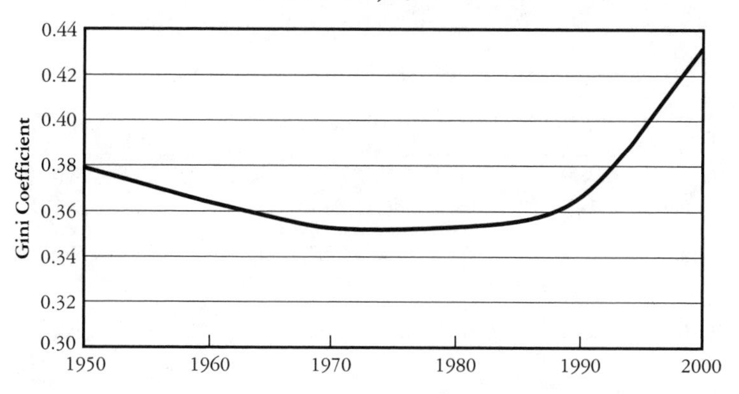


Adapted from "Historical Income Inequality Tables," by U.S. Bureau of the Census. Web site of U.S. Census Bureau: www.census.gov/income/histinc/.

Income inequality fell slowly but surely during the 1950s and 1960s, with the Gini coefficient moving from a value of 0.38 to one of about 0.35 by 1975. Over the same period, median income increased steadily as a rising economic tide indeed lifted all boats (Danziger and Gottschalk 1995). Inequality with respect to wealth—the ownership of assets that generate income—is always much greater than inequality with respect to income; and as Figure 6.4 shows, even after the relatively compressed years of the 1940s and 1950s, the Gini coefficient for wealth stood at 0.80 during the early 1960s, more than twice the level for income. Moreover, despite 15 more years of rising income and falling inequality with respect to income, the shape of the wealth distribution hardly moved, evincing only the slightest downward movement in the Gini coefficient by the mid-1970s.

**Figure 6.4**

**Gini Coefficient for Household Wealth Inequality in the United States, 1963–2000**

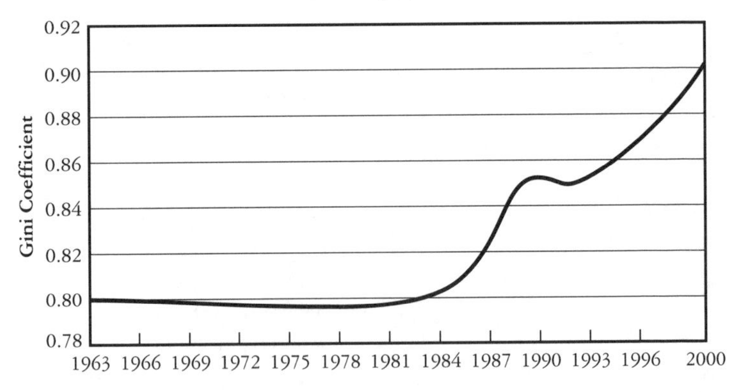


Adapted from *Wealth in America: Trends in Wealth Inequality*, by Lisa A. Keister, 2000. New York: Cambridge University Press, Table 3-2.

As the aforementioned trends indicate, it is generally quite difficult to achieve shifts in the distribution of income or wealth, as both are typified by considerable inertia over the short run. Hence, the transformation after 1980 is all the more remarkable. Returning to Figure 6.3, one can see that from a value of about 0.35 in 1985, the Gini coefficient for income underwent a remarkable rise through the end of the century to reach a value of 0.43 in the year 2000, the highest level recorded since the 1920s. And looking again at Figure 6.4, over essentially the same period, the Gini coefficient for wealth inequality rose from 0.80 to 0.90 from 1963 to 1997 (Keister 2000). Thus, whereas the largest private fortune stood at $3.6 billion in 1968, by 1999 it had reached $85 billion (Phillips 2002). The distance from the top to the bottom of the wealth distribution had increased 24 times in just 20 years! By the end of the twentieth century, the richest 1% of Americans controlled 40% of U.S. wealth, up from 20% in 1968 (Phillips 2002).

*Resurgent Family Differentiation*

This renewed differentiation of the United States and other countries in terms of socioeconomic status was accompanied by a simultaneous diversification of industrial societies with respect to household structure. During the nineteenth and early twentieth centuries, industrialization was associated with a wide-ranging demographic transition, as urban populations moved from a regime of high fertility and mortality to low levels of both demographic outcomes. In general, the decline in mortality preceded the decline in fertility to yield a period of rapid demographic growth during the transition era. The relative timing of the declines in mortality and fertility determined the length of the transition and the amount of population growth experienced within it.

The secular decline in fertility and mortality within the industrialized world might have been steady and monotonic were it not for the calamitous events of the twentieth century: a world war, a global depression, another world war, and then a long economic boom. These powerful macrostructural forces disrupted the normal rhythms of the demographic transition to create a unique demographic interregnum from 1945 to 1965. As noted above, births postponed during the years of warfare and depression burst forth to occur simultaneously with those accruing to people coming of age in the 1950s and 1960s, who themselves accelerated childbearing owing to the strong economy. The end result was a historically unique "baby boom" that temporarily reversed the diversification of society with respect to family status.

This phenomenon is documented in Figure 6.5, which shows trends in household structure from 1950 through 2000. Households are classified into one of seven categories: a married couple living together without children under age 18; a married couple living together with children under age 18; a single mother living with children under age 18; a single father living with children under age 18; some other kind of family household (containing members related to one another by blood or marriage); and two kinds of non-family households (containing unrelated members)—those headed by males and those headed by females. The latter two categories include single persons as well as people living with roommates or boarders.

In 1950, the baby boom was in full swing and 90% of U.S. households were composed of families. Indeed, three quarters of households comprised either a married couple with children

Figure 6.5

U.S. Family-Household Structure, 1950–2000

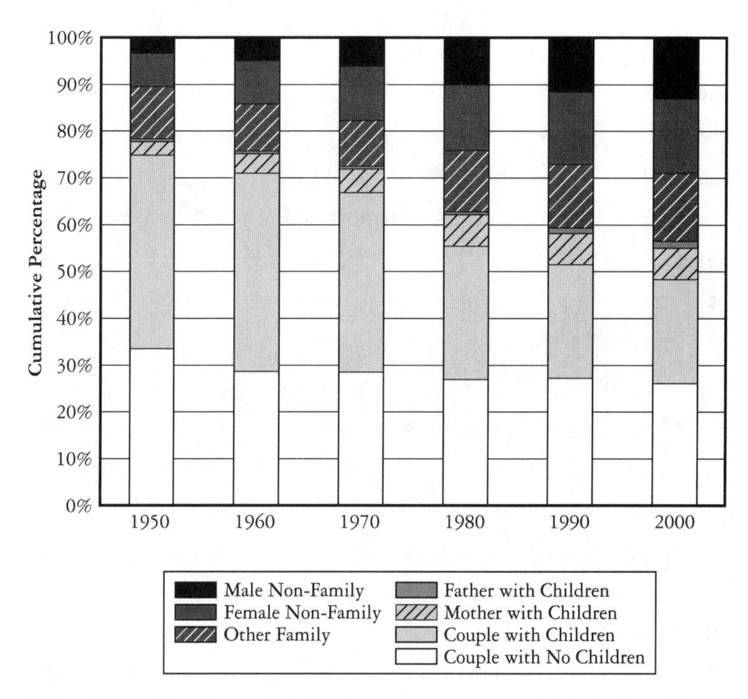


Adapted from "Families and Living Arrangements: Households by Type from 1940 to Present," by U.S. Bureau of the Census. U.S. Census Bureau Web site: www.census.gov/population/www/socdemo/hh-Fam.html.

(43%) or a childless couple (35%). In practice, the latter category included married couples whose children were already grown plus those who were about to begin having children. Single-parent families constituted only 3% of all households, and non-family households made up just 10% of the population. Thus, the 1950s and 1960s constituted an unusual historical period in which the large majority of households were occupied either directly or indirectly with family formation and child rearing.

The situation began to change radically in the 1970s as women's labor force participation rose, marriage rates fell, divorce and cohabitation increased, marital fertility declined, and non-marital fertility increased (Bianchi and Spain 1986, 1996). As a result, household structure underwent a renewed diversification over the next three decades (Farley 1995; Casper and Bianchi 2001). By the year 2000, married couples with children constituted less than one quarter of all households (24%) and married couples without children had fallen to 28% of the total. Unlike in 1950, moreover, many couples in the latter category could not be assumed to have had or be on the way to having children. A growing number of married couples were remaining permanently childless.

During the latter half of the twentieth century, single-parent households grew to account for 9% of the total (with 8 of 10 headed by single mothers); but the most remarkable growth was in the prevalence of non-family households. Between 1950 and 2000, the percentage of female-headed non-family households went from 7% to 17% and the share of male-headed non-family households grew from 4% to 14%. Moving out of the parental household at age 18 and establishing a new household by oneself or with a roommate became an established part of the life cycle, adding a new generation of "20- and 30-somethings" to the adolescent teenagers who rose to prominence in the 1950s and 1960s. At the other end of the age continuum, social security and improved retirement systems allowed widows and widowers to live independently after the death of their spouse. By the year 2000, only one third of households were directly involved in child rearing, yielding a distinct minority of citizens with an immediate interest in social arrangements relevant to the care and nurturing of children (Preston 1984).

*The Diversification of Ethnicity*

The renewed differentiation of society with respect to socioeconomic and family status was accompanied by a simultaneous revival in diversity with respect to ethnic status. As shown in Figure 6.6, the population of the United States was overwhelmingly white and of European origin in 1940. Although whites earlier in the century may have been differentiated by national origin, during the period 1940–1975 the second and third generations increasingly mixed together socially, culturally, and biologically to create a blended Euro-American population in which ancestry was complex, identity situational, and ethnicity more of an optional expression than an ascribed status (Alba 1985; Lieberson and Waters 1988; Waters 1990; Alba and Nee 2003).

The Eurocentric nature of American society in 1940 and 1950 is indicated by the fact that nearly 90% of the population was classified as white and most of the remaining Americans were classified as black. At mid-century, few inhabitants of the United States were of Asian, Caribbean, or Latin American origin, and the main contour of ethnic stratification was the "color line" that had long divided whites of European origin from blacks of African origin (Farley and Allen 1987). Despite a historical legacy of black-white miscegenation (much of it coerced), a "one drop rule" prevailed to define anyone with any trace of African ancestry as "black" (Higginbotham 1980, 1996).

Figure 6.6

Racial-Ethnic Composition of the United States, 1940–2000

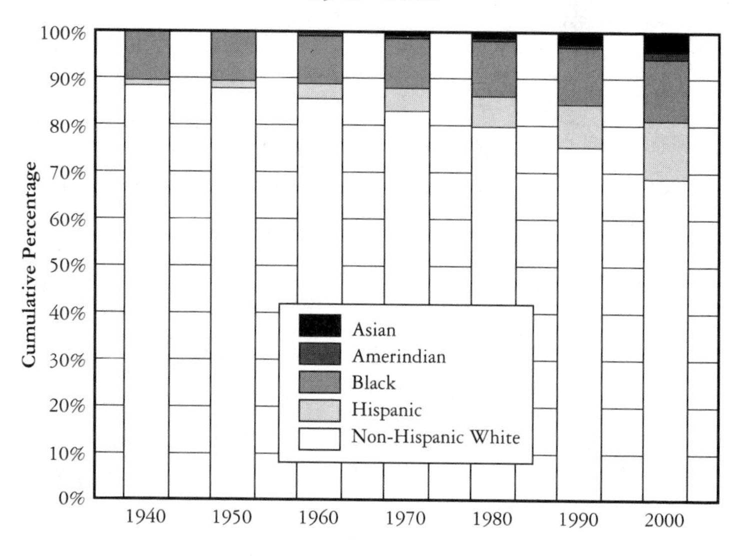


Adapted from "Historical Census Statistics on Population Totals by Race, 1790–1990, and by Hispanic Origin 1970 to 1990 for the United States," by Campbell Gibson and Kay Jung, 2002. Working Paper Series No. 56, Detailed Table 1, and "Census 2000 Briefs and Special Reports," by U.S. Bureau of the Census. U.S. Census Bureau Web site: www.census.gov/population/www/cen2000/briefs.html.

The basic composition of the United States with respect to race and ethnicity changed little until the 1960s. During that decade, however, nations throughout the industrial world modified their immigration policies to become less discriminatory on the basis of race, ethnicity, religion, and national origin. In many countries, immigration was also stimulated by the recruitment of foreign "guest workers." In the United States, nearly 5 million workers from Mexico were imported for temporary labor between 1942 and 1964, effectively reviving immigration from that country after a 10-year hiatus (Massey, Durand, and Malone 2002). Immigration to the United States was also stimulated by successive political-military failures in Latin America, the Caribbean, and Southeast Asia, which led to the entry of hundreds of thousands of refugees (Massey 1995).

By the mid 1970s, a clear revival of immigration was under way throughout the developed world. In the United States, most of the new arrivals came from countries outside of Europe. As a result, the share of Euro-Americans in the American population steadily fell and the relative number of Asians, Caribbeans, and Latin Americans correspondingly rose. From 1960 to 1990, the percentage of non-Hispanic whites dropped from 86% to 75% as the relative number of Asians went from 0.5% to 3% and that of Hispanics went from 3% to 9%.

By the year 2000, whites of European origin—who at this point were several generations removed from earlier waves of immigrants—had fallen to just two thirds of all Americans, while the number of Hispanics had mushroomed to equal the number of African Americans, constituting more than 12% of the population compared with 5% for Asians. Given forecasts for continuing immigration, the ongoing diversification of U.S. society by race and ethnicity is not expected to end anytime soon (Smith and Edmonston 1997, 1998). Figure 6.7 shows expected changes in the racial-ethnic structure of the U.S. population over the next 50 years, as projected by the U.S. Bureau of the Census.

As Figure 6.7 indicates, by 2050 non-Hispanic whites are expected to constitute barely 50% of the population, whereas

Figure 6.7

Projected Racial-Ethnic Composition of the United States, 2000–2050

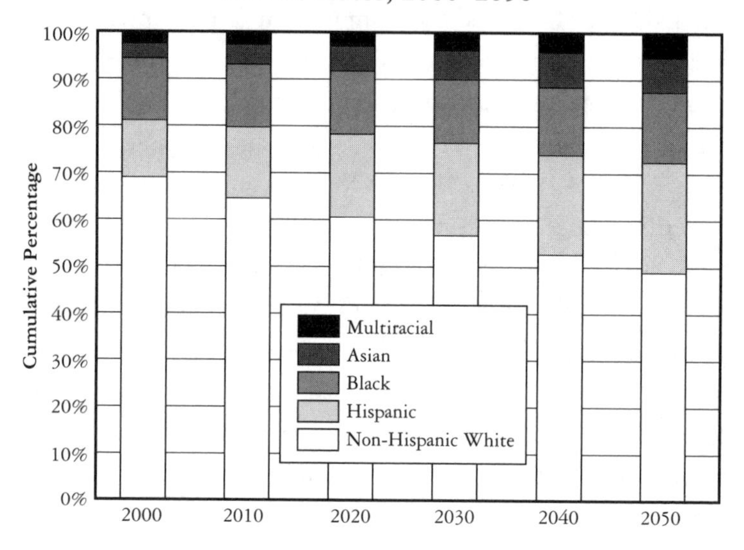


Adapted from "U.S. Interim Projections by Age, Sex, Race, and Hispanic Origin," by U.S. Bureau of the Census, 2004. Web site of U.S. Census Bureau: www.census.gov/ipc/www/usinterimproj/, Table 1.

Hispanics will make up 24%, blacks 14%, and Asians 8%. In addition, given ongoing intermarriage among these groups, the share of Americans classifying themselves as "multiracial" is expected to reach 5%. Shortly after mid-century, in other words, no single group will make up a majority in the United States. Of course, by the mid-twenty-first century the socially constructed categories of race and ethnicity used by future Americans are likely to be quite different from those in use today (Alba and Nee 2003).

## THE STRUCTURE OF POST-INDUSTRIALISM

The remarkable resurgence of economic inequality, family diversification, and racial-ethnic heterogeneity bespeak a profound transformation in underlying economic and ecological relations and a radical break from the past. Such widespread, wholesale, and rapid change simultaneously along all three of the fundamental dimensions of social space could not have occurred without an elemental restructuring of the very foundations of society. The net effect was a powerful reorganization of markets and the wholesale reconfiguration of urban geography within post-industrial cities (Scott 1988).

### *Fragmentation of Markets*

The ongoing revolutions in transportation, communication, computation, and production had particularly profound effects on the structure of markets throughout the world. During the 1970s and early 1980s, computerization swept through manufacturing. Older plants that employed thousands of well-paid, unionized workers were replaced by new, capital-intensive facilities where a few skilled workers operated mechanized, continuous-flow production lines controlled largely by computers and carried out increasingly by robots (Rifkin 1995). Manufacturing productivity soared, and plants that could not compete either closed or moved to low-wage areas in the developing world. Employment in manufacturing plummeted, especially in older urban areas (Kasarda 1995). As manufacturing dwindled, so did union membership, notably in the United States. Between 1969 and 1989, the share of unionized non-farm workers dropped from 29% to 16% of the U.S. workforce, and in the private sector the level of unionization reached 12%, a figure not seen since the 1920s (Freeman 1993).

Whereas manufacturing bore the brunt of the cybernetic revolution during the 1970s, during the 1980s and 1990s services took the hit. Large, bureaucratic organizations filled with mid-level white-collar workers gave way to re-engineered, downsized, and flattened structures that were "lean and mean," to employ a slogan of the day (Harrison 1995). Making use of new, ultra-fast silicon chips and fiber optics, engineers created smaller, cheaper, and steadily more powerful computers while programmers developed more efficient algorithms to routinize much white-collar work into canned subroutines with user-friendly interfaces.

Thanks to these new cybernetic tools, tasks that were formerly undertaken by a host of service workers (e.g., making an airline reservation) were shifted to consumers themselves, who performed the same functions at a fraction of the cost (e.g., using Web-based programs such as Travelocity or Expedia). Within the service bureaucracy itself, one well-trained operative sitting in front of a computer terminal could perform a series of tasks formerly carried out by scores of relatively expensive, white-collar workers located at multiple administrative layers, usually in a fraction of the time. During the 1990s, the era of the gray flannel suit gave way to the era of the pink slip, as corporations, governments, and nonprofits shed mid-level administrators by the thousands (Harrison 1995; Rifkin 1995).

At the same time that computers were transforming productivity in manufacturing and services, they were also facilitating another, geographic revolution. During the last decade of the twentieth century, markets for capital and labor became fully globalized, making possible a truly worldwide division of labor and production. The rising speed of communication, declining costs of transportation, increasing ease of international movement, and growing importance of smaller and lighter consumer products, when combined with the new centrality of knowledge and information in production, promoted the globalization of markets. If the owners of capital could find more attractive prospects in some other country, they were now able to shift billions of dollars across borders in a nanosecond; and if producers in developed nations needed to reduce labor costs, they could easily relocate factories overseas or simply wait for immigrants from developing countries to show up at their factory gates.

In this context, producers were able to improve efficiency and lower costs by combining low-wage and high-wage production using an international division of labor that concentrated capital-intensive activities in developed nations and labor-intensive activities in the developing world. As a result of these and other changes, post-industrial consumer markets increasingly fragmented, offering a stark contrast to the homogenous markets of the industrial era.

From 1870 through 1970, industrial nations generally prospered by manufacturing standardized goods cheaply and selling them at affordable prices on relatively homogenous mass markets patronized by middle-class consumers. Products were affordable because economies of scale and agglomeration reduced prices, and consumer markets grew because mass production required large numbers of well-paid workers to staff manufacturing plants and legions of salaried white-collar workers to control them (Maddrick 1995). After 1970, however, international competition, technological innovation, and the diversification of society upset this economic logic and led to a fragmentation of consumer markets.

Rather than catering to average tastes among millions of consumers, firms in the post-industrial era increasingly marketed to specialized niches of the population defined by the intersection of socioeconomic status, family status, and ethnic status. Rather than manufacturing huge quantities of similar products, stockpiling them in warehouses, and then shipping them via rail networks to centralized retail outlets where "everyone" shopped, producers came to use a range of new techniques such as "flexible production," "out-sourcing," "continuous-flow production," "just-in-time delivery," and "computerized inventory control" to make a variety of specialized products tailored individually to the tastes and needs of different market segments that were increasingly housed in different parts of the urban landscape.

Instead of selling the same goods to the same people in the same stores at the same prices, products came to be differentiated with respect to quality, price, and style and were sold in specialized stores in different locations that catered to different segments of the market—Bloomingdale's and Nordstrom's for the upper classes, and WalMart and Costco for the masses. Under the old industrial regime, companies were large, administrative hierarchies were deep, authority was rigid, markets were massive and homogeneous, and companies were slow to respond to shifts in consumer demand. In the new post-industrial order, companies became lean, hierarchies flattened, and authority diffused to serve populations that were diverse and whose tastes and buying power were heterogeneous. Successful companies were those able to move quickly to anticipate shifting and variable demands (Piore and Sabel 1984; Castells 1989; Harvey 1989; Sassen 1991, 1994, 2002).

*Segmentation of the Media*

Marketing of goods to diverse consumers differentiated from one another on the basis of economic status, life cycle stage, and ethnicity was facilitated by a parallel fragmentation of the mass media, in particular television. Whereas consumers in 1950 watched a limited number of TV shows produced by one of three networks and a small number of locally owned stations, by the year 2000 consumers could select from among thousands of programs broadcast daily on hundreds of channels. Advertisers and programmers appropriated the potential of this new media environment to segment consumers according to specific demographics, classifying consumers on the basis of socioeconomic, family, and ethnic status (Turow 1997). Ironically, now the most vigorous devotees of the Chicago School of Sociology were not social scientists, but market researchers.

Using survey research, focus groups, and intensive interviews, professional marketers have been able to discern with great accuracy the likes, desires, preferences, ambitions, and motivations of people in different sociodemographic categories. They have also determined which signs and symbols appeal to them emotionally. Armed with this knowledge, marketers deliberately place symbolic and subliminal messages in advertising and programming to attract viewers from certain social categories while repelling others. As a result of this deliberate manipulation of viewers, during the last quarter of the twentieth century consumption of the media and the consumer products they hawk was increasingly segmented, as people in different social circumstances came to watch entirely different programs, buy entirely different goods and services, and construct (through television) entirely different views of the world—a process that Turow (1997) calls "breaking up America."

The differentiation of markets and media has grown more acute over time. Drawing upon data and tools derived from the market research from Claritas, Weiss in 1988 was able to divide America into 40 meaningful sociodemographic clusters. When he revisited his classification a decade later, he discovered the number of relevant clusters had grown to 62, which he grouped under 15 basic social rubrics defined by the intersection of class, family status, race-ethnicity, and geography (see Weiss 1988, 2000). The 15 major groupings and the 62 subclusters developed by Weiss are listed in Table 6.1.

Table 6.1

America's Clustered Lifestyles Classified According to Claritas Corporation's PRIZM Cluster System, as Presented by Weiss (2000)

| Grouping and clusters | Brief description |
|---|---|
| **Elite Suburbs** | |
| Blue-Blood Estates | Elite super-rich families |
| Winner's Circle | Executive suburban families |
| Executive Suites | Upscale white-collar couples |
| Pools and Patios | Established empty-nesters |
| Kids and Cul-de-Sacs | Upscale suburban families |

| Grouping and clusters | Brief description |
|---|---|
| **Urban Uptown** | |
| Urban Gold Coast | Elite urban singles and couples |
| Money and Brains | Sophisticated townhouse couples |
| Young Literati | Upscale urban singles and couples |
| American Dreams | Established urban immigrant families |
| Bohemian Mix | Bohemian singles and couples |
| **Second-City Society** | |
| Second-City Elite | Upscale executive families |
| Upward Bound | Young upscale white-collar families |
| Gray Power | Affluent retirees in Sunbelt cities |
| **Landed Gentry** | |
| Country Squires | Elite exurban families |
| God's Country | Executive exurban families |
| Big Fish, Small Pond | Small-town executive families |
| Greenbelt Families | Young middle-class town families |
| **The Affluentials** | |
| Young Influentials | Upwardly mobile singles and couples |
| New Empty Nests | Upscale suburban fringe couples |
| Boomers and Babies | Young white-collar suburban families |
| Suburban Sprawl | Young suburban townhouse couples |
| Blue-Chip Blues | Upscale blue-collar families |
| **Inner Suburbs** | |
| Upstarts and Seniors | Middle-income empty-nesters |
| New Beginnings | Young mobile city singles |
| Mobility Blues | Young blue-collar and service families |
| Gray Collars | Aging couples in inner suburbs |
| **Urban Midscale** | |
| Urban Achievers | Mid-level white-collar urban couples |
| Big-City Blend | Middle-income immigrant families |
| Old Yankee Rows | Empty-nest middle-class families |
| Mid-City Mix | African American singles and families |
| Latino America | Hispanic middle-class families |

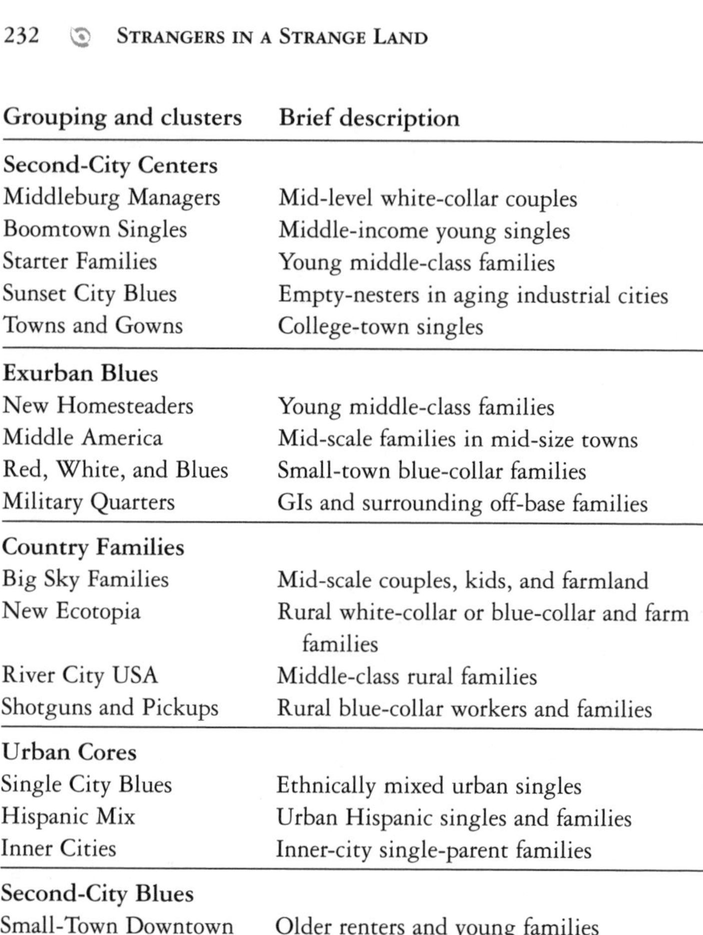

| Grouping and clusters | Brief description |
|---|---|
| **Second-City Centers** | |
| Middleburg Managers | Mid-level white-collar couples |
| Boomtown Singles | Middle-income young singles |
| Starter Families | Young middle-class families |
| Sunset City Blues | Empty-nesters in aging industrial cities |
| Towns and Gowns | College-town singles |
| **Exurban Blues** | |
| New Homesteaders | Young middle-class families |
| Middle America | Mid-scale families in mid-size towns |
| Red, White, and Blues | Small-town blue-collar families |
| Military Quarters | GIs and surrounding off-base families |
| **Country Families** | |
| Big Sky Families | Mid-scale couples, kids, and farmland |
| New Ecotopia | Rural white-collar or blue-collar and farm families |
| River City USA | Middle-class rural families |
| Shotguns and Pickups | Rural blue-collar workers and families |
| **Urban Cores** | |
| Single City Blues | Ethnically mixed urban singles |
| Hispanic Mix | Urban Hispanic singles and families |
| Inner Cities | Inner-city single-parent families |
| **Second-City Blues** | |
| Small-Town Downtown | Older renters and young families |
| Hometown Retired | Low-income older singles and couples |
| Family Scramble | Low-income Hispanic families |
| Southside City | African American service workers |
| **Working Towns** | |
| Golden Ponds | Retirement-town seniors |
| Rural Industrial | Low-income blue-collar families |
| Norma Rae-Ville | Young families in biracial mill towns |
| Mines and Mills | Older families in mine and mill towns |
| **The Heartlanders** | |
| Agri-Business | Rural farm-town and ranch families |
| Grain Belt | Farm owners and tenants |

| Grouping and clusters | Brief description |
|---|---|
| **Rustic Living** | |
| Blue Highways | Moderate blue-collar and farm families |
| Rustic Elders | Low-income older rural couples |
| Back-Country Folks | Remote rural or town families |
| Scrub Pine Flats | Older African American farm families |
| Hard Scrabble | Older families in poor isolated areas |

Adapted from *The Clustered World: How We Live, What We Buy, and What It All Means about Who We Are*, by Michael J. Weiss, Boston: Little, Brown, pp. 12-13.

These classifications represent a post-modern version of the natural areas originally described by Park (1925) for the city of Chicago. In a way that both Park and Burgess would readily appreciate, Weiss's major groupings are defined on the basis of class and geography, whereas the sub-clusters are distinguished on the basis of life cycle stage and ethnicity. All of American society, according to this scheme, can be neatly classified into cells of a social space defined succinctly by the intersection of three social dimensions: economic status, family status, and ethnicity.

Over the years market researchers have carried out extensive research on each grouping and cluster, and they have amassed vast amounts of data on the attitudes, tastes, consumption habits, viewing patterns, voting preferences, travel experiences, fertility intentions, mortality expectations, health outcomes, residential circumstances, and buying power of each one (Weiss 2000). These clusters may be mapped down to the block level, so that advertisements for magazines and newspapers can be tailored to specific residentially selected populations. As a consequence, not only do people in different clusters watch different television programs, but increasingly they browse different magazines, read different newspapers, see different billboards, and consume different products. Even when they nominally read the same magazine or newspaper, the content—both substantive and commercial—is systematically varied according to the target audience.

*Ecological Segregation*

As in the industrial and pre-industrial agrarian eras, changes in technology and social structure have been expressed spatially. Whereas industrialism favored the concentration of people in space, the technologies of post-industrialism favor decentralization, leading to a rapid expansion of the areal size of cities. In the United States in particular, heavy state spending on highways after 1950 enabled automobiles to eclipse trains and trolleys as the primary means of transport for short and medium distances, while trucks replaced trains in shipping all but the heaviest goods over any distance. Meanwhile, government investments in airports and air traffic control systems combined with public and private investments in aviation to make jet planes the preferred mode for moving passengers and lighter goods over long distances.

A key event in the spatial reconfiguration of U.S. urban areas was the creation in 1954 of the Interstate Highway System, which brought the federal government into partnership with states to build an integrated network of roads that connected central cities with one another. In addition to the transcontinental routes, over time each city came to be surrounded by successive "beltways" built to accommodate the rising volume of traffic within and among suburbs.

The systematic nature and planned quality of the U.S. highway grid is indicated by its numbering system. Interstate highways running north-south are numbered 5 through 95 in regular increments moving from east to west (so that I-5 is the principal Pacific Coast route and I-95 is the main route along the eastern seaboard). Highways running east-west are numbered 4 to 94 in regular increments from Mexico to Canada. Beltways surrounding central cities take the number of the interstate highway to which they are connected and precede it with an even integer (2, 4, 6) to indicate how closely they circle the central business district. Meanwhile, branch routes that do not encircle a central city are given three-digit numbers that begin with odd integers (1, 3, 5).

In addition to the Interstate Highway System, the U.S. government aided suburban expansion through the Federal Housing Administration (FHA), which put home ownership within reach of most families. From a level of 44% in 1940, home ownership rates rose steadily to reach 67% in the year 2000. The FHA achieved this feat by creating a loan program that insured privately held mortgages for up to 90% of home value and extended amortization periods for up to 30 years (Jackson 1985).

When combined with technological changes in transportation and communication, these federal policies dramatically increased the spatial size of American cities. The freeing of intraurban transportation from fixed routes, in particular, opened up vastly more land for urban settlement and led to the in-filling of undeveloped lands between rail lines and the rapid outward expansion of urban settlement, resulting in the formation of "edge cities"—office parks, commercial centers, and factory zones scatterd widely around the urban fringes (Garreau 1992; Duany, Plater-Zyberk, and Speck 2000). Figure 6.8

Figure 6.8
Area, Population, and Density of 34 Largest U.S. Urbanized Areas, 1950–2000

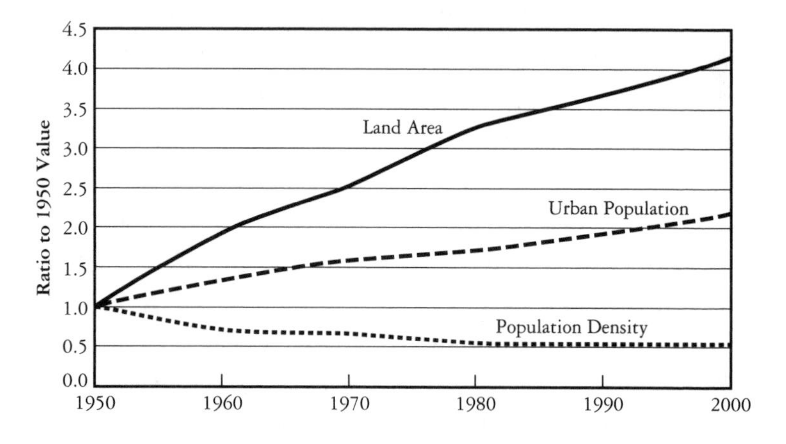


Adapted from "U.S. Urbanized Areas 1950–2000." Web site of *Demographia*: www.demographia.com/dm-uaix.htm.

shows changes in total land area occupied by the nation's largest urbanized areas from 1950 to 2000, along with corresponding changes in population size and density. To place all values on the same scale, each numerical series was divided by its value in 1950. The top line thus indicates the factor by which urbanized areas increased in areal size after this date.

In total, the land area occupied by U.S. urbanized areas more than quadrupled between 1950 and 2000, with a noticeable acceleration during the 1970s, just as the interstate system was being completed. Growth in the amount of urbanized land was roughly twice that of the urban population generally, which increased by a factor of just 2.2 (see the dashed line in the middle). As a result, population density within urbanized areas fell steadily during the last half of the twentieth century, and by the year 2000 it stood at just 50% of what it had been in 1950. Owing to changes in technology abetted by government policies, American cities consumed more space but used it less intensively, resulting in the permanent removal of large tracts of land from agricultural production (Vining, Plaut, and Bieri 1977).

At the same time, progress in telecommunications reduced the importance of central location and interpersonal accessibility. During the 1950s and 1960s, local telephone service grew to the point at which reliable and affordable voice communication was available to virtually all urban households. By the 1970s and 1980s, satellite communications were extending voice communication nationally and then internationally. Finally, during the 1990s, wireless technology increasingly replaced land lines and fixed communication stations to permit, at least in theory, any member of society to communicate with any other member at any point in space or time, effectively erasing the historical barrier of distance and definitively decoupling communication from transportation (Cairncross 1997). The efficient transmission of information over space no longer required anyone to move anywhere.

Not only the residential structure, but also the productive geography of cities was transformed by these technological changes. Whereas steam power favored the vertical orientation of production, electric motors were better suited to horizontal expansion, creating a need for large amounts of land on which to locate sprawling factories. Moreover, whereas rail transport encouraged the geographic concentration of productive activities at terminals and break-in-bulk points near waterways, automotive and truck transport favored the location of plants away from clogged central cities, near highway interchanges in more sparsely populated areas. Finally, wireless communication and computerized inventory control reduced the importance of physical closeness, allowing clerical, managerial, professional, and manufacturing operations to be separated from one another rather than concentrated in the central city.

The dramatic increase in the geographic size of urbanized areas and the steady decline in urban densities, when combined with the growing differentiation of metropolitan populations with respect to socioeconomic status, family status, and ethnic status, created a new potential for spatial separation among people and social groups. As income inequality rose, for example, so did residential segregation on the basis of social class. During the early postwar period, class-based segregation had been on the decline, like inequality generally (Simkus 1978; Massey 1996; Massey and Fischer 2003). After 1970, however, levels of segregation between rich and poor families began to rise as the nation grew more divided spatially as well as socially.

Figure 6.9 presents trends in the degree of residential dissimilarity between affluent and poor families in 60 U.S. metropolitan areas between 1970 and 2000 (taken from Massey and Fischer 2003). The upper bound defining family poverty is the federal poverty threshold for a family of four, and the lower bound of affluence is four times this value. These absolute cutpoints are inevitably subjective and arbitrary, so the figure also shows segregation between families within the top and bottom quintiles of the income distribution. No matter what definition is used, however, segregation on the basis of income clearly rose

Figure 6.9

Segregation between Affluent and Poor Families in 60 U.S. Metropolitan Areas, 1970–2000

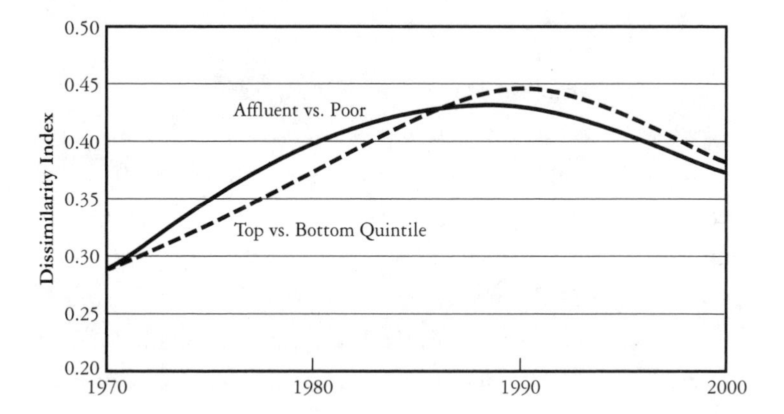


Adapted from "The Geography of Inequality in the United States, 1950–2000," by Douglas S. Massey and Mary J. Fischer, 2003. Pp. 1–40 in W. G. Gale and J. R. Pack, eds., *Brookings-Wharton Papers on Urban Affairs, 2003*. Washington, D.C.: Brookings Institution, Table 2.

between 1970 and 1990, as the affluent-vs.-poor dissimilarity index went from 0.29 to 0.43 and that between the top and bottom fifth of the income distribution grew from 0.29 to 0.45, an increase of more than 50% in just two decades.

During the 1990s, segregation on the basis of income moderated and dipped slightly to finish the decade at about 0.38. This moderation corresponds to a small reduction in income inequality and a slight increase in average incomes during the late 1990s. By the end of that decade, the longest sustained economic expansion in U.S. history had virtually eliminated unemployment and tight labor markets had produced the first rise in entry-level wages since the mid-1970s, yielding a moderation of both income inequality and class segregation. Nonetheless, the decline in class segregation during the 1990s counterbalanced only a portion of the previous increase, leaving segregation between affluent and poor families in 2000 still one third higher than it had been in 1970.

The differentiation of households with respect to family status was also expressed spatially, as indicated in Figure 6.10. Whereas the notable trend during the period 1960–1970 was the growing segregation between elderly and non-elderly households (see Cowgill 1978), the salient development after 1970 was the emergence of the twenties and early thirties as a distinct, identifiable stage in the life cycle, as evidenced by the growing number of non-family households containing unmarried men and women without children. Although census data do not permit the computation of segregation scores by household type, one can examine the spatial distribution of people age 20 to 34 to see whether it has changed over time.

Figure 6.10 shows dissimilarity indices computed between those age 20 to 35 and everyone else in 1970, 1980, 1990, and 2000 to determine trends over time in 60 U.S. metropolitan areas. From 1970 to 1990, the level of segregation between twenty- and thirty-somethings and the rest of urban society was essentially constant at around 0.13. Between 1990 and 2000, however, the segregation of young adults rose from 0.13 to 0.16. Although this shift may not seem like much, it represents an increase of 23% in just a decade and may serve as a harbinger of future trends in segregation by family status.

The period 1940-1970 was likewise characterized by a steady decline in levels of segregation among various European-origin groups that was linked to socioeconomic mobility and

Figure 6.10

Segregation of Persons Age 20 to 35 in 60 U.S. Metropolitan Areas, 1970–2000

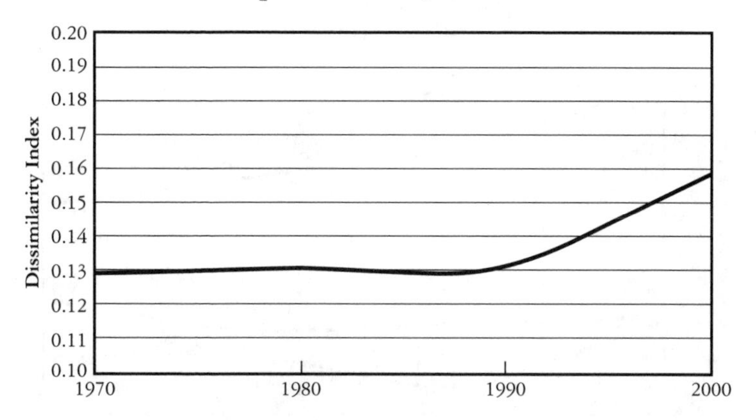


the succession of generations (Lieberson 1980; Massey 1985; Alba and Nee 2003). After 1970, the meaningful lines of spatial differentiation were no longer among groups of European origin, but among blacks, Asians, Hispanics, and whites (Massey and Denton 1987; Bobo et al. 2000). Figure 6.11 presents indices of dissimilarity to measure trends in the degree of black, Hispanic, and Asian segregation from non-Hispanic whites in the 60 largest metropolitan areas during the period 1970-2000.

Reflecting the enactment of fair housing and fair lending laws in the United States between 1968 and 1977, black-white segregation generally declined between 1970 and 1980, going from 0.80 to 0.70 in this decade. Thereafter the pace of change slowed to half its earlier rate, as average black-white segregation fell from 0.70 to 0.61 over the next two decades. As of the year 2000, the average segregation of blacks and whites in the

Figure 6.11

Segregation of Hispanics, Blacks, and Asians from Non-Hispanic Whites in 60 U.S. Metropolitan Areas, 1970–2000

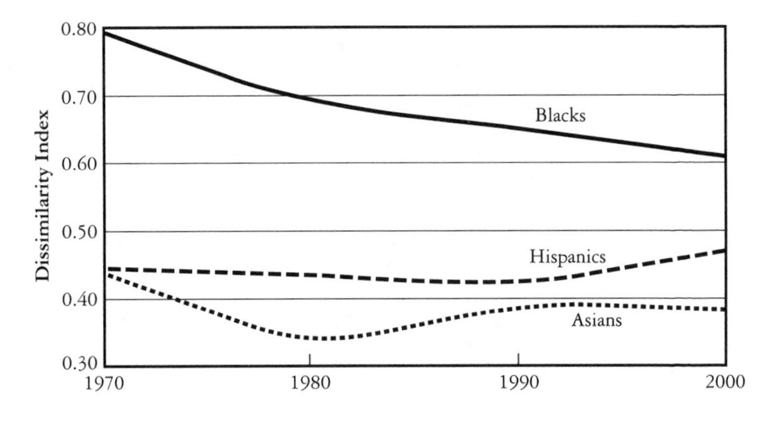


Computed by author using STF3 and STF4 Files, 1970–2000, U.S. Censuses of Population.

60 largest metropolitan areas still remained above the threshold defining a "high" level of segregation. In contrast, segregation between Hispanics and non-Hispanic whites remained fairly constant from 1970 through 1990 at around 0.43–0.44 and then increased to around 0.47 by the year 2000. Likewise, after declining from 0.44 to 0.34 in 1980, Asian-white segregation rose from 1980 to 1990 and then stabilized at around 0.39.

The dissimilarity index is insensitive to the relative size of the minority population and therefore cannot detect increases in the propensity of racial or ethnic groups to live in residential enclaves (Massey and Denton 1988). If Hispanic and Asian populations grew rapidly during a period of stable or rising residential dissimilarity, one would expect to observe a growing tendency for co-residence among both groups. Similarly, the modest increase in the size of the black population, when combined with recent stability in the index of black-white dissimilarity, predicts relative stasis in black residential isolation, or even a slight increase.

The tendency for different groups to form ethnically homogenous residental enclaves is appropriately measured using the P* isolation index (Massey and Denton 1988). For any particular minority group, the isolation index gives the proportion of in-group members within the neighborhood of the average group member. The isolation index among blacks, for example, gives the proportion of blacks within the neighborhood of the average African American living within any given urban area. Figure 6.12 presents isolation indices for blacks, Hispanics, and Asians for 1970 through 2000 in the 60 largest U.S. metropolitan areas.

Trends generally correspond to the expectations just described and paint a slightly different picture of the evolving system of racial-ethnic segregation in U.S. urban areas compared with that derived from trends in residential dissimilarity. As expected, black isolation declined significantly from 1970 to 1980 (going from 0.62 to 0.55) and then more slowly from 1980 to 1990 (falling from 0.55 to 0.51); but the decline halts thereafter, with racial isolation rising slightly to 0.52 by the year 2000. In other words, moves toward black-white desegregation appear largely to have come to an end by the decade of the 1990s, at least in the nation's largest metropolitan areas.

Figure 6.12

Isolation of Blacks, Hispanics, and Asians within 60 U.S. Metropolitan Areas, 1970–2000

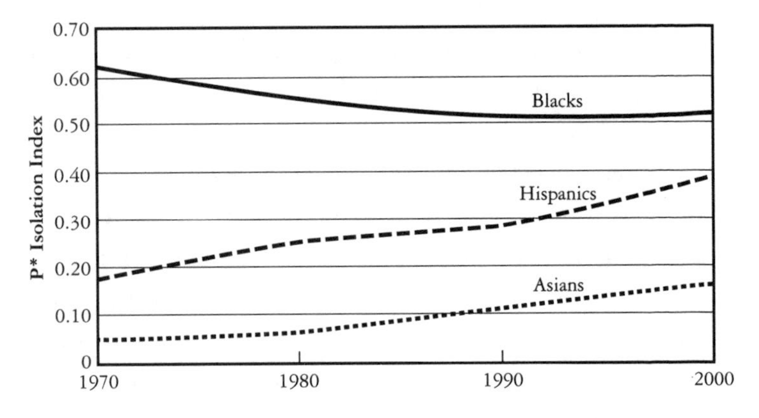


Computed by author using STF3 and STF4 Files, 1970–2000, U.S. Censuses of Population.

In contrast, isolation indices for Asians and Hispanics both displayed sustained increases throughout the latter part of the twentieth century, reflecting the resurgence of immigration and the formation of new immigrant enclaves. From 1970 to 2000, Asian isolation rose from an average of 0.05 to 0.16 while average Hispanic isolation increased from 0.17 to 0.39. Despite these increases, however, as of the turn of the twenty-first century black-white segregation and black isolation remained far more severe than that between whites and either Hispanics or Asians, underscoring African Americans' unique social and spatial position in American society.

## INTO THE AGE OF EXTREMES

The late twentieth century witnessed the transition from an industrial to a post-industrial way of life, a shift characterized by rising socioeconomic inequality, increasing heterogeneity with respect to family and household structure, and growing racial-ethnic diversity. The revival of international trade and the resurgence of technological innovation at once globalized and fragmented markets and transformed the ecological structure of cities. Peak city densities declined, the amount of urbanized territory increased, and the urban fringe expanded outward as functional activities were redistributed within the urban, suburban, and increasingly the ex-urban landscape. At the same time, urban residential space was increasingly segmented along the lines of class, life cycle, race, and ethnicity, corresponding to a broader segmentation of society along these dimensions.

At the dawn of the twenty-first century, therefore, urban dwellers are more separated from each other socially, economically, and spatially than ever before. Whether or not these trends continue into the future, one thing is clear: They will apply to a growing share of the human population. Figure 6.13 shows the level of urbanization for developing nations, developed nations, and the world from 1970 through 2030 as estimated and projected by the United Nations (2002). As of 1970, developed nations were already close to fully urbanized, with nearly 70% of their population living in cities, a share that is projected to rise above 80% by 2030.

In contrast, the developing world was still substantially rural in 1970, with only around 25% of its population living in cities. This percentage steadily rose over the next three decades

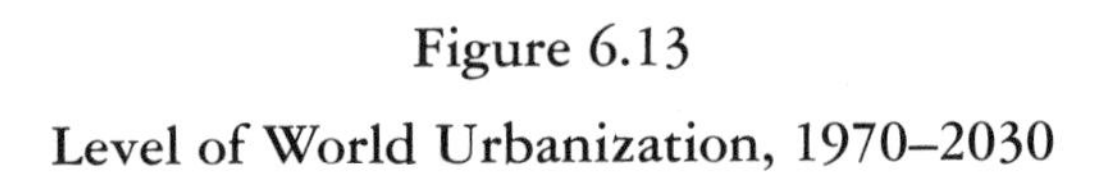

Figure 6.13

Level of World Urbanization, 1970–2030

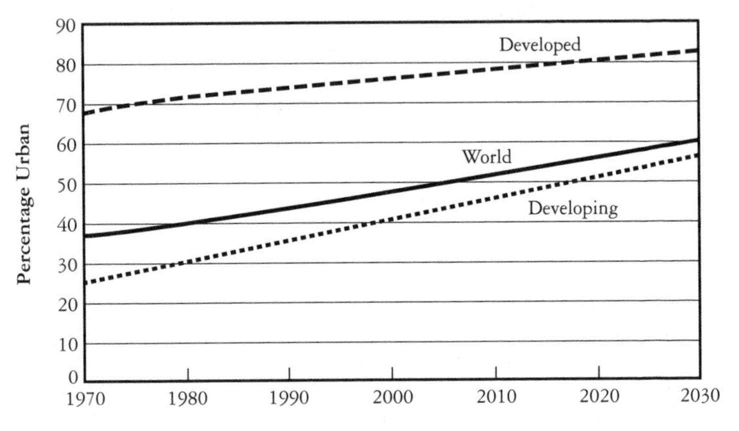


Adapted from *World Urbanization Prospects: The 2001 Revision*, United Nations, 2002. New York: United Nations, Table 10.

to reach 40% by the year 2000; somewhere around 2018, a majority of people in the developing world will live in cities. When this threshold is crossed, urbanized life will cease to be the exclusive province of people in the developed, industrialized world. Indeed, by 2030 the level of urbanization in the developing world is projected to reach 56%.

The growing degree of urbanization throughout the developing world means that sometime after 2005 the world will reach a milestone: For the first time in human experience, a majority of the world's people will live in urban settings. Not only will they live in cities, moreover; increasingly they will live in very large cities. Figure 6.14 shows trends in the number of people living in urban areas of 1 million or more from 1975 to 2015, again as estimated and projected by the United

## Figure 6.14
## Number of People Living in Large Urban Areas, 1975–2015

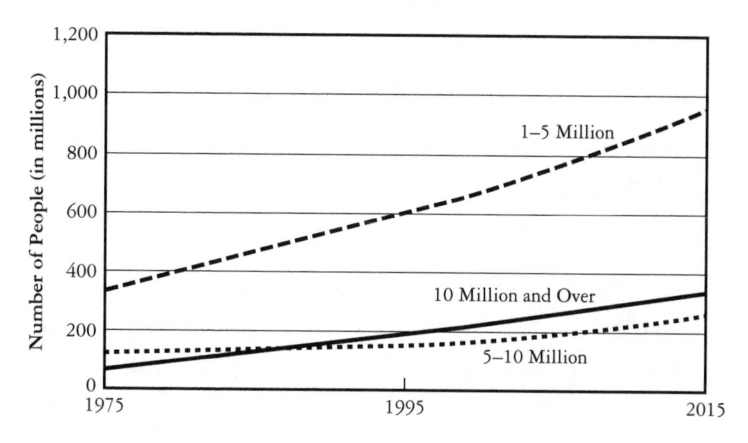


Adapted from *World Urbanization Prospects: The 2001 Revision*, Data Tables and Highlights, United Nations, 2002. New York: United Nations, Table 3.

Nations (2002). Over this period, the number of people living in megacities of 10 million or more is projected to increase from 68 million to 340 million; the number living in metropolitan areas of 5–10 million will go from 122 to 264 million; and the number residing in areas of 1–5 million will rise from 332 to 960 million. All told, 1.6 billion of the world's people are expected to live in cities of 1 million or more by 2015, constituting 22% of the world's population (United Nations, 2002).

Most of these new urbanites, whether in large cities or small, will be located in the developing world. As an illustration, Figure 6.15 shows the percentage people in the largest metropolitan areas who are estimated or projected to be from developing nations. As late as 1975, most people living in ur-

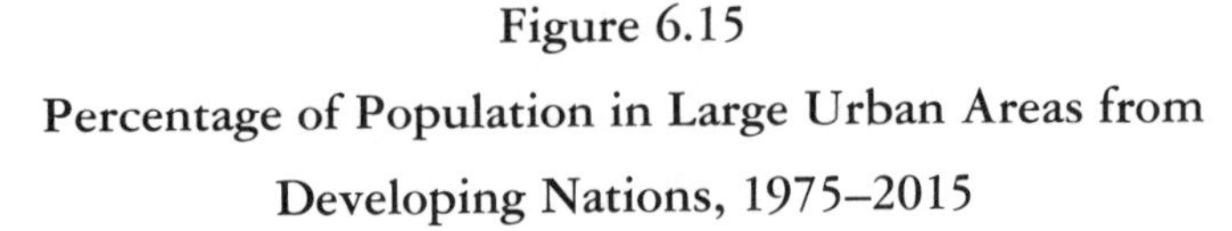

Figure 6.15

Percentage of Population in Large Urban Areas from Developing Nations, 1975–2015

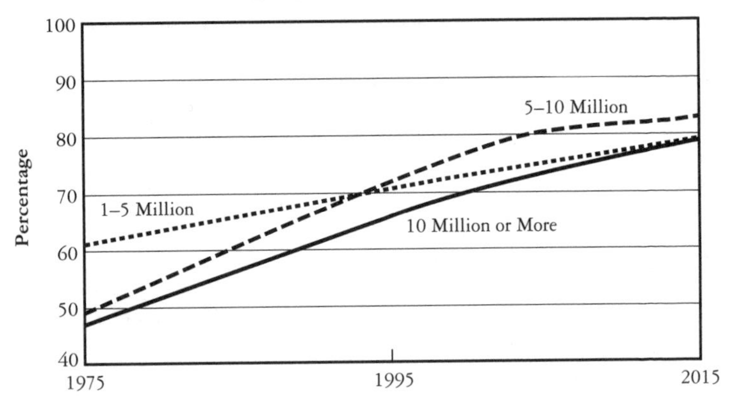


Adapted from *World Urbanization Prospects: The 2001 Revision*, Data Tables and Highlights, United Nations, 2002. New York: United Nations, Table 3.

ban areas of 5–10 million and 10 million or more were inhabitants of developing nations.

However, a harbinger of things to come is the fact that even at this date, more than 60% of those in urban areas of 1–5 million were inhabitants of the developing world. During the early twenty-first century, however, the vast majority of *all* the world's urbanites will come to reside in developing countries. As the figure shows, the percentage of developing country citizens among those living in cities of 1–5 million and 10 million or more is projected to reach 80%, while the percentage in cities of 5–10 million will substantially exceed this threshold. Simply put, over the twenty-first century the vast majority of the world's inhabitants will come to live in large urbanized areas, and most of the new urbanites will reside in poor nations of the developing world.

The long-run demographic structure likely to prevail in post-industrial metropolises, and certainly in those of the developed world, is indicated by Figure 6.16, which shows the population pyramid projected for the United States in the year 2050. Countries with very low fertility and more limited immigration, such as Japan and many countries of Europe, already

Figure 6.16

**Projected Age Distribution for Urban Population of the United States, 2050**

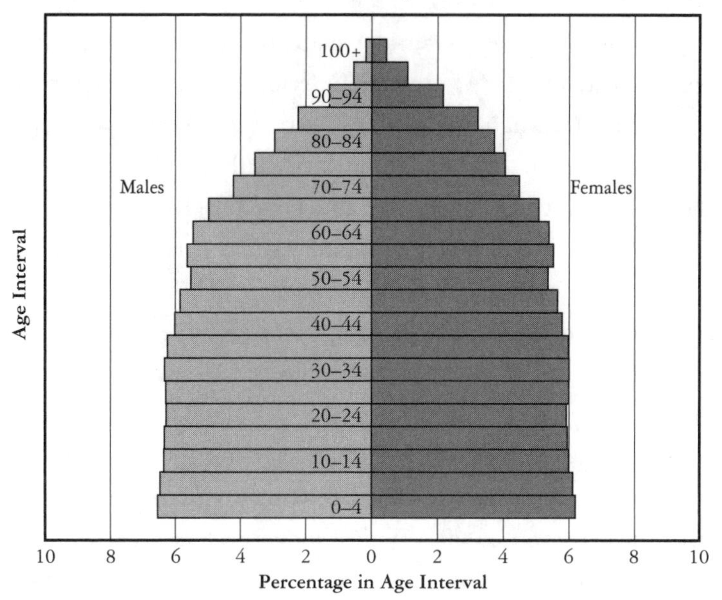


Adapted from "U.S. Interim Projections by Age, Sex, Race, and Hispanic Origin," by U.S. Bureau of the Census, 2004. Web site of U.S. Census Bureau: www.census.gov/ipc/www/usinterimproj/, Table 2a.

approximate this demographic structure. Although such a structure will take longer to achieve in the developing world, it will soon be the prevailing form in China and other nations that experienced sharp declines in fertility during the last decades of the twentieth century.

Ultimately, in the long term, the population composition shown in Figure 6.16 is the only structure that is environmentally sustainable, with low rates of fertility, high life expectancies, and little or no natural increase. Even if immigration persists into the foreseeable future, as long as it is characterized by a stable age distribution and a constant volume, urban populations will slowly revert to the stationary form shown in the figure (Espenshade 1986).

In contrast to the pyramidal shape of the past, the age and sex structure of future human populations will be characterized by a more rectangular, "beehive" structure. Very few people will die before the age of 60, and there will be little tapering of the age distribution before this age. Given higher rates of male mortality across all ages, moreover, the tapering will occur more abruptly among men than women. Above age 60, the population increasingly will comprise widows. Above age 80, for example, the Census Bureau projects 1.5 women for every man.

The radical nature of the shift in age structure is illustrated by dependency ratios computed for this population compared with those computed for a typical industrial-era urban population (see Figure 5.16). Recall that the age-sex distribution achieved under urban industrialism produced a total dependency burden of .39, indicating roughly 39 dependents for every 100 workers. Of these 39 dependents, moreover, 29 (or three quarters) were children under the age of 15.

In contrast, by 2050 the total dependency burden in the urban United States is projected to rise to around 0.697, indicating that there will be around 70 dependents for every 100 workers. Moreover, 39 or the 70 dependents (56%) will be age 65 or older. Indeed, whereas childhood dependency is projected to rise only about 15% over the next 50 years, old-age dependency is expected to rise by a startling 81%, portending a radically different pattern of social and economic organization.

Clearly, the generous retirement and health benefits funded by the welfare state during the latter half of the twentieth century will be impossible to sustain, at least using the same financial mechanisms employed to the present (Kotlikoff and Burns 2004). Until now, generous old-age benefits have been funded by redistributing tax revenues from current workers to current retirees, not by contributions from current retirees made earlier during their working years. Maintaining old-age benefits at current levels will require taxes so high that they will leave little money left over to sustain workers and their families.

In the long run, the only way out of this demographic dilemma is to shift from funding retirement and health care systems through direct transfers to an actuarial system whereby people make regular contributions during their working lives and then draw these funds down for living and health care expenses in their old age. The principal obstacle to making the shift is the exorbitant cost imposed on workers during the transition period. People now in the labor force and expecting to retire in the coming decades simply have not put enough aside to meet their retirement needs. During any transition period, working taxpayers will be called upon to set aside money not only for their own retirement, but also for the retirement of those who are already out of the labor force, a burden that would virtually eliminate discretionary income for at least an entire generation.

The conflict between the demography of post-industrialism and the generous social programs implemented during the industrial era is a fundamental factor behind the retreat from the welfare state and the downsizing of government. Over the next several decades, the most likely scenario is for retirement ages to rise, extending working lives well beyond the threshold of 65 years that has been the normative age for retirement until now. As a result, social and economic structures will increasingly be dominated by the needs, characteristics, and temperament of the elderly rather than the young. Although the average experience of workers—and whatever wisdom comes with it—will increase, so will fallible memories, diminished capacity, restricted dexterity, and social and psychological rigidity. Generational tensions will constitute a fundamental feature of post-industrial urban society, as the burdens on workers inevitably rise while the quality and quantity of services provided to seniors just as inevitably fall.

# Chapter Seven
## STRANGERS IN A STRANGE LAND

IN HIS CELEBRATED SCIENCE FICTION NOVEL *Stranger in a Strange Land*, Robert A. Heinlein describes the travails of Valentine Michael Smith, a human being who was born, orphaned, and raised on Mars and then brought to Earth as an adult. Although he is physically human, he is socially and culturally Martian and thus a complete stranger to the ways and thoughts of his ancestral people. He is a stranger in a strange land. We human beings in the twenty-first century likewise find ourselves in a situation of estrangement. The genome we possess leaves us physiologically, psychologically, and socially adapted to life in small groups spread thinly about an organic natural environment, but instead we find ourselves living in huge, densely packed settlements housed within an inorganic artificial environment. As biological organisms, we are indeed strangers in a strange land.

How we manage this contradiction over the next 100 years will determine much about our well-being and perhaps our survival as a species. The discrepancy between our organic heritage and our present material circumstances carries biological as well as social challenges. Socially, the most serious challenge stems from the ongoing consolidation of social and economic characteristics in urban space. Biologically, the most pressing problem arises from our physiological response to certain conditions of life within dense urban settings. In both cases, the net effect of recent changes has been to perpetuate social divisions, harden the lines of stratification, and expand the gulf between the haves and have-nots. Unless we reverse trends now well under way, the structure of post-industrial urban society might ultimately become so brittle as to break, with unknown but likely calamitous consequences for human welfare.

### THE CONSOLIDATION OF PARAMETERS

In his general theory of social structure, Blau (1977) introduced the concept of *multiform heterogeneity*, by which he meant diversity along multiple social dimensions simultaneously. What I have here labeled as dimensions of social differentiation, he calls *parameters* and notes that in combination they define the social space for any human community: "Actual social structures are characterized by multiform heterogeneity in terms of several and sometimes many intersecting nominal parameters. Differences in sex, race, national background, religion, and occupation do not coincide, although some are correlated. Multiform heterogeneity refers to the overlapping groups and numerous subgroups generated by such differences" (Blau 1977:83).

Blau anticipated that a full characterization of the social space of any society would involve the intersection of many different dimensions of differentiation, some graduated or ranked (e.g., income) and others nominal or categorical (e.g., ethnicity). The distribution of people simultaneously along $N$ separate axes of differentiation yields an $N$-dimensional hyperspace, a concept that most people have difficulty visualizing (although with matrix algebra the concept is mathematically tractable). Fortunately, contemporary human societies can be rather parsimoniously described by the intersection of three basic dimensions of variation, one graduated and two nominal.

All non-foraging societies display some degree of economic stratification defined by inequality with respect to material, emotional, and symbolic resources (graduated parameters). As societies increase in size and scale, separate axes of family differentiation and ethnic status emerge by which people can be categorized into discrete social groups (nominal parameters). Over the long run, as development proceeds and the scale of society increases, the absolute length of the graduated dimension grows and the number of categories in the two nominal parameters multiplies to produce growing diversity within an expanding, three-dimensional social space.

Any given human community may be characterized by the length of its socioeconomic dimension (the distance from the top to the bottom of the economic ladder) and by the number and range of categories it uses to define ethnicity and family structure. If one divides socioeconomic status into a series of ranked categories, then social position may be conceptualized as a cell within a three-dimensional space defined by the intersection of socioeconomic status, family status, and ethnic status (as depicted in Figure 5.13). Each community is characterized by a particular distribution of individuals among cells in this three-dimensional space, and the location of any particular individual within the space is precisely given by his or her position with respect to each of the three dimensions.

In theory, the only dimension that need imply a differential in well-being is socioeconomic status. Having more resources at one's disposal enables one to improve the quality of one's life by acquiring those goods and services that contribute to a longer and more enjoyable existence, such as more and better food, housing, clothing, education, entertainment, and medical care, as well as greater amounts of emotional support and symbolic validation. Rising inequality generally means that fewer people have access to these desirable resources, and falling inequality indicates greater and more widespread access to these good things.

Conceptually, the three dimensions of social space are independent of one another. Each is defined according to its own criteria, and in theory knowing a person's family status and ethnic status need not imply anything about his or her position in the socioeconomic hierarchy. In practice, however, location with respect to the three dimensions is often correlated, yielding what Blau calls a "consolidation of parameters."

When social parameters are consolidated—that is, correlated with one another—the process of stratification becomes sharper and more acute. Within the social space of any society, within-cell relations intensify and between-cell interactions attenuate. Over time, inter-cell mobility withers, social categories reify and reproduce themselves, and the social structure as a whole grows rigid. A society defined by consolidated parameters is one in which the categorical mechanisms of inequality operate very effectively and where social boundaries are very salient. It is difficult to implement strategies of exploitation and opportunity hoarding within a homogenous society where everyone is perceived and treated equally, without pejorative labeling. Once out-groups are socially defined by the privileged, however, categorical mechanisms can be implemented to produce what Tilly (1998) calls "durable inequality"—socioeconomic stratification that replicates and reproduces itself more or less automatically over time.

One of the most effective means of creating an association between social dimensions is by arranging their concordance in urban space. It is no coincidence that the construction of apartheid in South Africa after 1948 began with the Group Areas Act, which assigned whites, blacks, and "coloureds" to separate locations within the urban environment. The de facto apartheid of the United States has likewise created a strong association among race, poverty, and single parenthood (Massey and Denton 1993). The correlation of socioeconomic status, family status, and minority status—a consolidation of three fundamental parameters—creates a social structure wherein it is remarkably easy for the privileged to preserve opportunities for themselves while denying resources to others.

A sure sign that spatially based mechanisms of inequality have taken hold is the appearance of geographically concentrated affluence and poverty within the urban landscape. The mechanics by which poverty and affluence become concentrated geographically are quite simple and well understood (see Massey 1990; Massey and Denton 1993; Massey and Fischer 2000). Rising inequality creates the potential for spatially concentrated advantage and disadvantage by expanding the number of people at the top and bottom of the socioeconomic hierarchy. Larger and denser concentrations of poverty are more possible when there are 10,000 poor people in a city than when there are only 1,000. In general, as poor and affluent households proliferate during periods of rising inequality, the geographic concentration of poverty and affluence both increase as well. Periods of rising socioeconomic inequality are thus naturally prone to the concentration of privilege and disadvantage.

The potential for geographic concentration is exacerbated by class segregation. To the extent that affluent and poor families live in separate neighborhoods, increases in the number of each population will accrue in different parts of the urban environment. When disadvantaged families disproportionately inhabit their own neighborhoods, then any structural economic change that pushes more people into poverty will tend to affect neighborhoods that are already quite poor. Likewise, when privileged families are located within exclusive enclaves, increases in wealth and income accrue there. As the degree of spatial separation between rich and poor rises, therefore, poverty and affluence tend to become more geographically concentrated, regardless of the extent of income inequality in society.

Finally, when rising inequality and class segregation occur within a population that is also segregated on the basis of race or ethnicity, the potential for poverty concentration is magnified while the concentration of affluence is reduced, inflicting a "double whammy" on the segregated minority group. In such an ecology, the class disadvantages of the minority poor are reinforced and the class advantages of the minority rich are undermined. As a consequence, it is more likely that poor families pass their disadvantages on to their children and less likely that affluent members bequeath privileges to theirs.

Understanding the mechanisms by which poverty and affluence become spatially concentrated yields very clear predictions for the United States. Specifically, one can expect to observe growing concentrations of affluence and poverty during the period 1970–1990 when both inequality and class segregation were rising in American cities; and one can expect to encounter falling, or at least moderating, concentrations of poverty and affluence during the economic boom of 1990–2000 when inequality and class segregation peaked and edged slightly downward. Among African Americans, one can expect to observe the same trends, but at every date their poverty will be more concentrated and affluence less concentrated than for whites.

Figure 7.1 shows trends in the concentration of poverty for blacks and whites in the 60 largest U.S. metropolitan areas between 1970 and 2000. Given their predominance in the U.S. population, trends for the total population closely mirror those of whites. Concentration here is measured using the P* isolation index for poverty, which gives the proportion of poor people in the neighborhood of the average poor person (Massey and Eggers 1990). As the index increases, the poor display a greater tendency to live in and among other poor people. Poverty is defined according to the U.S. government's poverty threshold for a family of four, expressed in constant, inflation-adjusted dollars (see Massey and Fischer 2003).

The data generally bear out expectations. From 1970 to 1990, there was a sharp increase in the concentration of white poverty, which doubled from an index value of 0.13 to one of 0.26. During the 1990s, however, when inequality and class segregation both moderated (as shown in Chapter Six), the concentration of white poverty dropped slightly and ended the century at a level of 0.23, but still 77% above that observed in 1970. In addition, although trends for blacks and whites are parallel, at every date the degree of poverty concentration for blacks was higher than that of whites. Black poverty concentra-

Figure 7.1

The Spatial Concentration of Poverty in 60 U.S. Metropolitan Areas, 1970–2000

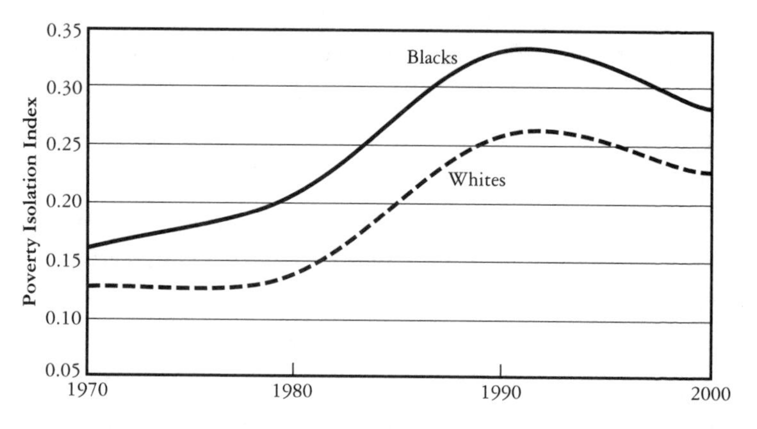


Adapted from "The Geography of Inequality in the United States, 1950–2000," by Douglas S. Massey and Mary J. Fischer, 2003. Pp. 1–40 in W. G. Gale and J. R. Pack, eds., *Brookings-Wharton Papers on Urban Affairs*. Washington, DC: Brookings Institution, Table 3.

tion rose from an average of 0.16 in 1970 to 0.33 in 1990. At the end of the economically tumultuous 1980s, in other words, the typical poor black family lived in an area where one third of neighboring families were also poor, compared with around one quarter for whites. By the year 2000, the degree of black poverty concentration had declined somewhat to 0.28 (compared with 0.23 for whites).

Figure 7.2 repeats the analysis for the concentration of affluence, where affluent households are defined as having incomes at least four times the poverty level for a family of four (following Smith 1988, and Massey and Eggers 1990). In general, the affluent are even more geographically concentrated than the poor. Whereas the white poor displayed concentration indices of 0.13 in 1970 and 0.23 in 2000, the white affluent evinced respective indices of 0.31 and 0.35. The time trend for concentrated affluence is at once simpler and more complicated than that observed for the concentration of poverty. It is simpler in the sense that the amplitude of shifts over time are less extreme than those observed for the concentration of poverty. It is more complex in the sense that there are more ups and downs in the series, which fell from 1970 to 1980, rose from 1980 to 1990, and then fell again between 1990 and 2000.

Consistent with predictions, the concentration of black affluence was systematically *less than* that observed for whites at

**Figure 7.2**

**The Spatial Concentration of Affluence in 60 U.S. Metropolitan Areas, 1970–2000**

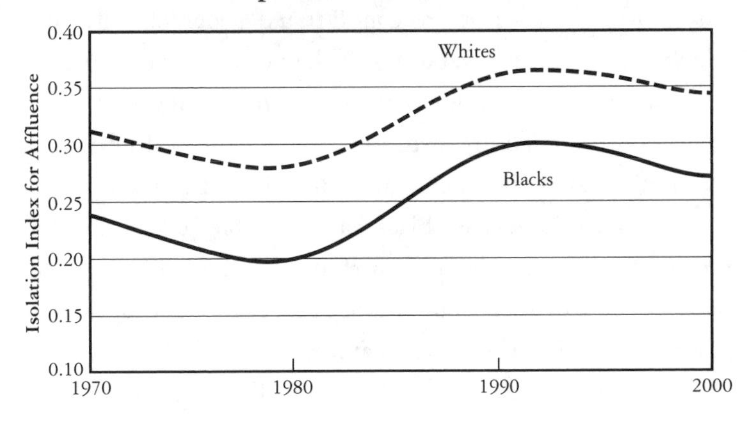


Adapted from "The Geography of Inequality in the United States, 1950–2000," by Douglas S. Massey and Mary J. Fischer, 2003. Pp. 1–40 in W. G. Gale and J. R. Pack, eds., *Brookings-Wharton Papers on Urban Affairs*. Washington, DC: Brookings Institution, Table 3.

every date, reflecting the effect of racial segregation, which forces blacks of all classes to live together. The concentration of black affluence reached a nadir of 0.20 in 1980 and a peak of 0.30 in 1990, compared with figures of 0.28 and 0.36 for affluent whites. Dollar for dollar, affluent white families are able to buy their way into higher-quality, more advantaged neighborhoods than comparably affluent black families, and overall middle-class white neighborhoods that are characterized by lower rates of poverty, fewer social problems, and richer amenities (Massey, Condran, and Denton 1987; Massey and Fong 1990; Logan and Alba 1993; Logan et al. 1996).

The geographic concentration of the poor forces them disproportionately to bear the negative externalities of their own poverty. They experience greater exposure to negative correlates of poverty such as higher rates of substance abuse, crime, delinquency, family disruption, poor health, and gang activity. Likewise, when the affluent are concentrated geographically they benefit from a greater exposure to the positive externalities of their privileged status: lower rates of crime, delinquency, substance abuse, and family disruption; and a more healthful physical and social environment. More insidious, because of racial segregation, middle-class blacks are less able to benefit from the positive externalities of their affluence while poor blacks are more likely to suffer from the negative externalities of their poverty, yielding the double whammy mentioned earlier.

Theorists such as Sassen (1991), Mollenkopf and Castells (1991), Scott (2001), and others have argued that social, economic, and spatial polarizations are particularly acute within certain "global cities" that serve as nodes of command, control, and finance in the global market economy. Figure 7.3 thus presents P* measures for the concentration of affluence and poverty in three U.S. metropolitan areas that have been universally identified as global cities (Chicago, Los Angeles, New York—see Friedman 1986), plus a fourth that represents an emerging hub for interchange in the global information economy (Atlanta, headquarters for CNN). Overall levels of concentrated poverty and affluence across all 60 metropolitan areas are shown for comparison (the data are taken from Massey and Fischer 2003).

In these metropolitan areas, both advantage and disadvantage appear to be more concentrated spatially than average. In

**Figure 7.3**

**Spatial Concentration of Poverty and Affluence in Four Metropolitan Areas in 2000**

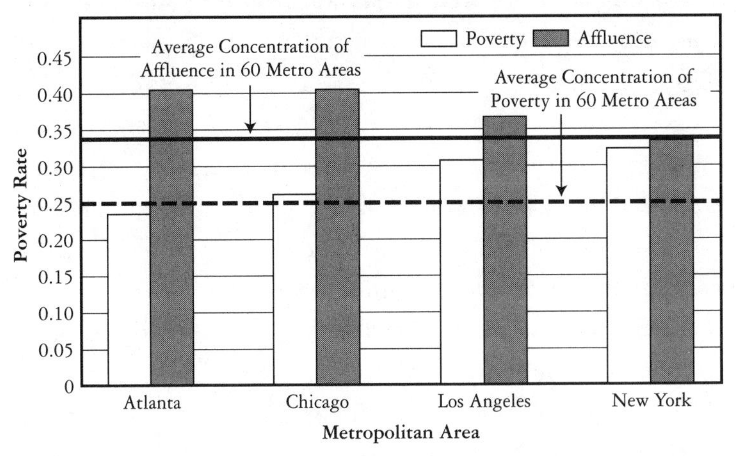


Adapted from "The Geography of Inequality in the United States, 1950–2000," by Douglas S. Massey and Mary J. Fischer, 2003. Pp. 1–40 in W. G. Gale and J. R. Pack, eds., *Brookings-Wharton Papers on Urban Affairs*. Washington, DC: Brookings Institution, Table 3.

each case, indices of concentrated affluence and concentrated poverty are higher than average in three of the four areas. In Atlanta and Chicago, for example, the concentration of affluence is around 0.40, meaning that in these metropolitan areas the typical affluent person lives in a neighborhood that is 40% affluent. The concentration of poverty is greatest in Los Angeles and New York, reaching a value of 0.31 in the former and 0.32 in the latter, meaning that the typical poor person lives in a neighborhood where nearly one-third of his or her neighbors are also poor. In these global cities, therefore, one can indeed observe a pattern of spatial polarization, which one would expect to see replicated in other global cities throughout the world (e.g., London, Tokyo, Frankfurt).

The fact that the concentration of poverty is so high in Los Angeles and New York is not coincidental, for they are the first and second most important destinations for immigration to the United States. Studies have shown that the higher the level of immigration, the greater the concentration of poverty within cities (Massey and Eggers 1990, 1993; Massey and Fischer 2000). In addition to the structural mechanisms of poverty concentration already described, therefore, an additional process of concentration is rural-urban migration. Of course, internal migration from rural to urban areas no longer contributes much to the concentration of poverty in developed countries, because they are already fully urbanized and migration from the countryside to the city has all but ceased. To the extent that they attract poor rural migrants from overseas, however, postindustrial cities continue to experience a growing concentration of poverty through rural-urban migration.

Rural-urban migration is more relevant to the concentration

of poverty within emerging metropolises of the developing world. As noted in Chapter Six, urban growth in the twenty-first century will occur primarily within poor countries of Asia, Latin America, and Africa, contributing to the growth of huge, densely populated megacities. Virtually all of the shift toward greater urbanization will occur because of rural-urban migration, which typically involves the movement of poor households from villages in sparsely settled rural areas to slums in densely populated cities (United Nations 1980, 2002). Within the poorest nations of the developing world, therefore, poor people will increasingly come to inhabit environments filled with dense concentrations of other poor people.

Although direct measures of spatially concentrated urban poverty in the third world are lacking, Figure 7.4 summarizes information taken from the United Nations Statistical Division, which provides data on rates of poverty within urban areas of the 50 developing nations that participate in its Millennium Project (http://millenniumindicators.un.org/unsd/mi/mi_series_xxx.asp?row_id=582). Poverty is defined according to each country's own poverty standards, so the data are potentially subject to political manipulation by national statistical offices. Given that the rates are likely to be biased downward (showing the country in a favorable light), these data provide a conservative indication of the potential for poverty concentration within the third world. The rate of urban poverty in the United States is shown for comparison.

The region with the greatest potential for poverty concentration is clearly Sub-Saharan Africa, where the average poverty rate in urban areas is estimated to be nearly 40%, meaning that four out of every ten African urbanites are poor. Knowing

Figure 7.4
Percentage of Urban Population in Poverty by Region Circa 2000

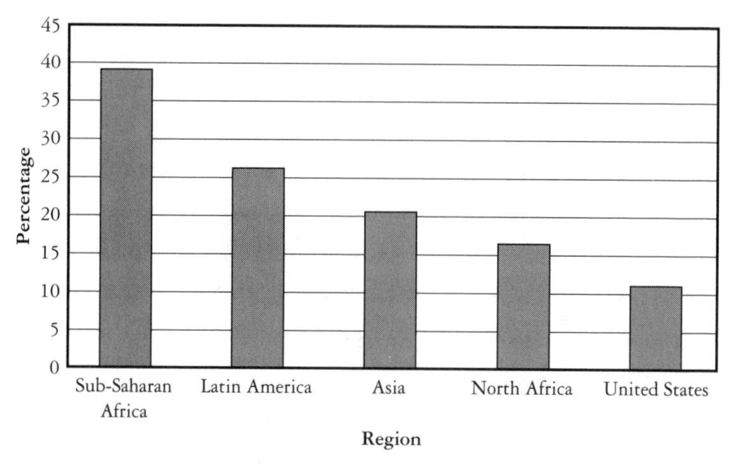


Millennium Project Web site:
http://millenniumindicators.un.org/unsd/mi/mi_series_xxx.asp?row_id-582.

nothing about the geographic distribution of poor and non-poor within cities, therefore, one would predict a poverty concentration index of around 0.40. This figure, however, would only result if poor and affluent were evenly distributed across neighborhoods; but most cities in the developing world are characterized by a high degree of class segregation, with poor families living in expansive slums and the elite being concentrated in protected enclaves (Montomery et al. 2003). If the *average* rate of poverty in African cities is 40%, therefore, the degree of poverty concentration must be much higher than 0.40.

In the United States, for example, the rate of urban poverty in 2000 was about 11%; but the index of poverty concentration stood at 0.25, reflecting the effect of segregation between income groups. Because class segregation is likely to be even higher in cities of the developing world than in the United States (see Rubalcava and Schteingart 2000; Sabatini and Arenas 2000; Torres 2001; Schifer 2003), an overall poverty rate of 40% suggests an isolation index of at least 0.80, meaning that the typical poor person living in the urban sector of Sub-Saharan Africa likely inhabits a neighborhood where eight out of ten neighbors are poor, a remarkable and alarming concentration of poverty by any standard.

Next in terms of urban poverty is Latin America, with an average poverty rate of 26% in the urban sector, followed by Asia at 21%, and North Africa at 17%. Applying the same rule of thumb (doubling the overall poverty rate) to conservatively predict the degree of urban poverty concentration in these regions, one derives respective figures of around 0.50, 0.40, and 0.30. These figures, if correct, suggest levels of poverty concentration in Latin America and Asia are well above those observed in the United States. Levels within northern Africa are also higher than in the United States, on average, although they do fall within the range of values encountered across U.S. metropolitan areas (see Massey and Fischer 2003).

The concentration of poverty brought about by the relocation of poor households from rural to urban areas need not be permanent, if by entering a city's labor force rural dwellers can place themselves on a path of upward mobility out of poverty. Such seems to have been the case in Latin America during the period of import substitution industrialization, with shantytowns steadily upgrading and transforming themselves into stable working-class neighborhoods as the economic fortunes of individual residents improved (Balán, Browning, and Jelin 1973; Muñoz, de Oliveira, and Stern 1977; Vélez-Ibáñez 1983). Implementation of the neoliberal economic program of export industrialization during the 1980s and 1990s, however, produced a substantial hollowing out of the urban middle class, a polarization of income, and the reversal of structural patterns of upward mobility (Portes and Hoffman 2003). In Africa, the in-migration of poor families from the countryside swamped socioeconomic mobility within cities during the 1980s and 1990s (van de Walle 2001). In Asia, the picture is more variable, with some nations (e.g., China, Singapore, Malaysia) displaying sustained increases in urban income and reductions in poverty while other nations (e.g., Myanmar, Vietnam) were not so fortunate (Dutt et al. 2004).

## THE NEW ECOLOGY OF INEQUALITY

A post-industrial ecology of concentrated affluence and poverty constitutes a radical departure from the past. Poverty itself is not new. For hundreds of thousands of years, the vast majority of human beings have lived and labored at low material standards of living. From the first hunter-gatherer societies that emerged on the savannahs of Africa, to the horticultural villages that later appeared in the highlands of the Fertile Crescent, to the great agrarian empires that ultimately arose in Mesopotamia, Europe, India, the Americas, and China, most people were very poor; and as prior chapters have shown, this basic fact of life prevailed in all human societies until quite recently.

Despite nearly universal material deprivation, human societies evolved cultures and social structures that permitted people to live and reproduce in relative peace. Social order was possible under conditions of pervasive poverty because the deprivation was shared equally and occurred at low geographic densities within small populations where everyone knew everyone else. As a result, the socially disruptive correlates of poverty occurred infrequently and could be managed informally through face-to-face interactions occurring within well-elaborated social networks. Individual behavior was shaped through systematic emotional contingencies, using positive reinforcers such as love, liking, and praise to encourage prosocial conduct and negative reinforcers such as dislike, ridicule, shaming, ostracism, and criticism to discourage antisocial behavior.

The Industrial Revolution of the nineteenth century upset the apple cart by creating and distributing wealth on a much larger scale, enabling affluence and poverty to become geographically concentrated for the first time. Through urbanization, the rich and the poor both came to inhabit large urban areas, and within industrial cities new transportation and communication technologies enabled the affluent to distance themselves spatially as well as socially from the poor, yielding rising levels of class segregation. For a short time after World War II, mass social mobility halted the geographic concentration of affluence and poverty in developed countries. After 1975, however, inequality and class segregation returned to usher in a new era when the privileges of the rich and the disadvantages of the poor were compounded geographically.

In the new geography of inequality, the means by which the negative externalities of poverty were managed in the past can no longer function. In an urban environment, where the vast majority of encounters are with strangers, informal emotional sanctions carry little weight. We have entered a new age of inequality in which mechanisms of socioeconomic stratification will be amplified and reinforced by geographic concentration.

*Political Mechanisms*

To the extent that the boundaries of governmental and administrative units can be arranged to approximate the geographic contours of concentrated affluence and poverty, and to the degree that the imposition of taxes and the delivery of services can be shifted down the administrative hierarchy, the potential for reifying class advantages and disadvantages is maximized. In an agrarian society where most people live in small towns and villages, affluent and poor families must mix socially, share the same public services, and inhabit the same political units. In such a geopolitical structure, the poor benefit from public institutions to which the rich are committed by reason of self-interest.

Once society becomes urbanized, however, and poverty and affluence become geographically concentrated in different parts of the urban environment, the affluent acquire the ability to separate themselves politically from the poor by judiciously drawing administrative lines. If they can create separate governmental districts that encompass concentrations of poverty, and if they can force these poor districts to supply and pay for their own services, then the affluent will be able to insulate themselves from the negative externalities of poor people while avoiding financial responsibility for ameliorating their plight (Orfield 2002).

In the contemporary United States, for example, the political isolation of the poor is accomplished by the segmentation of metropolitan regions into a patchwork of separate municipalities (Dreier, Mollenkopf, and Swanstrom 2001). The metropolitan area of Chicago, for example, contains 1,458 local governments, that of Boston 1,000, and that of Philadelphia 877 (Altshuler et al. 1999:23). The concentration of affluence in certain suburbs of these urban areas yields high real estate values that allow the affluent to tax themselves at low rates while offering generous, even lavish municipal services to residents. The concentration of poverty in central cities and inner suburbs, in contrast, generates a high demand for services but yields low property values, thereby requiring higher tax rates to support inferior services. The end result is a vicious cycle whereby city taxes are raised to maintain deficient services, driving out families of means, which lowers property values further, causing more tax increases and additional middle-class flight, which further exacerbates the concentration of poverty (Dreir, Mollenkopf, and Swanstrom 2001).

Under an ecological regime of concentrated affluence and poverty, efforts to decentralize government and shift the financing and provision of public services to lower administrative levels offer a remarkably efficient mechanism for enhancing the social and economic well-being of the rich at the expense of the poor. Political decentralization is progressive and democratic only in a world of small towns and villages, where the classes live together in small communities and share residential space, an antiquated model of society that no longer prevails. In today's world of large, dense urban agglomerations characterized by high income inequality and rising class segregation, political decentralization is punitive and regressive, forcing the poor to bear the costs of their own disadvantage.

The political mechanisms by which class position becomes institutionalized in the new ecology of inequality are many, but perhaps the most important occurs through schools. Education is one of the most important resources exchanged on global markets, and in recent years workers with college and post-graduate degrees have seen their earnings rise, while high school graduates and dropouts have seen their wages fall (see Bernhardt et al. 2001). Access to high-quality education has thus become the crucial factor determining one's position in the post-industrial pecking order (Massey 2000).

Because the emerging ecological structure concentrates the best-prepared students in areas of resource abundance while gathering the least-prepared students in areas of resource scarcity, it exacerbates class inequities and promotes a more rigid stratification of society. Students from low-income families with poorly educated parents, little experience reading books, and multiple social problems end up in schools with the fewest resources to help them learn, whereas students from affluent families with well-educated parents, extensive experience with books and reading, and few social problems attend well-funded schools that are in the best position to promote learning. This configuration of educational resources is precisely opposite that required to maximize human capital formation and promote equality. In the new ecology of inequality, the spatial concentration of both affluence and poverty raises the odds that affluent children will receive a superior education and that poor children will get inferior schooling, virtually guaranteeing the intergenerational transmission of class position.

*Economic Mechanisms*

Once an ecological order of concentrated affluence and poverty has emerged, and a political order has been structured spatially such that poor households are located systematically in separate revenue and service districts from affluent households, then private economic interests inevitably come into play to reinforce the ecology of inequality, making entirely rational decisions about the allocation of resources and investments. Producers of goods and services naturally seek to maximize profits and selectively locate offices and factories in municipalities where taxes are low, public services are good, and risks are minimal. Retailers likewise seek out zones where buying power is concentrated and the costs and risks of doing business are modest. Affluent households also selectively settle in communities where services are good, taxes are affordable, and safety is ensured.

The adjustment of private behaviors and expectations to existing social structures is what Tilly (1998) calls "adaptation"; over time, processes of adaptation lock in and institutionalize patterns of inequality. Consider the Philadelphia metropolitan area. If there were no separately incorporated suburbs and just a single municipal government responsible for taxes and services, then these factors would not loom large as factors in household decision making. Families would decide where to live using other criteria: distance to work or style of housing, for example. There would be sorting among households by income, life cycle, and ethnicity, of course; but selective migration and settlement would not be shaped by radically different structures of taxation and service provision in different segments of the urban environment. All households in the metropolitan area would pay the same taxes and receive the same services whether they lived near the center or at the fringe.

As already mentioned, however, the Philadelphia metropolitan area has 877 units of local government, two of which correspond to the City and County of Philadelphia, whose boundaries have been coterminous since 1854 (U.S. Bureau of the Census 2004). In 2000, the city housed a population in which 23% of families were poor and 18% spoke a foreign language at home, compared with statewide figures of 11% and 8%, respectively. In order to provide municipal and human services to this relatively disadvantaged population, the City of Philadelphia collects a lot of taxes. For example, it imposes a tax on wages earned in the city, a tax for the privilege of doing business in the city, a tax on the net business profits earned in the city, a tax on dividend and interest earned by city residents, plus taxes assessed on real estate within the city. Despite these heavy taxes, public services in the City of Philadelphia are insufficient to meet the demand; some, noteably education, are decidedly substandard.

In contrast, tax rates in most of the 875 surrounding municipalities are lower and the range and quality of services are better. No other municipality in the Philadelphia metropolitan area has a city wage tax, and most lack the deadly combination of business privilege and net profit taxes. Given this pattern of metropolitan fragmentation, over time families have "voted with their feet" based on their ability to pay. The poor have increasingly been trapped in the central city while the middle class have selectively moved to the suburbs, thereby reinforcing the lines of class advantage and disadvantage.

From the viewpoint of the business executive, the most efficient political organization for a post-industrial metropolis is to have municipal boundaries drawn to encompass as closely as possible the outline of specific office parks, shopping malls, or factory districts. Then the owners of these enterprises could tax themselves at very low rates to satisfy their minimal needs for public services (or pay for them privately) while forcing other municipalities to pay for the health, education, electricity, water, sewer, fire protection, and police services of the people who work in their offices, stores, and factories.

Often, business and political interests collude to produce just such an ecology. In Los Angeles, for example, there is an 18-mile-long worm-shaped municipality known as the City of Industry. Incorporated in 1958, it meanders through Los Angeles County and includes just 680 residents, many of them residents of a mental hospital. Despite its small population, however, the City of Industry houses 2,100 factories, warehouses, and shopping centers in addition to a luxury golf course and a resort hotel (Davis 1998). The original mayor of the City of Industry served for 40 years until passing the job on to his son, who, like his father, served at the pleasure of the business elite, the city's true "citizens." The costs of educating, housing, and protecting workers in the City of Industry fall on nearby suburbs, many of which are poor and heavily Latino.

Under this spatial configuration, employers are able to extract labor from workers without contributing anything to their maintenance as human beings. Similar ecological structures are observed in other U.S. metropolitan areas (Davis

1998; Dreier, Mollenkopf, and Swanstrom 2001; Orfield 2002). The imitation of this categorical form of inequality across metropolitan areas is what Tilly (1998) calls "emulation," and it likewise institutionalizes processes of stratification and makes them durable.

Like business interests, affluent households also attempt to isolate themselves within enclaves that systematically exclude the poor and their social problems, even though they court them as child care workers, house cleaners, gardeners, garbage haulers, and municipal employees. Poor people are welcome as workers, not as residents. Sometimes this exclusion is achieved through political means, as when a municipality adopts zoning restrictions, lot size requirements, density limitations, and construction standards that preclude the construction of housing for low-to-moderate income families.

Given the demand for low-level service workers in the community, it would be profitable for a developer to purchase a large lot and erect an apartment building that offered workers low rents and easy access to jobs in the community. But in exclusive residential communities developers are prevented from doing so by zoning restrictions, thereby forcing workers to commute from more distant neighborhoods and bear high transportation costs. The resulting ecology of inequality does not reflect the operation of the market, but the operation of categorical mechanisms of exploitation and opportunity hoarding.

Despite the ubiquity of political mechanisms, the process of exclusion is increasingly occurring under private auspices. As areas of concentrated poverty have become hothouses for the proliferation of social problems, developers have increasingly offered affluent consumers "gated communities" to protect themselves from the inevitable fallout, building exclusive enclaves that exclude the unwanted poor not only through invisible mechanisms such as lot sizes and density requirements, but more concretely through physical barriers such as walls, fences, and gates staffed by uniformed private security officers. Long a fixture in cities of the developing world (Montgomery et al. 2003), gated communities have become increasingly common in developed countries (Dreier, Mollenkopf, and Swanstrom 2001; Webster, Glasze, and Frantz 2002).

*Social Mechanisms*

Given the ease with which both information and people can move across space in the post-industrial era, some observers have claimed to foresee a "death of distance" (Cairncross 1997) and a "deterritorialization" of society (Papastergiadis 2000). As this book makes clear, however, space continues to matter very much in human affairs. It just matters in different ways as technologies and social organizations change. As noted earlier, all societies must grapple with problems of temporality and territoriality. Although the means by which the barriers of space and time are overcome may change over time and may be implemented within different social structures at different historical junctures, the people who inhabit those structures and use the technologies do not really change as organisms.

In the post-industrial era, people continue to be motivated to form interpersonal bonds, to belong to social groups, and to understand, predict, and control the behavior of others within the groups they encounter. Regardless of the social organization or level of technology, people expend time and energy building interpersonal networks and constructing social networks from which they derive emotional satisfaction and reap material and symbolic rewards. The only difference is that now networks are constructed and social bonds maintained within a highly differentiated urban environment characterized by dense concentrations of poverty and privilege that are correlated with ethnic status and family status.

At the low end of the income distribution, people lack the income necessary for the full enjoyment of post-modern technologies such as computers, the Internet, email, distant travel, and participation in transnational social networks. As a result, they tend to interact most intensively with other people in their immediate surroundings, meaning that their social networks connect them socially and spatially to a restricted set of people who themselves lack access to the full range of material, emotional, and symbolic resources of post-industrial society. In this way, their class disadvantages are socially compounded and their "underclass" identity solidified, thereby perpetuating poverty across the generations (Castells 1997). Not only do the poor lack material resources themselves, but because of the concentration of poverty their personal and extended networks also include people who lack resources.

At the other end of the continuum, people with high incomes increasingly live and work within residential and job settings with others of similar education, occupational status, and income. They not only possess the income to gain ready access to computers, the Internet, and various modalities of transportation and communication, but given their likely membership in transnational networks and organizations they are in a position to use these technologies to maintain interpersonal connections across a variety of social and geographic settings, thereby maximizing both the quantity and quality of their information and opportunities. They are well connected to many people at home and abroad who command formidable social, economic, and cultural resources, thereby reinforcing their identity as members of a privileged "overclass" and transmitting multiple advantages across the generations (Castells 1996).

Social networks are important to people at both the top and the bottom of the socioeconomic hierarchy, though in different ways. Social networks serve completely different functions in areas of concentrated poverty and affluence. Although people in all circumstances turn to those they know to get emotional satisfaction, material support, and symbolic rewards, for some people the circle of friends, relatives, and acquaintances has more capital—financial, social, cultural, and physical—to share. In areas of concentrated poverty, therefore, social networks serve more to ensure individual survival than to promote upward mobility (Stack 1974; Lomnitz 1975).

Poor people living in poor neighborhoods cultivate ties of kinship, friendship, and acquaintance and then draw on these social connections during times of emotional or economic stress in order to get by and make it to the next day. Network members are willing to provide support as part of a strategy of generalized reciprocity, because they know that given their precarious material circumstances they are quite likely to need assistance themselves at some point in the future. Social networks thus operate as a means of redistributing uncontrollable economic shocks and diversifying material risks across time and space.

Under these circumstances, network members who do manage to accumulate a small cushion of emotional, material, and symbolic resources are at constant risk of having their meager surplus disappear in response to the demands of friends, relatives, and acquaintances in desperate need of assistance. Under conditions of concentrated deprivation, therefore, networks function as a mechanism of social leveling and undermine the odds of individual advancement. The greater the local concentration of poverty, the more this fact holds true; and to the extent that marginal economic status coincides with single parenthood and fragmented families, the mobility-limiting effects of networks are further reinforced. Unstable households and transient pair bonding limit the possibilities for income pooling and risk diversification within households, making it more likely that during times of crisis people will be forced to fall back on extended networks.

Precisely the opposite set of circumstances prevails among people who are fortunate enough to live under conditions of concentrated affluence. For them, networks operate to consolidate an already privileged class position and enable them to acquire additional emotional, material, and symbolic resources (Mills 1956; Lomnitz and Pérez-Lizaur 1987). Once again, people within their networks provide support as part of a strategy of generalized reciprocity; but instead of using relationships of equality matching to ensure survival, which is already secured, these relationships are manipulated to accumulate further social and economic resources. The affluent grant assistance to friends, relatives, and associates as part of an emotional exchange that brings satisfaction to all parties but that also provides access to tangible material and symbolic benefits. A favor granted to an acquaintance pursuing an economic opportunity may be repaid at a later time and place when the grantor is pursuing his or her own opportunity. Rather than serving to redistribute income and diversify risks, therefore, conditions of concentrated privilege yield social networks that provide significant social, cultural, and financial capital; once again, the greater the concentration of affluence, the greater the utility of networks in accumulating additional resources.

*Cultural Mechanisms*

According to Fischer (1995:549), "subcultural theory seems really to be a theory of group concentration . . . [and] subcultural processes are revealed to be fundamentally about intragroup accessibility. Spatial agglomeration is . . . one way group members gain access to one another [and] in the end, [it] . . . is largely about the ability of subcultural members to communicate, to create 'moral density.' " In other words, the spatial concentration of people with similar traits gives rise to distinct subcultures, each corresponding to a specific ecological niche defined by the intersection of socioeconomic status, family status, and ethnic status and reflecting the circumstances of the people who live within it.

As poverty is concentrated spatially, anything correlated with poverty is also concentrated. As the density of poverty rises in cities, so does the density of joblessness, crime, family dissolution, substance abuse, disease, and violence. In an ecology of concentrated poverty, not only do the poor have to grapple with manifold problems stemming from their own lack of income, but they must also confront the social fallout that stems from living in an environment where most of their neighbors are poor as well. The concentration of affluence, in contrast, yields a social environment that is opposite in virtually every respect, surrounding already privileged people with low levels of joblessness, crime, family dissolution, substance abuse, disease, and violence.

The way that people grapple with the circumstances they encounter in daily life is through culture. They innovate attitudes, beliefs, values, and behaviors and tailor them to the conditions they encounter, constructing conceptual schemas and behavioral scripts that routinize commonly repeated thoughts and actions (Fiske 2003). Culture is not a fixed and invariant attribute of a group that replicates itself unchangingly over time, but a dynamic repertoire of patterned concepts, sentiments, and behaviors that develop in response to environmental conditions and change over time as those conditions change (Kuper 1999). Just as the human brain is incredibly plastic and adaptive, so too is the culture that it enables.

In the emerging ecology of inequality, therefore, the behavioral and conceptual repertoires of the poor and the affluent may be expected to diverge increasingly from one another to yield distinct and often opposing subcultures. Among those at the low end of the income distribution, the spatial concentration of poverty will create a harsh and destructive environment perpetuating values, attitudes, and behaviors that, while adaptive within a geographic niche of intense poverty, are injurious to society at large and destructive of the poor themselves. At the upper end of the hierarchy, a contrasting subculture of privilege will emerge from the spatial niche of concentrated affluence to confer additional advantages on the rich, thereby consolidating their social and economic dominance of society.

Figure 7.5
Linear Relationship between Crime and Poverty in Philadelphia

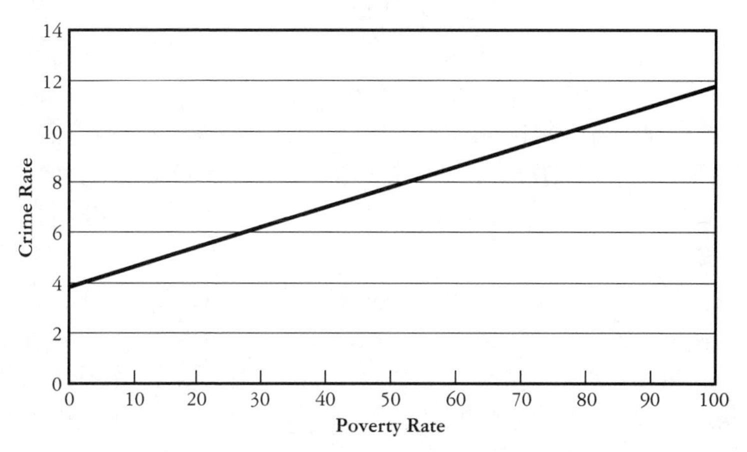


Perhaps no consequence of concentrated poverty is as destructive as the proliferation of crime and violence. Because criminal behavior is strongly associated with income deprivation, the geographic concentration of poverty yields a concentration of crime, delinquency, and violence in poor neighborhoods (Massey, Condran, and Denton 1987). According to estimates developed for Philadelphia, each point increase in the neighborhood poverty rate raises the major crime rate by 0.8 points (Fig. 7.5; Massey 2001). In Columbus, Ohio, the crime rate for neighborhoods with a poverty rate under 20% is just 7 per 1,000, but in neighborhoods where the poverty rate is 40% or over, it is 23 per 1,000 (Krivo and Peterson 1996). A resident of the latter neighborhood experiences three times the likelihood of criminal victimization as a resident of the former neighborhood. Clearly, the greater the concentration of poverty in one's neighborhood, the greater the chances of becoming a victim of crime or violence.

How do the poor adapt culturally to an environment in which violence is endemic and the risk of victimization great? At the level of behavior, a logical adaptation is to become violent oneself. Anderson (1999) has discovered through his ethnographic fieldwork that by adopting a threatening demeanor, cultivating a reputation for the use of force, and backing up that reputation with selective violence, residents of low-income neighborhoods deter potential criminals and increase the odds of their own survival. In a social world characterized by rampant violence, an obsessive concern with respect becomes an important adaptive strategy (Bourgois 1995) in much the same way it does for people in herding and horticultural societies.

Given the concentration of poverty, therefore, some poor people are sure to adopt violent attitudes and behavior as survival strategies (Massey 2001). As increasing numbers of people adopt more violent strategies for self-preservation, the average level of violence within poor neighborhoods rises, leading others to adopt still more violent behavior. As the average level of violence rises over time, more people adopt increasingly violent strategies to protect themselves from the growing threat of victimization, yielding a self-perpetuating upward spiral of violence.

The fundamental need to adapt to conditions of endemic violence that are structurally imbedded leads to the emergence of a "code of the streets" that encourages and promotes the use of force. Asking residents of poor neighborhoods to choose a less violent path or to "just say no" to the temptation of violence is absurd, given the threatening character of the ecological niche in which they live. To survive in such areas, one must learn—and to a significant extent, internalize—the code of violence described by Anderson (1999), and in this way aggression is passed from person to person in a self-feeding, escalating fashion.

High rates of violence within neighborhoods give rise to a particular cultural style characterized by a reluctance to intervene publicly for the common good, a belief in one's inability to influence one's social environment, and a fatalistic acceptance of social disorder and decline. Whereas individuals living in areas of concentrated affluence expect people they encounter to be civil, to treat them with respect, and to be responsible, trustworthy human beings, those who reside in areas of concentrated poverty cannot make these assumptions. As a result, they are very guarded in their public behavior and cautious in their attitudes and poor neighborhoods come to lack a sense of "collective efficacy" (Sampson 2004). The absence of this intangible social resource contributes to the escalation of social disorder and decline by lowering the degree of public vigilance and limiting the willingness of residents to assume responsibility for conditions in the public sphere (Sampson, Raudenbush, and Earls 1997; Sampson, Morenoff, and Earls 1999).

The contrasting ecologies of affluence and poverty also breed opposing peer subcultures. As the concentration of affluence grows, the children of the privileged increasingly socialize with other children of well-educated and successful parents. Knowledge of what one does to prepare for college and an appreciation of the connection between schooling and socioeconomic success is widespread in the schools of the affluent.

Students arrive in the classroom well prepared and ready to learn. School officials need only build on this base of knowledge and motivation by using their ample resources to hire well-informed guidance counselors and enthusiastic, talented teachers.

The children of the poor, meanwhile, attend schools with children from other poor families, who themselves are beset by multiple difficulties stemming from a lack of income. Their parents are poorly educated and lack adequate knowledge about how to prepare for college, and the children do not fully appreciate the connection between education and later success. Supervision and monitoring of students is difficult because so many come from single-parent families, and schools are in a poor position to make up for this deficit because of funding limitations. Students arrive in the classroom poorly prepared, and neither dispirited guidance counselors nor overworked and underpaid teachers expect much from them.

Within such settings an alternative status system is likely to develop. Under circumstances where it is difficult to succeed according to conventional standards, the usual criteria of success are often inverted to create an oppositional identity (Ogbu, 1978). Children formulate oppositional identities in order to preserve self-esteem when expectations are low and failure by conventional norms is likely. In areas of concentrated poverty, therefore, students from poor families legitimize their educational failures by attaching positive value and meaning to outcomes that affluent children label as deviant and unworthy. In this type of adaptation to the environment created by concentrated poverty, success in school is devalued, hard work is seen as a sell-out, and any display of learning is viewed as distinctly uncool.

At the same time that the concentration of poverty and violence produces distinct subcultures of poverty and affluence, their juxtaposition within a single urban ecology also heightens class awareness and promotes social stereotyping. High rates of crime, delinquency, and social disorder within poor neighborhoods are all too evident to the affluent, reinforcing their negative stereotypes about the poor while inculcating a deep sense of fear of people who exhibit visible markers associated with poverty, which may be physical (e.g., height, skin color, hair texture) or cultural (e.g., speech, clothing, bearing). In post-industrial societies, such stereotypical fears are exaggerated by their over-representation in the media (Fishman and Cavender 1998; Glassner 2000).

The juxtaposition of affluence and poverty also serves to heighten the sense of relative deprivation experienced by the poor and hone their envy of the rich. Although the vast majority of people in agrarian societies may have been peasants, most never came into contact with members of the nobility and had few opportunities to observe directly the discrepancy in living standards. As the poor urbanize and concentrate in post-industrial cities, however, they acquire new opportunities to observe the lifestyles of the privileged, not only through personal observation but through the media as well. As a result, the concentration of affluence and poverty in cities increases the poor's sense of relative deprivation, which is in turn associated with strong feelings of grievance toward the affluent (Sweeney, McFarlin, and Inderrieden 1990; Walker and Smith 2002) and a high likelihood of acting out these sentiments through crime (Blau and Blau 1982), thereby reinforcing the negative stereotypes of the rich and further hardening the lines of stratification.

*Biological Mechanisms*

Significant differences in lifetime exposure to disorder and violence within neighborhoods also carry important physiological consequences because of the over-activation of the human stress response. To understand the manifold effects of stress on human beings, biomedical researchers have developed the concept of *allostasis*, which refers to the tendency of organisms to maintain stability through bodily changes in response to events in the environment (Sterling and Ayer 1988; McEwen and Lasley 2002). Whenever a person perceives an external threat, a brain organ known as the *hypothalamus* triggers an allostatic response—a complex interaction among the brain, the endocrine system, and the immune system.

Upon perceiving the threat, the hypothalamus signals the drenal glands to release *adrenaline* (McEwen and Lasley 2002), which accelerates the heartbeat, constricts blood vessels in the skin, increases the flow of blood to internal organs, dilates the bronchial tubes, triggers the release of fibrinogen into the circulatory system (to promote clotting), releases glucose and fatty acids into the bloodstream from stored fats (to provide a ready source of energy), and signals the brain to produce endorphins (to mitigate pain). These physiological changes ready the organism for aggressive or evasive action.

While all this is going on, the hypothalamus simultaneously signals the pituitary gland to release *adrenocorticotropic hormone*, which in turn causes the glands to secrete *cortisol* into the blood (McEwen and Lasley 2002). Cortisol acts to replace the energy stores depleted by adrenaline, converting them into glycogen and fat. It also promotes the conversion of muscle protein to fat, blocks insulin from taking up glucose, removes minerals from bones, and changes the external texture of white blood cells to make them "stickier" and more adhesive.

This hypothalamic-pituitary-adrenal (HPA) axis is common to all mammals and is designed for infrequent and sporadic use. Unlike most mammals, however, humans are capable of keeping the HPA axis turned on indefinitely because they are capable of experiencing stress from ideas in addition to actual events. Human beings can anticipate threatening circumstances *mentally*—imagining events that might occur or recalling past traumas (McEwen and Lasley 2002; Bremner 2002).

Repeated triggering of the allostatic response through chronic exposure to stressful events—as when someone is compelled by poverty to live in a dangerous and violent neighborhood—yields a condition known as *allostatic load*. As allostatic load increases and persists over time, it has powerful negative effects on a variety of bodily systems (McEwen and Lasley 2002).

One important set of effects is cardiovascular. Chronically elevated levels of adrenaline increase blood pressure and raise the risk of hypertension. Elevated fibrinogen levels increase the likelihood of blood clots and thrombosis. The build-up of "sticky" white blood cells causes the formation of arterial plaques that contribute to atherosclerosis. Elevated cortisol levels, meanwhile, cause the production of excess glycogen and fat, raising the risk of obesity, while the suppression of insulin leads to excessive blood sugar and a greater risk of Type II diabetes (McEwen and Lasley 2002).

Chronically elevated levels of adrenaline also disrupt the functioning of the *vagal nervous system*. This system is responsible for slowing down the heart rate and reducing bodily tension, acting as a "brake" for the HPA axis. Disruption of the vagal system contributes to the expression of a Type A personality, which is associated with aggressiveness, impulsiveness, frustration, and a low threshold for anger. People with Type A personalities often try to reduce tension by self-medicating with drugs, alcohol, and tobacco, and through these poor coping choices they end up exacerbating allostatic load and causing secondary damage to vital organs such as the liver, lungs, and heart (McEwen and Lasley 2002).

Allostatic load also compromises the human *immune system*. Long-term exposure to elevated cortisol usually lowers the immune response to increase susceptibility to illness and infection (Schulz et al. 1998). In some circumstances, however, it appears to overstimulate the immune system to mistakenly goad it into attacking targets within the body that do not normally pose a threat, leading to the expression of inflammatory conditions such as asthma and autoimmune diseases such as multiple sclerosis, arthritis, and Type I diabetes (McEwen and Lasley 2002).

Finally, allostatic load has serious consequences for a variety of *brain systems* and hence influences cognitive functioning. The organ of the brain that is primarily responsible for the consolidation and storage of memory is the hippocampus (Carter 1998). Because stressful events are important to remember, the hippocampus is rich in cortisol receptors and people are indeed more likely to remember things that are associated with strong emotions (McEwen and Lasley 2002). After all, our ancestors who recalled where and under what circumstances danger occurred were more likely to survive and pass on their genes. Chronically elevated cortisol, however, cause the receptors to become permanently saturated, leading to atrophy of the hippocampus and an impairment of memory, both short-term and long-term (Bremner 2002).

Excessive cortisol also appears to interfere with the normal operation of neurotransmitters such as glutamate, which is a critical ingredient in the formation of synaptic connections. By disrupting the production and operation of glutamate at the synapse, allostatic load inhibits *long-term potentiation*—the formation of a relatively permanent neural connection—which is the fundamental chemical event in human learning. In this way, chronic exposure to disorder and violence may compromise the very process of learning itself (McEwen and Lasley 2002).

Finally, the hippocampus plays an important role in shutting down the HPA axis by reducing cortisol production. As a result, damage to it is doubly detrimental. Through its effect on the hippocampus, chronic stress creates a vicious cycle whereby excessive cortisol causes shrinkage of the hippocampus, which causes less inhibition of cortisol production, which causes more hippocampal shrinkage (McEwen and Lasley 2002). Over the long run, this cycle leads to *dendritic remodeling*, wherein neurons become shorter and sprout fewer branches, as well as the *suppression of neurogenesis*, or the creation of new brain cells (Gould et al. 1998). Simply put, people who are exposed to high levels of stress over a prolonged period of time are at risk of experiencing a "re-wiring" of their brains in a way that leaves them with fewer cognitive resources with which to work (Bremner 2002).

## BRAVE NEW WORLD

Over the past 10,000 years, human society has evolved in stages from tiny populations of mobile foragers circulating through natural environments, to small populations of settled horticulturalists exploiting narrow ecological niches, to moderately sized cities presiding over large agrarian hinterlands, to densely settled industrialized cities within an urbanizing world, to the present configuration of populous, geographically expansive metropolitan areas containing nearly all members of post-industrial society. In the course of this evolution, people did not change physiologically as organisms; what changed were the social structures they created and the technologies they deployed.

The schematic representation of social change depicted in Figure 1.1 presents a conceptualization of societal evolution as an interplay among three clusters of interacting factors operating within the environment (temperature, water, terrain), microsocial structures (which link individuals to households and small groups), and macrosocial relations (defined by population, technology, and larger social structures). For most of human history, the impetus for social change came from fluctuations in the environment that occurred over time and space. As groups encountered different ecological conditions in different locations and in historical epochs, they innovated social structures and technologies to adapt.

Since the emergence of the first human beings, the various stages of societal evolution have unfolded at an accelerating rate and the impetus for change has shifted from the environment to the microsocial cluster and finally to the macrosocial structure, which dominates today. The symbolic revolution that occurred around 50,000 years ago led to the flowering of mythic culture as an adaptive tool, which led to innovations in technology and microsocial organization that in turn promoted the domestication of plants and animals. Around 10,000 years ago the first cities emerged, which made possible a new kind of theoretic culture, which further accelerated rates of social and technological innovation that combined to produce, just 200 years ago, an industrial revolution that accelerated population growth and enabled societies finally to surpass the urbanization threshold of 5%. The subsequent industrialization and urbanization of society led to exponential accumulations of wealth, knowledge, and technology to give birth, a mere 25 years ago, to a post-industrial order based on the production and manipulation of information within large, deconcentrated urban agglomerations scattered throughout the globe.

At each step in the process of social evolution, human beings sought to satisfy core social motivations, and in doing so they constructed interpersonal networks and built larger social institutions. All human social structures are constructed from four basic types of relationships: communal sharing, equality matching, authority ranking, and market pricing. What has changed over time has been the relative prevalence of these relations. Foraging societies were dominated by communal sharing and equality matching, agrarian societies by equality matching and authority ranking, and industrial and post-industrial societies by authority ranking and market pricing.

In the twenty-first century, a growing majority of human

beings will come to live in large, densely populated urban agglomerations. In this environment, most interpersonal associations will be impersonal and will occur in the context of markets and anonymous public settings. The inhabitants of post-industrial urban societies will not lose their ability to form lasting bonds of intense emotion, of course. While continuing to cultivate such primary relationships to achieve emotional satisfaction, they will increasingly engage in fleeting, superficial relationships to attain material and symbolic rewards. In quantitative terms, these secondary role relationships will increasingly dominate society, leading to the expansion of extended and global networks relative to personal and effective networks. Although humans will not cease forming multiplex social ties, the number of such ties that any human can manage is ultimately limited, implying that the size of personal and effective networks will also be limited.

What has changed most dramatically in the last 100 years is the setting within which the core social motivations play out. Increasingly, human social interactions will be shaped by exposure to an urban environment of great size, density, and social heterogeneity. Within this brave new urban world, the character of the ecological setting in which people find themselves—and the nature of their psychological, social, cultural, and physiological adaptations to it—will vary dramatically depending on whether they are rich or poor, and whether they live in areas of concentrated affluence or poverty.

Evidence suggests that a remarkable and widespread geographic concentration of deprivation and advantage occurred within post-industrial cities during the final decades of the twentieth century. This concentration was brought about by the combination of rising socioeconomic inequality with growing class segregation, a pernicious interaction whose effects were exacerbated by segregation on the basis of race or ethnicity. Post-industrial societies are increasingly differentiated socially along three fundamental axes—socioeconomic status, ethnic status, and family status—and the geographic intersection of these axes within the urban landscape has produced a consolidation, or correlation, among these fundamental social dimensions.

A growing body of urban research suggests that people who grow up under conditions of concentrated poverty and deprivation display higher rates of joblessness, educational failure, single parenthood, income deprivation, family disruption, poor health, and cognitive impairment as adults, compared with those who grow up in areas of concentrated affluence (Brooks-Gunn, Duncan, and Aber 1997; Sampson, Morenoff, and Gannon-Rowley 2002). Inequality, class segregation, and the resulting concentration of affluence and poverty have thus produced a reification of the fundamental mechanisms of stratification, leading to a tighter intergenerational transmission of socioeconomic advantage and disadvantage. These stratifying mechanisms are especially potent for members of any group that is segregated on the basis of race or ethnicity (Massey and Denton 1993; Massey 2004b).

Ultimately, avoiding the creation of a hardened stratification system of "durable inequality" requires preventing further concentrations of affluence and poverty and rolling back those that emerged during the period 1975–1995 (Tilly 1998). Such a reduction ultimately requires the effective implementation of policies to reduce inequalities with respect to income and wealth, lower levels of class segregation, and reduce segregation on the basis of ascriptive traits such as race, ethnicity, and gender, which are the proximate determinants of ecologically concentrated wealth and poverty.

Although some inequality in the distribution of material resources is inevitable within market-based societies, the high levels of inequality that typify society in the United States are neither necessary nor inevitable. Markets are social constructions that people have built to facilitate the exchange of material, symbolic, and emotional resources (Massey 2005). Market participants are allocated certain rights and obligations by formal and informal social mechanisms; they make exchanges within manufactured arenas defined by specific physical infrastructures, social institutions, and cultural practices; and they compete with one another according to agreed-upon rules.

In defining the rights and obligations of market participants, building the necessary social, physical, and cultural infrastructures, and writing the rules of competition, societies constitute markets and determine outcomes, including the degree of inequality they produce. During the period 1930–1975 industrialized societies wrote rules, built infrastructures, and defined rights so as to minimize socioeconomic inequality and reduce disparities in social, economic, and physical well-being. After 1975, national and international markets were systematically reconfigured to favor the interests of owners and professionals rather than those of employees and manual workers. Given appropriate political will, markets can just as easily be reconfigured to restore more of a balance in the interests served by post-industrial markets.

Because markets tend to produce inequalities, some societies have adopted non-market mechanisms to promote social and economic inequality. Specifically, governments seeking to achieve greater equality impose taxes on those who have benefitted most from markets and redistribute the revenues to those who, for whatever reason, achieve less success in markets. Even in this age of rising inequality, societies differ dramatically in the degree to which they tax and redistribute income earned from markets. Of all developed countries, the United States attempts by far the least in redistribution (Smeeding 2002, 2003). The implementation of more progressive systems of taxation and social welfare is one sure way to ameliorate the concentration of poverty and affluence that built up in the United States during the late twentieth century.

Although some degree of inequality may follow from the nature of markets, most of the inequality that has existed historically has stemmed not from market mechanisms per se, but from the categorical mechanisms of exploitation and opportunity hoarding. To operate effectively, these mechanisms of stratification require the social construction of out-groups, which are then prevented by social institutions, cultural conventions, and individual practices from realizing the full value of their own labor. At the same time, opportunities for material improvement are monopolized by the socially constructed in-group.

The way to prevent categorical mechanisms from exacerbating inequalities produced by the market is by clearly defining the rights and privileges of citizenship and using the power of government to guarantee those rights for all members of all social groups. The history of human progress has involved (1) an extension of greater social and economic rights to more people through the dismantling of systems of hereditary privilege, and (2) the deployment of governmental power to ensure that these rights are respected regardless of a person's social status. Among industrialized nations, rights wrested from the aristocracy were first allocated to male property owners, then to all adult males, then to women, and finally to racial and ethnic minorities.

Guaranteeing the fair operation of markets—which tend to break down categorical distinctions—requires the vigorous enforcement of anti-discrimination laws. Protected groups must be legally constituted (e.g., women, blacks, Latinos, gay men and lesbians, the disabled, gypsies). Then acts of discrimination must be defined and penalties for unlawful discrimination established. Finally, government agencies must be created, empowered, and funded to enforce anti-discrimination statutes through a combination of active policing (regular monitoring of market transactions) and passive response (acting on complaints). It is no coincidence that in the United States the period 1945–1975 (one of declining inequality) was characterized by the implementation of stronger civil rights policies and more vigorous enforcement mechanisms, whereas the period 1975–2000 (one of rising inequality) was characterized by a weakening of civil rights policies and a scaling back of enforcement (Orfield 1994; Klinker and Smith 2002).

In many respects, the most important way to combat the geographic concentration of poverty and affluence is to promote greater access to decent housing in high-quality neighborhoods for the poor. This outcome may be achieved by eliminating legal and regulatory barriers that prevent poor families from being able to settle in middle-class or affluent neighborhoods, such as restrictive zoning that forbids the construction of multi-family housing, size restrictions that limit density to prevent the intensive use of residential land, and building codes that unfairly favor the construction of luxury homes and expensive condominiums.

Finally, given the uniquely powerful effect of racial-ethnic segregation in concentrating minority poverty, progress in reducing geographically based mechanisms of stratification requires the reduction of segregation by eliminating racial and ethnic discrimination within urban housing markets. In the United States, considerable evidence suggests that racial discrimination continues to occur at relatively high levels and that blacks remain uniquely segregated in American society (Massey 2004). As of the year 2000, nearly half of all black urbanites live in metropolitan areas that are segregated so severely they are said to be hypersegregated (Wilkes and Iceland 2004). The only other case in which a minority group has experienced such a profound level of segregation is that of South Africa under apartheid (Massey 2004).

Although human males and females may not be residentially segregated from one another in most societies, they are often segregated from one another in other areas of social life, such as schools and jobs. As discussed in earlier chapters, across human societies the segregation of males from females is generally associated with higher rates of male violence and social disorder. When they are isolated with one another, men tend to reinforce and encourage male tendencies toward aggression to produce a kind of hypermasculinity (Mosher and Sirkin 1984). Greater social integration between men and women has considerable potential to moderate societal violence and reduce gender inequality by making the sexes more alike, with men becoming less violent and more cooperative and women becoming more aggressive and assertive, to the benefit of both sexes and the overall improvement of society.

Levels of gender segregation with respect to education and occupation generally fell in developed nations during the final decades of the twentieth century (Jacobs 1989, 1995; Jacobs and Gerson 2004). In the United States, however, the degree of segregation between men and women has dramatically increased for one segment of the population: African Americans. Because of massive incarceration, there was an increasing separation of black men from black women during the late twentieth century (Collins 2004). At present rates, at any point in time around 8% of black males age 18 to 65 are in jail or prison, a level eight times that observed among whites (Western, Patillo, and Weiman 2004). Overall, roughly one quarter of all black males age 20 to 29 are under the supervision of the criminal justice system at any point in time (Tonry 1995).

This glaring racial differential in sex segregation stems from punitive policies enacted during the 1980s, such as mandatory minimum sentences, "three strikes" laws, and harsh penalties on certain kinds of drug use. As a result, a large number of nonviolent male offenders have found themselves imprisoned with violent criminals (Tonry 1995). The socially imposed segregation of nonviolent black men with criminal offenders can only produce more violence and social disarray in the black community. This particularly insidious form of gender segregation erodes bonds between men and their families (Western, Lopoo, and McLanahan 2004; Edin, Nelson, and Paranal 2004), estranges them from their children (Nurse 2004), lowers their odds of eventual re-employment (Western and Pettit 2000; Holzer, Raphael, and Stoll 2004; Pager 2003), and weakens processes of social control within black communities (Lynch and Sabol 2004). Rather than promoting greater social stability, the American mania for incarceration appears to be undermining it significantly, particularly within the black community.

Addressing difficult issues such as rising income inequality, growing class segregation, ongoing racial prejudice and discrimination, and the geographic concentration of poverty will inevitably require sacrifice. The immediate path of least resistance for affluent leaders and the fearful middle class will be to raise the walls of social, economic, and geographic segregation higher in order to protect themselves from the rising tide of social pathology and violence from below.

If the status quo continues, however, inequality will increase and racial-ethnic divisions will grow, yielding a volatile and unstable society for the twenty-first century. Urban areas in developed countries and the third world can expect to experience escalating crime and violence punctuated by sporadic riots and increased terrorism as class and communal tensions rise. The poor will become disenfranchised and alienated from mainstream political and economic institutions, while the middle classes will grow increasingly angry, frustrated, and politically conservative. The affluent will continue to withdraw socially and spatially from the rest of society and seek to placate middle-class anger with quick fixes and demagogic excesses that do not change the underlying structure responsible for their problems.

This scenario is by no means inevitable, and one can only

hope that it will not come to pass. Yet this is the path down which we are headed unless self-conscious actions are undertaken to change course. We still have time. At this point, neither the nature of the new ecological order nor its stratifying consequences have been fully realized. What this book has sought to offer is not so much a solution to a difficult problem as a call to begin a process of thought, reflection, and debate on the new ecology of inequality, out of which solutions may ultimately emerge. One thing is clear: Until we face up to the reality of rising inequality and its geographic expression, no solution will be possible.

# References

Aielo, L. C., and Robin I. M. Dunbar. 1993. "Neocortex Size, Group Size, and the Evolution of Language." *Current Anthropology* 34:184–93.

Alba, Richard D. 1985. *Italian Americans: Into the Twilight of Ethnicity.* Englewood Cliffs, NJ: Prentice-Hall.

Alba, Richard, and Victor Nee. 2003. *Remaking the American Mainstream: Assimilation and Contemporary Immigration.* Cambridge, MA: Harvard University Press.

Alonso, William. 1964. *Location and Land Use: Toward a General Theory of Land Rent.* Cambridge, MA: Harvard University Press.

Altshuler, Alan, William Morrill, Harold Wolman, and Faith Mitchell, eds. 1999. *Governance and Opportunity in Metropolitan America.* Washington, DC: National Academy Press.

Anderson, Elijah. 1978. *A Place on the Corner.* Chicago: University of Chicago Press.

———. 1999. *The Code of the Street: Decency, Violence, and the Moral Life of the Inner City.* New York: Norton.

Atkinson, Anthony B., Lee Rainwater, and Timothy M. Smeeding. 1995. *Income Distribution in OECD Countries: Evidence from the Luxembourg Income Study.* Paris: Organization for Economic Cooperation and Development.

Axelrod, Robert. 1985. *The Evolution of Cooperation.* New York: Basic Books.

Axtell, Roger E. 1998. *Gestures: The Do's and Taboo's of Body Language around the World.* New York: Wiley.

Balán, Jorge, Harley L. Browning, and Elizabeth Jelin. 1973. *Men in a Developing Society: Geographic and Social Mobility in Monterrey, Mexico.* Austin: University of Texas Press.

Balter, Michael. 2001. "In Search of the First Europeans." *Science* 291(5509):1722–25.

Bargh, John A. 1996. "Automaticity in Social Psychology." In *Social Psychology: Handbook of Basic Principles*, eds. E. Tory Higgins and Arie W. Kruglanski, 169–83. New York: Guilford.

———. 1997. "The Automaticity of Everyday Life." In *The Automaticity of Everyday*

*Life: Advances in Social Cognition,* ed. Robert S. Weyer Jr., 1–61. Mahwah, NJ: Erlbaum.

Bargh, John A., M. Chen, and L. Burrows. 1996. "Automaticity of Social Behavior: Direct Effects of Trait Construct and Stereotype Activation on Action." *Journal of Personality and Social Psychology* 71:230–44.

Barrett, Louise, Robin Dunbar, and John Lycett. 2002. *Human Evolutionary Psychology.* Princeton: Princeton University Press.

Baumeister, Roy F. 1991. *Meanings of Life.* New York: Guilford.

Bernhardt, Annette, Martina Morris, Mark S. Handcock, and Marc Scott. 2001. *Divergent Paths: Economic Mobility in the New American Labor Market.* New York: Russell Sage.

Berry, Brian J. L., and Philip H. Rees. 1969. "The Factorial Ecology of Calcutta." *American Journal of Sociology* 74:445–91.

Bianchi, Suzanne, and Daphne Spain. 1986. *American Women in Transition.* New York: Russell Sage Foundation.

———. 1996. *Balancing Act: Motherhood, Marriage, and Employment among American Women.* New York: Russell Sage Foundation.

Black-Michaud, J. 1975. *Cohesive Force: Feud in the Mediterranean.* Oxford: Basil Blackwell.

Blau, Peter M. 1977. *Inequality and Heterogeneity: A Primitive Theory of Social Structure.* New York: Free Press.

Blau, Peter M., and Judith R. Blau. 1982. "The Cost of Inequality: Metropolitan Structure and Violent Crime." *American Sociological Review* 47:114–29.

Bleda, Sharon E. 1978. "Intergenerational Differences in Patterns and Bases of Ethnic Residential Dissimilarity." *Ethnicity* 5:91–107.

———. 1979. "Socioeconomic, Demographic, and Cultural Bases of Ethnic Residential Segregation." *Ethnicity* 6:47–67.

Bobo, Lawrence D., Melvin Oliver, James H. Johnson Jr., and R. Abel Alenzuela. 2000. *Prismatic Metropolis: Inequality in Los Angeles.* New York: Russell Sage Foundation.

Bodenhausen, Galen V., and M. Lichtenstein. 1987. "Social Stereotypes and Information Processing Strategies: The Impact of Task Complexity." *Journal of Personality and Social Psychology* 52:871–80.

Bodenhausen, G. V., and Robert S. Wyer. 1985. "Effects of Stereotypes on Decision Making and Information Processing Strategies." *Journal of Personality and Social Psychology* 48:267–82.

Bogin, Barry. 2001. *The Growth of Humanity.* New York: Wiley-Liss.

Bogucki, Peter. 1999. *The Origins of Human Society.* Malden, MA: Blackwell.

Boserup, Ester. 1981. *Population and Technological Change: A Study of Long-Term Trends.* Chicago: University of Chicago Press.

———. 1990. *Economic and Demographic Relationships in Development*. Baltimore: Johns Hopkins University Press.

Bourdieu, Pierre. 1986. "The Forms of Capital." In *Handbook of Theory and Research for the Sociology of Education*, ed. John G. Richardson, 241–58. New York: Greenwood.

Bourgois, Philippe I. 1995. *In Search of Respect: Selling Crack in El Barrio*. New York: Cambridge University Press.

Bowlby, John. 1982. "Attachment and Loss: Retrospect and Prospect." *American Journal of Orthopsychiatry* 52:664–78.

Brain, Charles K. 1983. "Evidence of Fire in Swartkrans Cave." In *Swartkrans*, ed. Charles K. Brain, 229–42. Pretoria: Transvaal Museum, Monograph No. 8.

Braudel, Fernand. 1982. *The Wheels of Commerce: Civilization and Capitalism 15th–18th Century*, Vol. 2. New York: Harper & Row.

Bremner, J. Douglas. 2002. *Does Stress Damage the Brain? Understanding Trauma-Related Disorders from a Neurological Perspective*. New York: Norton.

Breese, Gerald W. 1949. *The Daytime Population of the Central Business District of Chicago*. Chicago: University of Chicago Press.

Brooks-Gunn, Jeanne, Greg Duncan, and J. Lawrence Aber. 1997. *Neighborhood Poverty: Context and Consequences for Children*. New York: Russell Sage Foundation.

Brown, Donald E. 1991. *Human Universals*. New York: McGraw-Hill.

———. 2000. "Human Universals and Their Implications." In *Being Humans: Anthropological Universality and Particularity in Transdisciplinary Perspectives*, ed. Neil Roughley, 156–74. New York: Walter de Gruyter.

Bruner, Jerome. 1986. *Actual Minds, Possible Worlds*. Cambridge, MA: Harvard University Press.

Bulmer, Martin. 1984. *The Chicago School of Sociology: Institutionalization, Diversity, and the Rise of Sociological Research*. Chicago: University of Chicago Press.

Burenhult, Goran, Peter Rowley-Conwy, Wulf Schiefenhovel, David H. Thomas, and J. Peter White, eds. 1993. *People of the Stone Age: Hunter-Gatherers and Early Farmers*. New York: HarperCollins.

Burgess, Ernest W. 1925. "The Growth of the City: An Introduction to a Research Project." In *The City*, eds. Robert E. Park and Ernest W. Burgess, 47–62. Chicago: University of Chicago Press.

———. 1928. "Residential Segregation in American Cities." *Annals of the American Academy of Political and Social Science* 140:105–15.

Byrne, Richard W. 2001. "Social and Technical Forms of Primate Intelligence." Pp. 145–72 in *Tree of Orgin: What Primate Behavior Can Tell Us about Human Social Evolution*, ed. Frans B. M. de Waal. Cambridge: Harvard University Press.

Cairncross, Frances. 1997. *The Death of Distance: How the Communications Revolution Will Change Our Lives*. Boston: Harvard Business School Press.

Caldwell, John C. 1982. *Theory of Fertility Decline*. New York: Academic Press.

Campbell, Arthur A. 1978. "Baby Boom to Birth Dearth and Beyond." *Annals of the American Academy of Political and Social Science* 435:40–60.

Campbell, Joseph. 1995. *The Masks of God: Creative Mythology*. New York: Penguin.

Carneiro, Robert L. 1970. "A Theory of the Origin of the State." *Science* 169:733–38.

Carter, Rita. 1998. *Mapping the Mind*. Berkeley: University of California Press.

Casper, Lynn, and Suzanne M. Bianchi. 2001. *Continuity & Change in the American Family*. Newbury Park, CA: Sage.

Castells, Manuel. 1989. *The Informational City: Information Technology, Economic Restructuring, and the Urban-Regional Process*. New York: Blackwell.

———. 1996. *The Rise of the Network Society*. Cambridge: Blackwell.

———. 1997. *The Power of Identity*. Cambridge: Blackwell.

———. 1998. *End of Millennium*. Cambridge: Blackwell.

Cavalli-Sforza, L. Luca, Paolo Menozzi, and Alberto Piazza. 1994. *The History and Geography of Human Genes*. Princeton: Princeton University Press.

Cavalli-Sforza, L. Luca, and Francesco Cavalli-Sforza. 1995. *The Great Human Diasporas: The History of Diversity and Evolution*. Cambridge, MA: Perseus Books.

Chagnon, Napoleon A. 1968. *Yanomamo: The Fierce People*. New York: Holt, Rinehart, and Winston.

Chandler, Tetrius, and Gerald Fox. 1974. *3000 Years of Urban Growth*. New York: Academic Press.

Chant, Colin, and David Goodman. 1999. *Pre-Industrial Cities and Technology*. London: Routledge.

Chase, Philip G. 1999. "Symbolism as Reference and Symbolism as Culture." In *The Evolution of Culture*, eds. Robin Dunbar, Chris Knight, and Camilla Power, 34–49. New Brunswick, NJ: Rutgers University Press.

Chayanov, Alexander V. 1966. *Theory of Peasant Economy*. Homewood, IL: Richard D. Irwin.

Childe, V. Gordon. 1951. *Social Evolution*. London: Watts & Co.

Choldin, Harvey M. 1978. "Urban Density and Pathology." *Annual Review of Sociology* 4:91–113.

Chomsky, Noam. 1975. *Reflections on Language*. New York: Pantheon Books.

Cipolla, Carlo M. 1969. *Literacy and Development in the West*. Baltimore: Penguin.

Clark, Richard B. 1970. *Planning Import Substitution*. Amsterdam: North-Holland Publishing.

Clarke, David B. 2002. *Consumer Society and the Postmodern City*. New York: Routledge.

Coale, Ansley J. 1974. "The History of the Human Population." *Scientific American* 231(3):15–28.

Coale, Ansley J., and Paul Demeny. 1966. *Regional Model Life Tables and Stable Populations*. Princeton: Princeton University Press.

Coale, Ansley J., and Susan C. Watkins. 1986. *The Decline of Fertility in Europe*. Princeton: Princeton University Press.

Collins, Patricia Hill. 2004. *Black Sexual Politics: African Americans, Gender, and the New Racism*. New York: Routledge.

Collins, Randall. 2004. *Interaction Ritual Chains*. Princeton: Princeton University Press.

Colson, E. 1978. "A Redundancy of Actors." In *Scale and Social Organization*, ed. Frederick Barth, 150–62. Oslo: Universitets Forlaget.

Cooper, Joel, and Grant Cooper. 2002. "Subliminal Motivation: A Story Revisited." *Journal of Applied Social Psychology* 32:2213–27.

Cosmides, Leda, and John Tooby. 1989. "Evolutionary Psychology and the Generation of Culture: II. Case Study: A Computational Theory of Social Exchange." *Ethnology and Sociobiology* 10:51–97.

———. 1992. "Cognitive Adaptations for Social Exchange." In *The Adapted Mind: Evolutionary Psychology and the Generation of Culture*, eds. Jerome H. Barkow, Leda Cosmides, and John Tooby, 163–228. New York: Oxford University Press.

Cowgill, Donald O. 1978. "Residential Segregation by Age in American Metropolitan Areas." *Journal of Gerontology* 33:446–53.

Crane, Diana. 2000. *Fashion and Its Social Agendas: Class, Gender, and Identity in Clothing*. Chicago: University of Chicago Press.

Cumliffe, B. 1979. *The Celtic World*. New York: McGraw-Hill.

Damasio, Antonio R. 1994. *Descartes' Error: Emotion, Reason, and the Human Brain*. New York: Putnam.

———. 1999. *The Feeling of What Happens: Body and Emotion in the Making of Consciousness*. New York: Harcourt Brace.

Danziger, Sheldon, and Peter Gottschalk. 1995. *America Unequal*. New York: Russell Sage Foundation.

Davidio, John F., and Samuel L. Gaertner. 1986. *Prejudice, Discrimination, and Racism*. Orlando, FL: Academic Press.

Davies, Glynn. 2002. *A History of Money: From Ancient Times to the Present Day*. Cardiff: University of Wales Press.

Davis, Mike. 1998. *Ecology of Fear: Los Angeles and the Imagination of Disaster*. New York: Metropolitan Books.

Dawes, Robyn M. 1998. "Behavioral Decision Making and Judgment." Pp. 497–548 in Daniel T. Gilbert, Susan T. Fiske, and Gardner Lindzey, eds., *The Handbook of Social Psychology*, Vol. 1. Boston: McGraw-Hill.

Dawes, Robyn M., and Reid Hastie. 2001. *Rational Choice in an Uncertain World: The Psychology of Judgement and Decision Making*. Newbury Park, CA: Sage.

Deaux, Kay, and Marianne LaFrance 1998. "Gender." In *Handbook of Social Psychology*, eds. Daniel Gilbert, Susan T. Fiske, and Gardner Lindzey, 788–828. New York: McGraw-Hill.

De Jorio, Andrea. 2002. *Gesture in Naples and Gesture in Classical Antiquity*. Trans. Adam Kendon. Bloomington: Indiana University Press.

Devine, Patricia G. 1989. "Stereotypes and Prejudice: Their Automatic and Controlled Components." *Journal of Personality and Social Psychology* 56:5–18.

de Waal, Frans B. M. 1996. *Good Natured: The Origins of Right and Wrong in Humans and Animals*. Cambridge: Harvard University Press.

———. 1998. *Chimpanzee Politics: Power and Sex among the Apes*. Baltimore: Johns Hopkins University Press.

Diamond, Jared. 1992. *The Third Chimpanzee: The Evolution and Future of the Human Animal*. New York: HarperCollins.

———. 1997. *Guns, Germs, and Steel: The Fates of Human Societies*. New York: Norton.

Donald, Merlin. 1991. *Origins of the Modern Mind: Three States in the Evolution of Culture and Cognition*. Cambridge, MA: Harvard University Press.

Draper, Patricia, and Henry C. Hardpending. 1982. "Father Absence and Reproductive Strategy: An Evolutionary Perspective." *Journal of Anthropological Research* 38:255–73.

Dreier, Peter, John Mollenkipf, and Todd Swanstrom. 2001. *Place Matters: Metropolitics for the Twenty-First Century*. Lawrence: University of Kansas Press.

Duany, Andres, Elizabeth Plater-Zyberk, and Jeff Speck. 2000. *Suburban Nation: The Rise of Sprawl and the Decline of the American Dream*. New York: North Point Press.

Dunbar, Robin I. 1988. *Primate Social Systems*. London: Croom Helm.

———. 1996. *Grooming, Gossip, and the Evolution of Language*. London: Faber and Faber.

———. 2001. "Brains on Two Legs: Group Size and the Evolution of Intelligence." In *Tree of Origin: What Primate Behavior Can Tell Us about Human Social Evolution*, ed. Frans B. M. de Waal, 173–92. Cambridge, MA: Harvard University Press.

Duncan, Otis D. 1964. "Social Organization and the Ecosystem." In *Handbook of Modern Sociology*, ed. Robert E. L. Farris, 36–82. Chicago: Rand McNally.

Duncan, Otis D., and Beverly Duncan. 1955. "Residential Distribution and Occupational Stratification." *American Journal of Sociology* 60:493–503.

Duncan, Otis Dudley, and Stanley Lieberson. 1959. "Ethnic Segregation and Assimilation." *American Journal of Sociology* 64:364–74.

Durkheim, Emile. 1933. *The Division of Labor in Society*. Glencoe, IL: Free Press.

Dutt, Ashok K., Allen G. Noble, G. Venugopal, and S. Subbiah. 2004. *Challenges to Asian Urbanization in the 21st Century*. Amsterdam: Kluwer.

Easterlin, Richard A. 2004. "The Economics of Happiness." *Daedalus* (Spring):26–33.

Edin, Kathy, Timothy J. Nelson, and Rechelle Paranal. 2004. "Fatherhood and Incarceration as Potential Turning Points in the Criminal Careers of Unskilled Men." In *Imprisoning America: The Social Effects of Mass Incarceration*, eds. Mary Patillo,

David Weiman, and Bruce Western, 46–75. New York: Russell Sage Foundation.

Eibl-Eibesfeld, Irenaus. 1989. *Human Ethnology*. New York: Aldine de Gruyter.

Ekman, Paul, and Erika Rosenberg. 1997. *What the Face Reveals: Basic and Applied Studies of Spontaneous Expression Using the Facial Action Coding System*. Oxford: Oxford University Press.

Ellison, Peter. 2001. *On Fertile Ground: A Natural History of Human Reproduction*. Cambridge, MA: Harvard University Press.

Espenshade, Thomas J. 1986. "Population Dynamics with Immigration and Low Fertility." *Population and Development Review* 12:248–61.

Esping Anderson, Gosta. 1990. *The Three Worlds of Welfare Capitalism*. Princeton: Princeton University Press.

———. 1996. *Welfare States in Transition: National Adaptations in Global Economies*. Newbury Park, CA: Sage.

Farley, Reynolds. 1995. *State of the Union: America in the 1990s*. Vol. 2: *Social Trends*. New York: Russell Sage Foundation.

Farley, Reynolds, and Walter B. Allen. 1987. *The Color Line and the Quality of Life in America*. New York: Russell Sage Foundation.

Ferenczi, Imre. 1929. *International Migration*. Vol. 1: *Statistics*. New York: National Bureau for Economic Research.

Ferguson, Niall. 1999. *The Pity of War*. New York: Basic Books.

Fischer, Claude S. 1972. "Urbanism as a Way of Life: A Review and Agenda." *Sociological Methods and Research* 1:187–242.

———. 1975. "Toward a Subcultural Theory of Urbanism." *American Journal of Sociology* 80:1319–41.

———. 1981. "The Public and Private Worlds of City Life." *American Sociological Review* 46:306–16.

———. 1982. *To Dwell among Friends: Personal Networks in Town and City*. Chicago: University of Chicago Press.

———. 1995. "The Subcultural Theory of Urbanism: A Twentieth-Year Assessment." *American Journal of Sociology* 101:543–77.

Fisek, Güler O. 1983. "Turkey: Understanding and Altering Family and Political Violence." In *Aggression in Global Perspective*, eds. A. P. Goldstein and M. J. Segall, 122–38. New York: Pergamon.

Fishman, Mark, and Gray Cavender, eds. 1998. *Entertaining Crime: Television Reality Programs*. New York: Aldine de Gruyter.

Fiske, Alan P. 1991. *Structures of Social Life: The Four Elementary Forms of Human Relations*. New York: Free Press.

Fiske, Susan T. 1992. "Thinking Is for Doing: Portraits of Social Cognition from Daguerreotype to Laserphoto." *Journal of Personality and Social Psychology* 63:877–89.

———. 1993. "Social Cognition and Social Perception." *Annual Review of Psychology* 44:155–94.

———. 1998. "Stereotyping, Prejudice, and Discrimination." In *The Handbook of Social Psychology,* Vol. 1, 4th ed., eds. Daniel T. Gilbert, Susan T. Fiske, and Gardner Lindzey, 357–414. New York: McGraw-Hill

———. 2003. *Social Beings: A Core Motives Approach to Social Psychology*. New York: Wiley.

Fiske, Susan T., and Shelly E. Taylor. 1991. *Social Cognition,* 2nd ed. New York: McGraw-Hill.

Fitzpatrick, R. 1989. *God's Frontiersmen: The Scots-Irish Epic*. London: Weidenfeld and Nicolson.

Fligstein, Neil. 2001. *The Architecture of Markets: An Economic Sociology of Twenty-First Century Capitalist Societies*. Princeton: Princeton University Press.

Folbre, Nancy. 2001. *The Invisible Heart: Economics and Family Values*. New York: New Press.

Fredrickson, George M. 2002. *Racism: A Short History*. Princeton: Princeton University Press.

Freeman, Richard B. 1993. "How Much Has De-Unionization Contributed to the Rise in Male Earnings Inequality?" In *Uneven Tides: Rising Inequality in America*, eds. Sheldon Danziger and Peter Gottschalk, 133–63. New York: Russell Sage Foundation.

Friedman, John. 1986. "The World City Hypothesis." *Development and Change* 17:69–83.

Galaty, J. G., and P. Bonte. 1991. *Herders, Warriors, and Traders: Pastoralism in Africa*. Boulder: Westview.

Galbraith, John Kenneth. 1958. *The Affluent Society*. Boston: Houghton Mifflin.

Gallup, Gordon G. 1970. "Chimpanzees: Self-Recognition." *Science* 167:86–87.

———. 1982. "Self-Awareness and the Emergence of Mind in Primates." *American Journal of Primatology* 2:237–48.

Gamble, Clive. 1999. *The Paleolithic Societies of Europe*. Cambridge: Cambridge University Press.

Gans, Herbert J. 1962. *The Urban Villagers: Group and Class in the Life of Italian-Americans*. New York: Free Press.

———. 1967. *The Levittowners: Ways of Life and Politics in a New Suburban Community*. New York: Vintage Books.

Garnsey, Peter, and Richard Saller. 1987. *The Roman Empire: Economy, Society, and Culture*. London: Duckworth.

Garreau, Joel. 1992. *Edge City: Life on the New Frontier*. New York: Anchor.

Gazzaniga, Michael S. 1992. *Nature's Mind: The Biological Roots of Thinking, Emotions, Sexuality, Language, and Intelligence*. Harmondsworth: Penguin Books.

Gibbons, Ann. 2001. "The Peopling of the Pacific." *Science* 291(5509):1735–37.

———. 2004. "Chimpanzee Gang Warfare." *Science* 304(5672):818–19.

Gibson, Campbell. 1998. "Population of the 100 Largest Cities and Other Urban Places in the United States: 1790–1990." Population Division Working Paper 27. Washington, DC: U.S. Bureau of the Census.

Giddens, Anthony. 1984. *The Constitution of Society: Introduction of the Theory of Structuration*. Berkeley : University of California Press.

Glassner, Barry. 2000. *The Culture of Fear: Why Americans Are Afraid of the Wrong Things*. New York: Basic Books.

Goldin, Claudia, and Robert Margo. 1992. "The Great Compression: The U.S. Wage Structure at Mid-Century." *Quarterly Journal of Economics* 62:1–34.

Goleman, Daniel. 1995. *Emotional Intelligence*. New York: Bantam.

Goodall, Jane. 1986. *The Chimpanzees of Gombe: Patterns of Behavior*. Cambridge, MA: Harvard University Press.

———. 1999. *Jane Goodall: 40 Years at Gombe*. New York: Stewart, Tabori & Chang.

Goody, Jack. 1977. *The Domestication of the Savage Mind*. Cambridge: Cambridge University Press.

———. 1986. *The Logic of Writing and the Organization of Society*. Cambridge: Cambridge University Press.

Gould, Elizabeth, P. Tanapat, Bruce S. McEwen, G. Flugge, and E. Fuchs (1998). "Proliferation of Granule Cell Precursors in the Dentate Gyrus of Adult Monkeys Is Diminished by Stress." *Proceedings of the National Academy of Sciences USA*, 95:3168–71.

Graff, Harvey J. 1987. *The Legacies of Literacy: Continuities and Contradictions in Western Culture and Society*. Bloomington: Indiana University Press.

Granovetter, Mark S. 1974. *Getting a Job: A Study of Contacts and Careers*. Cambridge, MA: Harvard University Press.

———. 1985. "Economic Action and Social Structure: The Problem of Embeddedness." *American Journal of Sociology* 91:481–510.

Gregory, Richard L. 1981. *Mind in Science*. London: Penguin.

Haggett, Peter. 1977. *Locational Analysis in Human Geography*. London: Palgrave Macmillan.

Hajnal, John. 1982. "Two Kinds of Preindustrial Household Formation Systems." *Population and Development Review* 8:449–94.

Hall, Peter A., and David Sockice. 2001. *Varieties of Capitalism: The Institutional Foundations of Comparative Advantage*. Oxford: Oxford University Press.

Halpern, Carolyn T., J. Richard Udry, Benjamin C. Campbell, and Chirayath Suchindran. 1994. "Relationships between Aggression and Pubertal Increases in Testosterone: A Panel Analysis." *Social Biology* 40:8–24.

Harris, Chauncy D., and Edward L. Ullman. 1945. "The Nature of Cities." *Annals of the American Academy of Political and Social Science* 242:7–17.

Harris, Julie A. 1999. "Review and Methodological Considerations in Research on Testosterone and Aggression." *Aggression and Violent Behaviour* 4:273–91.

Harris, Roy. 1986. *The Origin of Writing*. London: Duckworth.

Harrison, Bennett. 1995. *Lean and Mean: The Changing Landscape of Corporate Power in the Age of Flexibility*. New York: Basic Books.

Harvey, David. 1989. *The Condition of Postmodernity*. Cambridge: Blackwell.

Hatton, Timothy J., and Jeffrey G. Williamson. 1998. *The Age of Mass Migration: Causes and Economic Impact*. Oxford: Oxford University Press.

Hawley, Amos H. 1950. *Human Ecology: A Theory of Community Structure*. New York: Ronald Press.

Hayden, Brian. 1981. "Subsistence and Ecological Adaptations of Modern Hunter-Gatherers." In *Omnivorous Primates: Hunting and Gathering in Human Evolution*, eds. Geza Teleki and Robert S. O. Harding, 344–422. New York: Columbia University Press.

Hayden, Brian, Michael Deal, Aubrey Cannon, and Joanna Casey. 1986. "Ecological Determinants of Women's Status among Hunter-Gatherers." *Human Evolution* 1:449–74.

Henry, Louis. 1972. *On the Measurement of Human Fertility: Selected Writings of Louis Henry*. Trans. and eds. by Mindel C. Sheps and Evelyne Lapierre-Adamcyk. Amsterdam and New York: Elsevier.

Hershberg, Theodore, Alan N. Burstein, Eugene P. Ericksen, Stephanie W. Greenberg, and William L. Yancey. 1981. "A Tale of Three Cities: Blacks, Immigrants and Opportunity in Philadelphia 1850–1880, 1930, 1970." In *Philadelphia: Work, Space, Family, and Group Experience in the Nineteenth Century*, ed. Theodore Hershberg, 461–91. New York: Oxford University Press.

Higginbotham, A. Leon. 1980. *In the Matter of Color: The Colonial Period*. New York: Oxford University Press.

———. 1996. *Shades of Freedom: Racial Politics and Presumptions of the American Legal Process*. New York: Oxford University Press.

Higham, John. 1955. *Strangers in the Land: Patterns of American Nativism, 1860–1925*. New Brunswick, NJ: Rutgers University Press.

Hobbes, Thomas. 1982 [1651]. *Leviathan*. Ed. C. MacPherson. London: Penguin Classics.

Hochschild, Arlie R. 2001. *The Time Bind: When Work Becomes Home and Home Becomes Work*. New York: Henry Holt.

———. 2003. *The Commercialization of Intimate Life: Notes from Home and Work*. Berkeley: University of California Press.

Holzer, Harry, Steven Raphael, and Michael J. Stoll. 2004. "Will Employers Hire Former Offenders?" In *Imprisoning America: The Social Effects of Mass Incarceration*, eds. Mary Patillo, David Weiman, and Bruce Western, 205–46. New York: Russell Sage Foundation.

House, James S., Karl R. Landis, and Debra Umberson. 1988. "Social Relationships and Health." *Science* 241: 540–45.

Howell, Nancy. 1979. *Demography of the Dobe !Kung*. New York: Academic Press.

Hoyt, Homer. 1939. *The Structure and Growth of Residential Neighborhoods in American Cities*. Washington, DC: Federal Housing Administration.

Hunter, Albert. 1974. *Symbolic Communities: The Persistence and Change of Chicago's Local Communities*. Chicago: University of Chicago Press.

Hurd, Robert M. 1903. *Principles of City Land Values*. New York: The Record and Guide.

Ignatiev, Noel. 1995. *How the Irish Became White*. New York: Routledge.

Jackson, Kenneth T. 1985. *Crabgrass Frontier: The Suburbanization of the United States*. New York: Oxford University Press.

Jacobs, Jerry A. 1989. *Revolving Doors: Sex Segregation and Women's Careers*. Stanford: Stanford University Press.

———. 1995. *Gender Inequality at Work*. Thousand Oaks, CA: Sage.

Jacobs, Jerry A., and Kathleen Gerson. 2004. *The Time Divide: Work, Family, and Gender Inequality*. Cambridge, MA: Harvard University Press.

James, Harold. 2001. *The End of Globalization: Lessons from the Great Depression*. Cambridge, MA: Harvard University Press.

Janoff-Bulman, Ronnie, 1985. "The Aftermath of Victimisation." Pp. 15–35 in *Trauma and Its Wake: The Study and Treatment of Post-Traumatic Stress Disorder*, ed. Charles R. Figley. New York: Brunner/Mazel.

Jerison, Harry J. 1973. *Evolution of the Brain and Intelligence*. New York: Academic Press.

Johnson, Allen W., and Timothy Earle. 2000. *The Evolution of Human Societies: From Foraging Group to Agrarian State*, 2nd ed. Stanford: Stanford University Press.

Jones, Edward E. 1990. *Interpersonal Perception*. New York: Freeman.

Jones, Edward E., and Richard E. Nisbett. 1972. "The Actor and the Observer: Divergent Perceptions of the Causes of Behavior." In *Attribution: Perceiving the Causes of Behavior*, eds. Edward E. Jones, S. Valin, and B. Weiner, 79–94. Morristown, NJ: General Learning Press.

Kahneman, Daniel, and Amos Tversky. 1973. "On the Psychology of Prediction." *Psychological Review* 80:237–51.

———. 1979. "Prospect Theory: An Analysis of Decisions under Risk." *Econometrica* 47:313–27.

———. 2000. *Choices, Values, and Frames*. New York: Cambridge University Press.

Kantrowitz, Nathan. 1969. "Ethnic and Racial Segregation in the New York Metropolis, 1960." *American Journal of Sociology* 74:685–95.

———. 1973. *Ethnic and Racial Segregation in the New York Metropolis: Residential Patterns among White Ethnic Groups, Blacks, and Puerto Ricans*. New York: Praeger.

Kasarda, John D. 1995. "Industrial Restructuring and the Changing Location of Jobs." In *State of the Union: America in the 1990s*, ed. Reynolds Farley, 215–68. New York: Russell Sage Foundation.

Kassin, Saul M. 1979. "Consensus Information, Prediction, and Causal Attribution: A Review of the Literature and Issues." *Journal of Personality and Social Psychology* 37:1966–81.

Keister, Lisa A. 2000. *Wealth in America: Trends in Inequality*. New York: Cambridge University Press.

Kelly, Robert L. 1995. *The Foraging Spectrum: Diversity in Hunter-Gatherer Lifeways*. Washington, DC: Smithsonian Institution Press.

Kenwood, A. George, and Alan L. Lougheed. 1992. *The Growth of the International Economy 1820–2000* Third Edition. London: Routledge.

Keverne, E. B., N. Martensz, and B. Tuite. 1989. "Beta Endorphin Concentrations in CSF of Monkeys Are Influenced by Grooming Relationships." *Psychoneuroendocrinology* 14:155–61.

Klein, Herbert S. 1999. *The Atlantic Slave Trade*. New York: Cambridge University Press.

Klein, Richard G. 1999. *The Human Career: Human Biological and Cultural Origins*. Chicago: University of Chicago Press.

Klein, Richard G., and Blake Edgar. 2002. *The Dawn of Human Culture*. New York: Wiley.

Klinkner, Philip A., and Rogers M. Smith. 2002. *The Unsteady March: The Rise and Decline of Racial Equality in America*. Chicago: University of Chicago Press.

Knight, Chris, Robin Dunbar, and Camilla Power. 1999. "An Evolutionary Approach to Culture." In *The Evolution of Culture: An Interdisciplinary View*, eds. Robin Dunbar, Chris Knight, and Camilla Power, 1–15. New Brunswick, NJ: Rutgers University Press.

Konner, Melvin. 2002. *The Tangled Wing: Biological Constraints on the Human Spirit*. New York: Henry Holt.

Kotlikoff, Laurence J., and Scott Burns. 2004. *The Coming Generational Storm: What You Need to Know about America's Economic Future*. Cambridge, MA: MIT Press.

Krivo, Lauren J., and Ruth D. Peterson. 1996. "Extremely Disadvantaged Neighborhoods and Violent Crime." *Social Forces* 75:619–48.

Kuczynski, Pedro-Pablo, and John Williamson. 2003. *After the Washington Consensus: Restarting Growth and Reform in Latin America*. Washington, DC: Institute for International Economics.

Kuper, Adam. 1999. *Culture: The Anthropologists' Account*. Cambridge, MA: Harvard University Press.

Landers, John. 1992. "Reconstructing Ancient Populations." In *The Cambridge Ency-*

*clopedia of Human Evolution*, eds. Steve Jones, Robert Martin, and David Pilbeam, 402–5. Cambridge: Cambridge University Press.

Laslett, Peter. 1971. *The World We Have Lost*. London: Methuen.

Lawler, Andrew. 2001. "Writing Gets a Rewrite." *Science* 292(5526):2418–20.

LeDoux, Joseph. 1996. *The Emotional Brain: The Mysterious Underpinnings of Emotional Life*. New York: Simon & Schuster.

———. 2002. *Synaptic Self: How Our Brains Become Who We Are*. New York: Viking.

LeDoux, Joseph, D. H. Wilson, and Michael Gazzaniga. 1977. "A Divided Mind." *Annals of Neurology* 2:417–21.

Lee, Richard B., and Irven Devore, eds. 1968. *Man the Hunter*. Hawthorne, NY: Aldine de Gruyter.

Lenneberg, Eric. 1980. "Of Language, Knowledge, Apes, and Brains." In *Speaking of Apes: A Critical Anthology of Two-Way Communication with Man*, eds. T. A. Sebeok and J. Sebeok, 115–44. New York: Plenum Press.

Lestage, Andre. 1982. "Literacy and Illiteracy." Educational Studies and Documents No. 42. Paris: United Nations Educational Scientific, and Cultural Organization.

Levine, David. 2001. *At the Dawn of Modernity: Biology, Culture, and Material Life in Europe after the Year 1000*. Berkeley: University of California Press.

Levy, Frank. 1998. *The New Dollars and Dreams: American Incomes and Economic Change*. New York: Russell Sage Foundation.

Lewin, Marion E., and Stuart Altmann. 2000. *America's Health Care Safety Net: Intact but Endangered*. Washington, DC: National Academies Press.

Lieberman, Philip. 1975. *On the Origins of Language: An Introduction to the Evolution of Human Speech*. New York: Macmillan.

———. 1984. *The Biology and Evolution of Language*. Cambridge, MA: Harvard University Press.

Lieberson, Stanley. 1961. "The Impact of Residential Segregation on Ethnic Assimilation." *Social Forces* 40:52–57.

———. 1963. *Ethnic Patterns in American Cities*. New York: Free Press.

———. 1980. *A Piece of the Pie: Blacks and White Immigrants since 1980*. Berkeley: University of California Press.

Lieberson, Stanley, and Mary C. Waters. 1988. *From Many Strands: Ethnic and Racial Groups in Contemporary America*. New York: Russell Sage Foundation.

Livi-Bacci, Massimo. 1992. *A Concise History of World Population*. Oxford: Blackwell.

Lofland, Lyn H. 1973. *A World of Strangers: Order and Action in Urban Public Space*. New York: Basic Books.

Logan, John R., and Richard Alba. 1993. "Locational Returns to Human Capital: Minority Access to Suburban Community Resources." *Demography* 30:243–68.

Logan, John R., Richard Alba, Tom McNulty, and Brian Fisher. 1996. "Making a

Place in the Metropolis: Locational Attainment in Cities and Suburbs." *Demography* 33:443–53.

Lomnitz, Larissa. 1975. *Como Sobreviven los Marginados*. Mexico: Siglo Veintiuno.

Lomnitz, Larissa, and Marisol Pérez-Lizaur. 1987. *A Mexican Elite Family, 1820–1980: Kinship, Class, and Culture*. Princeton: Princeton University Press.

Lovejoy, C. O. 1980. "Hominid Origins: The Role of Bipedalism." *American Journal of Physical Anthropology* 52:250.

Low, Bobbi S. 2000. *Why Sex Matters: A Darwinian Look at Human Behavior*. Princeton: Princeton University Press.

Lowell, B. Lindsay. 1987. *Scandinavian Exodus: Demography and Social Development of 19th-Century Rural Communities*. New York: Perseus.

Lynch, James P., and William J. Sabol. 2004. "Effects of Incarceration on Informal Social Control in Communities." In *Imprisoning America: The Social Effects of Mass Incarceration*, eds. Mary Patillo, David Weiman, and Bruce Western, 135–64. New York: Russell Sage Foundation.

MacDonald, John S., and Leatrice D. MacDonald. 1974. "Chain Migration, Ethnic Neighborhood Formation, and Social Networks." In *An Urban World*, ed. Charles Tilly, 226–36. Boston: Little, Brown.

MacLean, Paul D. 1973. *A Triune Concept of the Brain and Behavior*. Toronto: University of Toronto Press.

———. 1990. *The Triune Brain in Evolution: Role in Paleocerebral Functions*. New York: Plenum.

Macoby, Eleanor E. 1998. *The Two Sexes: Growing Up, Coming Apart*. Cambridge, MA: Harvard University Press.

Macoby, Eleanor E., and Carol N. Jacklin. 1987. *The Psychology of Sex Differences*. Stanford: Stanford University Press.

Maddison, Angus. 2001. *The World Economy: Historical Statistics*. Paris: Organization for Economic Cooperation and Development.

Maddrick, Jeffrey. 1995. *The End of Affluence: The Causes and Consequences of America's Economic Dilemma*. New York: Random House.

Malthus, Thomas R. 1798. *An Essay on the Principle of Population as It Affects the Future Improvement of Society.* London: J. Johnson.

Mandelbaum, D. G. 1988. *Women's Seclusion and Men's Honor: Sex Roles in North India*. Tucson: University of Arizona Press.

Marks, Jonathan. 2002. *What It Means to Be 98% Chimpanzee: Apes, People, and Their Genes*. Berkeley: University of California Press.

Martel, Gordon. 1996. *The Origins of the First World War*. New York: Longman.

Maryanski, Alexandra. 1987. "African Ape Social Structure: Is There Strength in Weak Ties?" *Social Networks* 9:191–215.

———. 1992. "The Last Ancestor: An Ecological-Network Model on the Origins of Human Sociality." *Advances in Human Ecology* 2:1–32.

———. 1993. "The Elementary Forms of the First Proto-Human Society: An Ecological/Social Network Approach." *Advances in Human Ecology* 2:215–41.

———. 1996. "Was Speech an Evolutionary Afterthought?" In *Communicating Meaning: The Evolution and Development of Language*, eds. B. M. Vlechkousky and D. M. Rumbaugh, 121–31. Hillside, NJ: Erlbaum.

Maryanski, Alexandra, and Jonathan H. Turner. 1992. *The Social Cage: Human Nature and the Evolution of Society*. Stanford: Stanford University Press.

Massey, Douglas S. 1985. "Ethnic Residential Segregation: A Theoretical Synthesis and Empirical Review." *Sociology and Social Research* 69:315–50.

———. 1988. "International Migration and Economic Development in Comparative Perspective." *Population and Development Review* 14:383–414.

———. 1990. "American Apartheid: Segregation and the Making of the Underclass." *American Journal of Sociology* 95:1153–88.

———. 1995. "The New Immigration and the Meaning of Ethnicity in the United States." *Population and Development Review* 21:631–52.

———. 1996. "The Age of Extremes: Concentrated Affluence and Poverty in the 21st Century." *Demography* 33:395–412.

———. 2000. "Higher Education and Social Mobility in the United States, 1940–1998." In *America's Research Universities: Quality, Innovation, Partnership*, ed. Ann Leigh Speicher, 45–55. Washington, DC: Association of American Universities.

———. 2001. "Segregation and Violent Crime in Urban America." In *Problem of the Century: Racial Stratification in the United States*, eds. Elijah Anderson and Douglas S. Massey, 317–46. New York: Russell Sage Foundation.

———. 2002. "A Brief History of Human Society: The Origin and Role of Emotion in Social Life." *American Sociological Review* 67:1–29.

———. 2003. "Mondialisation et Migrations: L'Exemple des Etats-Unis." *Futuribles* 284:1–9.

———. 2004. "Segregation and Stratification: A Biosocial Approach." *The DuBois Review: Social Science Research on Race* 1:3–26.

———. 2005. *Return of the L-Word: A Liberal Vision for the New Century*. Princeton, NJ: Princeton University Press.

Massey, Douglas S., Gretchen A. Condran, and Nancy A. Denton. 1987. "The Effect of Residential Segregation on Black Social and Economic Well-Being." *Social Forces* 66:29–56.

Massey, Douglas S., Rafael Alarcon, Jorge Durand, and Humberto Gonzalez. 1987. *Return to Aztlan: The Social Process of International Migration from Western Mexico.* Berkeley: University of California Press.

Massey, Douglas S., Jorge Durand, and Nolan J. Malone. 2002. *Beyond Smoke and Mirrors: Mexican Immigration in an Age of Economic Integration*. New York: Russell Sage Foundation.

Massey, Douglas S., and Nancy A. Denton. 1987. "Trends in the Residential Segregation of Blacks, Hispanics, and Asians." *American Sociological Review* 52:802–25.

———. 1988. "The Dimensions of Residential Segregation." *Social Forces* 67:281–315.

———. 1993. *American Apartheid: Segregation and the Making of the Underclass*. Cambridge: Cambridge University Press.

Massey, Douglas S., and Mitchell E. Eggers. 1990. "The Ecology of Inequality: Minorities and the Concentration of Poverty 1970–1980." *American Journal of Sociology* 95:1153–88.

———. 1993. "The Spatial Concentration of Affluence and Poverty during the 1970s." *Urban Affairs Quarterly* 29:299–315.

Massey, Douglas S., and Mary J. Fischer. 2000. "How Segregation Concentrates Poverty." *Ethnic and Racial Studies* 23:670–91.

———. 2003. "The Geography of Inequality in the United States: 1950–2000." In *Brookings-Wharton Papers on Urban Affairs 2003*, eds. William G. Gale and Janet Rothenberg Pack, 1–40. Washington, DC: Brookings Institution Press.

Massey, Douglas S., and Eric Fong. 1990. "Segregation and Neighborhood Quality: Blacks, Hispanics, and Asians in the San Francisco Metropolitan Area." *Social Forces* 69:15–32.

Massey, Douglas S., and J. Edward Taylor. 2004. "Back to the Future: Immigration Research, Immigration Policy, and Globalization in the 21st Century." In *International Migration: Prospects and Policies in a Global Market*, eds. Douglas S. Massey and J. Edward Taylor, 373–88. Oxford: Oxford University Press.

Matlin, Margaret W., and David J. Stang. 1978. *The Pollyanna Principle*. Cambridge, MA: Schenkman.

Mauss, Marcel. 1967. *The Gift: The Form and Reason for Exchange in Archaic Societies*. New York: Norton.

Mayer, Karl Ulrich, and Urs Schoepflin. 1989. "The State and the Life Course." *Annual Review of Sociology* 15:187–209.

McClellan, James E. III, and Harold Dorn. 1999. *Science and Technology in World History: An Introduction*. Baltimore: Johns Hopkins University Press.

McEwen, Bruce, and Elizabeth N. Lasley, 2002. *The End of Stress as We Know It*. Washington, DC: Joseph Henry Press.

McNeill, William H. 1976. *Plagues and Peoples*. Garden City, NY: Anchor Press.

McWhiney, G. 1988. *Cracker Culture: Celtic Ways in the Old South*. Tuscaloosa: University of Alabama Press.

Meehan, Betty, and Neville White. 1990. *Hunter Gatherer Demography: Past and Present*. Sydney: University of Sydney Press.

Mellars, Paul. 1996. *The Neanderthal Legacy: An Archaeological Prospective from Western Europe*. Princeton: Princeton University Press.

Messing, Lynn S., and Ruth Campbell, eds. 1999. *Gesture, Speech, and Sign*. New York: Oxford University Press.

Milardo, Robert M. 1992. "Comparative Methods for Delineating Social Networks." *Journal of Social and Personal Relationships* 9:447–61.

Miller, George A. 1956. "The Magical Number Seven Plus or Minus Two: Some Limits on the Capacity for Processing Information." *Psychological Review* 63:81–97.

Mills, C. Wright. 1956. *The Power Elite*. New York: Oxford University Press.

Mills, Edwin S. 1972. *Urban Economics*. Glenview, Il: Scott, Foresman.

Mollenkopf, John H., and Manuel Castells. 1991. *Dual City: Restructuring New York*. New York: Russell Sage Foundation.

Mombauer, Annika. 2002. *The Origins of the First World War: Controversies and Consensus*. New York: Longman.

Montgomery, Mark R., Richard Stren, Barney Cohen, and Holly E. Reed, eds. 2003. *Cities Transformed: Demographic Change and Its Implications in the Developing World*. Washington, DC: National Academies Press.

Moscovici, Serge. 1988. "Notes toward a Description of Social Representations." *European Journey of Social Psychology* 18:211–50.

Mosher, D. L., and M. Sirkin. 1984. "Measuring a Macho Personality Constellation." *Journal of Research and Personality* 18:150–63.

Muñoz, Humberto, Orlandina de Oliveira, and Claudio Stern. 1977. *Migración y Desigualdad Social en la Ciudad de México*. Mexico City: Instituto de Investigaciones Sociales, Universidad Nacional Autónoma de México.

Naim, Moises. 2000. "Washington Consensus or Washington Confusion?" *Foreign Policy* (Spring) 118:86–103.

Napier, John R., and Prue H. Napier. 1985. *The Natural History of the Primates*. Cambridge, MA: MIT Press.

Newell, Allen, and Herbert A. Simon. 1972. *Human Problem Solving*. Englewood Cliffs, NJ: Prentice-Hall.

Nisbett, Richard E., and Dov Cohen. 1996. *Culture of Honor: The Psychology of Violence in the South*. Boulder: Westview.

Nisbett, Richard E., and Timothy D. Wilson. 1977. "Telling More Than We Know: Verbal Reports on Mental Processes." *Psychological Review* 84:231–59.

Nurse, Anne M. 2004. "Returning to Strangers: Newly Paroled Young Fathers and Their Children." In *Imprisoning America: The Social Effects of Mass Incarceration*, eds. Mary Patillo, David Weiman, and Bruce Western, 76–96. New York: Russell Sage Foundation.

Ogbu, John. 1978. *Minority Education and Caste: The American System in Cross Cultural Perspective*. New York: Academic Press.

Olzak, Susan. 1992. *The Dynamics of Ethnic Competition and Conflict*. Stanford: Stanford University Press.

Orfield, Gary. 1994. *Turning Back the Clock: The Reagan-Bush Retreat for Civil Rights in Higher Education*. Lanham, MD: Rowman & Littlefield.

Orfield, Myron. 2002. *American Metropolitics: The New Suburban Reality*. Washington, DC: Brookings Institution Press.

O'Rourke, Kevin H., and Jeffrey G. Williamson. 1999. *Globalization and History: The Evolution of a Nineteenth Century Atlantic Economy*. Cambridge, MA: MIT Press.

Pager, Devah. 2003. "The Mark of a Criminal Record." *American Journal of Sociology* 108:937–75.

Panksepp, Jaak. 1998. *Affective Neuroscience: The Foundations of Human and Animal Emotions*. New York: Oxford University Press.

Papastergiadis, Nikos. 2000. *The Turbulence of Migration: Globalization, Deterritorialization and Hybridity*. New York: Polity Press.

Park, Robert E. 1925. "The City: Suggestions for the Investigation of Human Behavior in the Urban Environment." In *The City*, eds. Robert E. Park and Ernest W. Burgess, 1–46. Chicago: University of Chicago Press.

———. 1926. "The Urban Community as a Spatial Pattern and a Moral Order." In *The Urban Community*, ed. Ernest W. Burgess, 3–18. Chicago: University of Chicago Press.

———. 1952. *Human Communities: The City and Human Ecology*. Glencoe, IL: Free Press.

Passingham, R. E., and G. Ettlinger. 1974. "A Comparison of Cortical Functions." Pp. 233–99 in C. C. Pfieffer and J. R. Smythies, eds., *International Review of Neurobiology*, Vol. 16. New York: Academic Press.

Pedersen, Susan. 1995. *Family, Dependence, and the Origins of the Welfare State: Britain and France, 1914–1945*. Cambridge: Cambridge University Press.

Pennington, Renee. 2001. "Hunter-Gatherer Demography." In *Hunter-Gatherers: An Interdisciplinary Perspective*, eds. Catherine Panter-Brick, Robert H. Layton, and Peter Rowley-Conwy, 170–204. Cambridge: Cambridge University Press.

Peristiany, Jean G., ed. 1966. *Honour and Shame: The Values of Mediterranean Society*. London: Weidenfeld and Nicolson.

Pfeiffer, John. 1982. *The Emergence of Culture*. New York: Harper & Row.

Phillips, Kevin. 2002. *Wealth and Democracy: A Political History of the American Rich*. New York: Broadway Books.

Philpott, Thomas L. 1978. *The Slum and the Ghetto: Neighborhood Deterioration and Middle-Class Reform, Chicago, 1880–1930*. New York: Oxford University Press.

Pinker, Steven. 1994. *The Language Instinct: How the Mind Creates Language*. New York: HarperCollins.

———. 2002. *The Blank Slate: The Modern Denial of Human Nature*. New York: Viking.

Piore, Michael, and Charles F. Sabel. 1984. *The Second Industrial Divide: Possibilities for Prosperity*. New York: Basic Books.

Pirenne, Henri. 1925. *Medieval Cities*. Princeton: Princeton University Press.

Plutchik, Robert. 1980. *Emotion: A Psychoevolutionary Synthesis*. New York: Harper & Row.

Portes, Alejandro, and Kelly Hoffman. 2003. "Latin American Class Structures: Their Composition and Change during the Neoliberal Era." *Latin American Research Review* 38:41–82.

Preston, Samuel H. 1979. "Urban Growth in Developing Countries: A Demographic Reappraisal." *Population and Development Review* 5:195–216.

———. 1984. "Children and the Elderly: Divergent Paths for America's Dependents." *Demography* 21:435–57.

Preston, Samuel H., and Michael R. Haines. 1991. *Fatal Years: Child Mortality in Late Nineteenth-Century America*. Princeton: Princeton University Press.

Redfield, Robert. 1934. *Chan Kom: A Maya Village*. Washington, DC: Carnegie Institution.

Relethford, John H. 2001. *Genetics and the Search for Modern Human Origins*. New York: Wiley-Liss.

Restak, Richard M. 2001. *The Secret Life of the Brain*. Washington, DC: Joseph Henry Press.

Rifkin, Jeremy. 1995. *The End of Work: The Decline of the Global Labor Force and the Dawn of the Post-Market Era*. New York: Putnam.

Rodseth, Lars, Richard W. Wrangham, Alisa M. Harrigan, and Barbara B. Smuts. 1991. "The Human Community as Primate Society." Current Anthropology 32:221–54.

Rogers, Richard G., Robert A. Hummer, and Charles B. Nam. 2000. *Living and Dying in the USA: Behavioral, Health, and Social Differentials of Adult Mortality*. San Diego: Academic Press.

Rosaldo, Renato. 1980. *Ilongot Headhunting 1883–1974: A Study in Society and History*. Stanford: Stanford University Press.

Ross, L. R., D. Greene, and P. House. 1977. "The False Consensus Effect: An Egocentric Bias in Social Perception and Attribution Processes." *Journal of Experimental Social Psychology* 13:279–301.

Ross, Lee. 1977. "The Intuitive Psychologist and His Shortcomings: Distortions in the Attribution Process." *Advances in Experimental Social Psychology* 10:174–221. Ed. L. Berkowitz. New York: Academic Press.

Rothschild, Babette. 2000. *The Body Remembers: The Psychophysiology of Trauma and Trauma Treatment*. New York: Norton.

Roughley, Neil. 2000. *Being Humans: Anthropological Universality and Particularity in Transdisciplinary Perspectives*. New York: Walter de Gruyter.

Rubalcava, Rosa María, and M. Schteingart. 2000. "Segregación Socioespacial." In La *Ciudad de México en el Fin del Segundo Milenio*, ed. Gustavo Garza, 287–96. Mexico City: El Colegio de México.

Ruhlen, Merritt. 1994. *The Origin of Language: Tracing the Evolution of the Mother Tongue*. New York: Wiley.

Rumbaugh, Duane M., and David A. Washburn. 2003. *Intelligence of Apes and Other Rational Beings*. New Haven: Yale University Press.

Runciman, Walter G. 1966. *Relative Deprivation and Social Justice*. Berkeley: University of California Press.

Sabatini, Francisco, and Federico Arenas. 2000. "Entre el Estado y el Mercado: Resonancias Geográficos y Sustentabilidad Social en Santiago de Chile." *Revista Latinoamericano de Estudios Urbanos y Regionales* 27(11):1917–38.

Sahlins, Marshall D. 1972. *Stone Age Economics*. Chicago: Aldine-Atherton.

Saller, Richard. 1996. *Patriarchy, Property and Death in the Roman Family*. Cambridge: Cambridge University Press.

Sampson, Robert J. 2004. "Neighborhood and Community: Collective Efficacy and Community Safety." *New Economy* 11:106–13.

Sampson, Robert J., Jeffrey Morenoff, and Felton Earls. 1999. "Beyond Social Capital: Spatial Dynamics of Collective Efficacy for Children." *American Sociological Review* 64:633–60.

Sampson, Robert J., Jeffrey D. Morenoff, and Thomas Gannon-Rowley. 2002. "Assessing 'Neighborhood Effects': Social Processes and New Directions in Research." *Annual Review of Sociology* 28:443–78.

Sampson, Robert J., Stephen Raudenbush, and Felton Earls. 1997. "Neighborhoods and Violent Crime: A Multilevel Study of Collective Efficacy." *Science* 277:918–24.

Sanday, Peggy R. 1981. *Female Power and Dominance: On the Origins of Sexual Inequality*. Pittsburgh: University of Pittsburgh Press.

Sanderson, Stephen K. 1999. *Social Transformations: A General Theory of Historical Development*. Lanham, MD: Rowman and Littlefield.

Sassen, Saskia. 1991. *The Global City: New York, London, Tokyo*. Princeton: Princeton University Press.

———. 1994. *Cities in a World Economy*. Thousand Oaks, CA: Pine Forge Press.

———. 2002. *Global Networks, Linked Cities*. New York: Routledge.

Savage-Rumbaugh, Sue, and Roger Lewin. 1994. *Kanzi: The Ape at the Brink of the Human Mind*. New York: Wiley.

Schiffer, Sueli Ramos. 2003. "Economic Restructuring and Urban Segregation in Sao Paolo." In *Of States and Cities: The Partitioning of Urban Space*, eds. Peter Marcuse and Ronald van Kempen, 143–69. Oxford: Oxford University Press.

Schiraldi, Glenn R. 2000. *Post-Traumatic Stress Disorder Sourcebook*. New York: McGraw-Hill.

Schulz, P., C. Kirschbaum, J. Prüssner, and D. Hellhammer. 1998. "Increased Free Cortisol Secretion After Awakening in Chronically Stressed Individuals Due to Work Overload." *Stress Medicine* 14:91–97.

Scott, Allen J. 1988. *Metropolis: From the Division of Labor to Urban Form.* Berkeley: University of California Press.

———. 2001. *Global City-Regions: Trends, Theory, Policy*. New York: Oxford University Press.

Scott, Allison M. 1994. *Gender Segregation and Social Change: Men and Women in Changing Labour Markets*. Oxford: Oxford University Press.

Sears, David O. 1983. "The Person-Positivity Bias." *Journal of Personality and Social Psychology* 44:233–50.

Sebba, Mark. 1997. *Contact Languages: Pidgins and Creoles*. New York: St. Martin's Press.

Senghas, Ann. 2003. "Intergenerational Influence and Ontogenetic Development in the Emergence of Spatial Grammar in Nicaraguan Sign Language." *Cognitive Development* 18:511–31.

Service, Elman R. 1962. *Primitive Social Organization: An Evolutionary Perspective*. New York: Random House.

———. 1975. *Origins of the State and Civilization*. New York: Norton.

Shevky, Eshref, and Wendell Bell. 1955. *Social Area Analysis: Theory, Illustrative Application, and Computational Procedures.* Stanford: Stanford University Press.

Shevky, Eshref, and Marylin Williams. 1949. *The Social Areas of Los Angeles: Analysis and Typology*. Los Angeles: University of California Press.

Simkus, Albert A. 1978. "Residential Segregation by Occupation and Race in Ten Urbanized Areas, 1950–1970." *American Sociological Review* 43:81–93.

Simon, Herbert A. 1981. *Sciences of the Artificial*. Cambridge, MA: MIT Press.

Simpson, Katherine, 2001. "The Role of Testosterone in Aggression." *McGill Journal of Medicine* 6:32–40.

Sjoberg, Gideon. 1960. *The Pre-Industrial City: Past and Present.* Glencoe, IL: Free Press.

Smeeding, Timothy. 2002. "Globalisation, Inequality, and the Rich of the G-20: Evidence from the Luxembourg Income Study." In *Globalisation, Living Standards, and Inequality: Recent Progress and Continuing Challenges*, eds. D. Gruen, T. O. O'Brien, and J. Lawson, 179–206. Sydney: Macmillan.

———. 2003. "Government Programs and Social Outcomes: The United States in Comparative Perspective." Paprer presented at the Conference on Poverty, the

Distribution of Income, and Public Policy. University of California, Berkeley, December 2003.

Smith, Eric A. 1981. "The Application of Optimal Foraging Theory to the Analysis of Hunter-Gatherer Group Size." In *Hunter-Gatherer Foraging Strategies*, eds. Bruce Winterhalder and Eric A. Smith, 36–65. Chicago: University of Chicago Press.

Smith, Eric A., and Bruce Winterhalder. 1992. *Evolutionary Ecology and Human Behavior*. Hawthorne, NY: Aldine de Gruyter.

Smith, James P. 1988. "Poverty and the Family." In *Divided Opportunities: Minorities, Poverty, and Social Policy*, eds. Gary D. Sandefur and Marta Tienda, 141–72. New York: Plenum.

Smith, James P., and Barry Edmonston. 1997. *The New Americans: Economic, Demographic, and Fiscal Effects of Immigration*. Washington, DC: National Academies Press.

———. 1998. *The Immigration Debate: Studies on the Economic, Demographic, and Fiscal Effects of Immigration*. Washington, DC: National Academies Press.

Smith, Thomas S., and David D. Franks. 1999. "Introduction: Emergence, Reduction, and Levels of Analysis in the Neurosociological Paradigm." In *Mind, Brain, and Society: Toward the Neurosociology of Emotion*, eds. David D. Franks and Thomas S. Smith, 3–18. Social Perspectives on Emotion, Vol. 5. Stamford, CT: JAI Press.

Snow, Charles P. 1959. *Two Cultures and the Scientific Revolution*. Cambridge: Cambridge University Press.

Snowdon, Charles T. 2001. "From Primate Communication to Human Language." In *Tree of Origin: What Primate Behavior Can Tell Us about Human Social Evolution*, ed. Frans B. M. de Waal, 193–228. Cambridge, MA: Harvard University Press.

Stack, Carol B. 1974. *All Our Kin: Strategies for Survival in a Black Community*. New York: Harper & Row.

Stansfeld, Stephen A., H. Bosma, Harry Hemingway, and Michael G. Marmot. 1998. "Psychosocial Work Characteristics and Social Support as Predictors of SF-36 Health Functioning: The Whitehall III Study." *Psychosomatic Medicine* 60:247–55.

Stephan, J. Edward. 2004. *The Division of Territory in Society*. Retrieved 10/20/2004, from http://www.ac.wwu.edu/~stephan/Book/contents.html.

Stepan-Norris, Judith, and Maurice Zeitlin. 1995. *Talking Union*. Urbana: University of Illinois Press.

Sterling, P., and J. Ayer. 1988. "Allostatis: A New Paradigm to Explain Arousal Pathology." In *Handbook of Life Stress, Cognition, and Health*, eds. S. Fischer and J. Reason, 629–49. New York: Wiley.

Steward, Julian C. 1955. *Theory of Culture Change*. Urbana: University of Illinois Press.

Stiglitz, Joseph E. 2002. *Globalization and Its Discontents*. New York: Norton.

Stringer, Chris B. 1992. "Evolution of Early Humans." In *The Cambridge Encyclopedia of Human Evolution*, eds. Steven Jones, Robert Martin, and David Pilbeam, 241–54. Cambridge: Cambridge University Press.

Suttles, Gerald D. 1968. *The Social Order of the Slum: Ethnicity and Territory in the Inner City*. Chicago: University of Chicago Press.

Swann, William B., J. G. Hixon, Alan Stein-Seroussi, and Daniel T. Gilbert. 1990. "The Fleeting Gleam of Praise: Cognitive Processes Underlying Behavior Reactions to Self-Relevant Feedback." *Journal of Personality and Social Psychology* 59:17–26.

Swedberg, Richard. 2003. *Principles of Economic Sociology*. Princeton: Princeton University Press.

Sweeney, Paul D., Dean B. McFarlin, and Edward J. Inderrieden. 1990. "Using Relative Deprivation Theory to Explain Satisfaction with Income and Pay Level: A Multistudy Examination." *Academy of Management Journal* 33:423–36.

Taeuber, Karl E., and Alma F. Taeuber. 1964. "The Negro as an Immigrant Group: Recent Trends in Racial and Ethnic Segregation in Chicago." *American Journal of Sociology* 69:374–82.

Tattersall, Ian. 1995. *The Last Neanderthal: The Origin, Success, and Mysterious Extinction of Our Closest Human Relative*. New York: Macmillan.

———. 1998. *Becoming Human: Evolution and Human Uniqueness*. New York: Harcourt Brace.

———. 1999. *The Last Neanderthal: The Rise, Success, and Mysterious Extinction of Our Closest Human Relatives*, 2nd ed. Boulder: Westview.

Taylor, Shelly E., and Jonathan D. Brown. 1988. "Illusion and Well-Being: A Social Psychological Perspective on Mental Health." *Psychological Bulletin* 103:193–210.

TenHouten, Warren D. 1980. "Social Dominance and Cerebral Hemisphericity: Discriminating Social Groups by Performance on Two Lateralized Tests." *International Journal of Neuroscience* 10:223–32.

———. 1985. "Right Hemisphericity of Australian Aboriginal Children: Effects of Culture, Sex, and Age on Performances of Cluster and Similarities Tests." *International Journal of Neuroscience* 28:125–46.

———. 1986. "Right Hemisphericity of Australian Aboriginal Children II: Conjugate Lateral Eye Movements." *International Journal of Neuroscience* 30:255–60.

———. 1999. "Explorations in Neurosociological Theory: From the Spectrum of Affect to Time Consciousness." In *Mind, Brain, and Society: Toward a Neurosociology of Emotion*, eds. David D. Franks and Thomas S. Smith, 41–80. Stamford, CT: JAI Press.

TenHouten, Warren D., A. L. Thompson, and D. O. Walter. 1976. "Discriminating Social Groups by Performance on Two Laterlized Tests." *Bulletin of the Los Angelés Neurological Societies* 42:99–108.

Thaler, Richard H. 1994. "Psychology and Savings Policies." *American Economic Review* 84:186–92.

Thomas, Brinley. 1973. *Migration and Economic Growth: A Study of Great Britain and the Atlantic Economy*. Cambridge: Cambridge University Press.

Thomas, Dorothy S. 1941. *Social and Economic Aspects of Swedish Population Movements: 1750–1933*. New York: Macmillan.

Tierney, Patrick. 2000. *Darkness in El Dorado: How Scientists and Journalists Devastated the Amazon*. New York: Norton.

Tilly, Charles. 1998. *Durable Inequality*. Berkeley: University of California Press.

Tilly, Charles, and C. H. Brown. 1967. "On Uprooting, Kinship, and the Auspices of Migration." *International Journal of Comparative Sociology* 8:139–64.

Timms, Duncan W. G. 1971. *The Urban Mosaic: Towards a Theory of Residential Differentiation*. Cambridge: Cambridge University Press.

Tönnies, Ferdinand. 1940. *Fundamental Concepts of Sociology (Gemeinschaft und Gesellschaft)*. New York: American Book Co.

Tonry, Michael. 1995. *Malign Neglect: Race, Crime, and Punishment in America*. New York: Oxford University Press.

Torres, Horacio A. 2001. "Cambios Socioterritoriales en Buenos Aires Durante la Década de 1990." *Revista Latinoamericana de Estudios Urbanos y Regionales* 27(80):33–56.

Trattner, Walter I. 1998. *From Poor Law to Welfare State: A History of Social Welfare in America*. 6th ed.: New York: Free Press.

Turner, Jonathan H. 1997. "The Evolution of Morality." *Critical Review* 11:211–32.

———. 1999. "The Neurology of Emotion: Implications for Sociological Theories of Interpersonal Behavior." *Social Perspectives on Emotion* 5:81–108.

———. 2000. *On the Origins of Human Emotions: A Sociological Inquiry into the Evolution of Human Affect*. Stanford: Stanford University Press.

Turner, Jonathan H., and Alexandra Maryanski. 1991. "Network Analysis." In *The Structure of Social Theory*, ed. Jonathan H. Turner, 540–72. Belmont: Wadsworth.

Turow, Joseph. 1997. *Breaking Up America: Advertisers and the New Media World*. Chicago: University of Chicago Press.

Tversky, Amos, and Daniel Kahneman., 1974. "Judgment under Uncertainty: Heuristics and Biases." *Science* 185:1124–31.

———. 1986. "Rational Choice and the Framing of Decisions." *Journal of Business* 59:S251–0S278.

United Nations. 1980. *Patterns of Urban and Rural Population Growth*. New York: United Nations Department of International Economic and Social Affairs.

———. 2002. *World Urbanization Prospects: The 2001 Revision*. New York: United Nations.

U.S. Bureau of the Census. 2004. "Pennsylvania Quick Facts, Philadelphia County." Census Bureau Web site: http://quickfacts.census.gov/gFd/states/42/42101.html.

van de Walle, Nicolas. 2001. *African Economies and the Politics of Permanent Crisis: 1979–1999*. Cambridge: Cambridge University Press.

Vélez-Ibáñez, Carlos G. 1983. *Rituals of Marginality: Politics, Process, and Culture Change in Urban Central Mexico, 1969–1974*. Berkeley: University of California Press.

Vining, Daniel R., Jr., T. Plaut, and K. Bieri. 1977. "Urban Encroachment on Prime Agricultural Land." *International Regional Science Review* 3:49–73.

Wagner, Daniel A. 1993. "Literacy and Development: Rationales, Assessment, and Innovation." LRC/NCAL International Paper IP93-1. Philadelphia: National Center on Adult Literacy, University of Pennsylvania.

Walker, Iain, and Heather J. Smith. 2002. *Relative Deprivation: Specification, Development, and Integration*. Cambridge: Cambridge University Press.

Wallerstein, Immanuel. 1974. *The Modern World-System I: Capitalist Agriculture and the Origins of the European World-Economy in the Sixteenth Century*. Orlando: Academic Press.

Waters, Mary C. 1990. *Ethnic Options: Choosing Identities in America*. Berkeley: University of California Press.

Watson, Robert T., ed. 2002. *Climate Change 2001: Sysnthesis Report. Third Assessment Report of the Intergovernmental Panel on Climate Change*. Cambridge: Cambridge University Press.

Watts, Ian. 1999. "The Origin of Symbolic Culture." In *The Evolution of Culture: An Interdisciplinary View*, eds. Robin Dunbar, Chris Knight, and Camilla Power, 113–46. New Brunswick, NJ: Rutgers University Press.

Weber, Max. 1968. *Economy and Society*. New York: Bedminster Press.

Webster, Chris, Georg Glasze, and Klaus Frantz. 2002. "The Global Spread of Gated Communities." *Environment and Planning B* 29:315–20.

Wegner, Daniel. 2002. *The Illusion of Conscious Will*. Cambridge, MA: MIT Press.

Weiss, Michael J. 1988. *The Clustering of America*. New York: Harper & Row.

———. 2000. *The Clustered World: How We Live, What We Buy, and What It All Means about Who We Are*. Boston: Little, Brown.

Western, Bruce, and Becky Pettit. 2000. "Incarceration and Racial Inequality in Men's Employment." *Industrial and Labor Relations Review* 54:3–16.

Western, Bruce, Leonard M. Lopoo, and Sara McLanahan. 2004. "Incarceration and the Bonds between Parents in Fragile Families." In *Imprisoning America: The Social Effects of Mass Incarceration*, eds. Mary Patillo, David Weiman, and Bruce Western, 21–45. New York: Russell Sage Foundation.

Western, Bruce, Mary Patillo, and David Weiman. 2004. "Introduction." In *Imprison-*

*ing America: The Social Effects of Mass Incarceration*, eds. Mary Patillo, David Weiman, and Bruce Western, 1–20. New York: Russell Sage Foundation.

White, Robert W. 1959. "Motivation Reconsidered: The Concepts of Competence." *Psychological Review* 66:297–333.

Whiting, Beatrice, and Carolyn P. Edwards. 1988. *Children of Different Worlds: The Formation of Social Behavior*. Cambridge, MA: Harvard University Press.

Whitley, Richard. 1999. *Divergent Capitalisms: The Social Structuring and Change of Business Systems*. Oxford: Oxford University Press.

Whyte, William F. 1943. *Street Corner Society: The Social Structure of an Italian Slum*. Chicago: University of Chicago Press.

Wilkes, Rima, and John Iceland. 2004. "Hypersegregation in the Twenty-First Century," *Demography* 41:23–36.

Williams, Kipling D., Kyong Won Cheung, and W. Choi. 2000. "Cyber-Ostracism: Effects of Being Ignored over the Internet." *Journal of Personality and Social Psychology* 79:748–62.

Winant, Howard. 2001. *The World Is a Ghetto: Race and Democracy since World War II*. New York: Basic Books.

Winterhalder, Bruce, and Eric A. Smith. 1981. *Hunter-Gatherer Foraging Strategies: Ethnographic and Archaeological Analyses*. Chicago: University of Chicago Press.

Wirth, Louis. 1928. *The Ghetto*. Chicago: University of Chicago Press.

———. 1938. "Urbanism as a Way of Life." *American Journal of Sociology* 44:1–24.

Wood, B. A. 1992. "Origin and Evolution of the Genus Homo." *Nature* 355:783–90.

Woodward, C. Vann. 1955. *The Strange Career of Jim Crow*. New York: Oxford University Press.

Wrangham, Richard W. 2001. "Out of the *Pan*, Into the Figure: How Our Ancestors Depended on What They Ate." In *Tree of Origin: What Primate Behavior Can Tell Us about Human Social Evolution*, ed. Frans B. M. de Waal, 121–43. Cambridge, MA: Harvard University Press.

Wright, Robert. 2000. *Nonzero: The Logic of Human Destiny*. New York: Vintage.

Yancey, William L., Eugene P. Ericksen, and Richard N. Juliani. 1976. "Emergent Ethnicity: A Review and Reformulation." *American Sociological Review* 41:391–403.

Yerkes, Robert M. 1943. *Chimpanzees: A Laboratory Colony*. New Haven: Yale University Press.

Zajonc, Robert B. 1998. "Emotions." Pp. 591–634 in Daniel T. Gilbert, Susan T. Fiske, and Gardner Lindzey, eds., *The Handbook of Social Psychology*. Boston: McGraw Hill.

Zajonc, Robert B., and Pamela K. Adelmann. 1987. "Cognition and Communication: A Story of Missed Opportunities." *Social Science Information* 26:3–30.

# Index